LIES MY PROFESSOR TOLD ME ABOUT AMERICAN POLITICS

For comments or questions about this book,
visit our website: *The Lost Stories Channel*, at
loststorieschannel.com

© 2024 by W. Kent Smith – All Rights Reserved
Published in the United States by
Lodestar Cinema Creations,
in association with Staten House
West Covina, California
Smith, W. Kent (1959-)

Front Cover and Title Page Painting:
Declaration of Independence,
John Trumbull, 1819

Book Exterior and Interior
Designed and Executed
by W. Kent Smith

All the artwork for this book is in the public
domain and is therefore not subject to copyright
infringement.

ISBN: 979-8-89686-016-7

Manufactured in the U.S.A.
November 2024

Lies My Professor Told Me About American Politics

Questions Concerning the Original Vision of the Founding Fathers

by

W. Kent Smith

Lodestar
Cinema
Creations

in association with

Staten House

Books by W. Kent Smith

Lies My Professor Told Me About American Politics: Questions Concerning the Original Vision of the Founding Fathers

Conquering Cynicism in a Modern Age: How The Bible in Nature Provides an Antidote to Doubt and Despair

On Earth as It is On Heaven: The Promise of America, Technology, and the New Earth, Book One: The Promise of America

The Book of Days: In Search of the 5,500-year Prophecy Given to Adam About the Coming of Christ

The Book of Tales: Stories That Confirm the 5,500-year Prophecy Given to Adam About the Coming of Christ

Fish Tales (From the Belly of the Whale): Fifty of the Greatest Misconceptions Ever Blamed on The Bible, Reel One, The Hook #50-34

Fish Tales (From the Belly of the Whale): Fifty of the Greatest Misconceptions Ever Blamed on The Bible, Reel Two, The Line #33-18

Fish Tales (From the Belly of the Whale): Fifty of the Greatest Misconceptions Ever Blamed on The Bible, Reel Three, The Sinker #17-1

Fish Tales (From the Belly of the Whale): Fifty of the Greatest Misconceptions Ever Blamed on The Bible, The Complete Edition, Hook, Line, and Sinker #50-1

Tales of Forever: The Unfolding Drama of God's Hidden Hand in History, Book One: The Analyses – Part One

Tales of Forever: The Unfolding Drama of God's Hidden Hand in History, Book Two: The Tales – Part One

Tales of Forever: The Unfolding Drama of God's Hidden Hand in History, Book Three: The Tales – Part Two

Tales of Forever: The Unfolding Drama of God's Hidden Hand in History, Book Four: The Analyses – Part Two

Tales of Forever: The Unfolding Drama of God's Hidden Hand in History, The Complete Edition

For Scott,

My Other Best Friend and Fellow Instigator

CONTENTS

THE PREAMBLE

"I've lived a long time, and the longer I live, the more convinced I am of this truth—that God governs the affairs of men. And if a sparrow doesn't fall to the ground without Him noticing, then how is it possible that an Empire can rise without His aid?"

Benjamin Franklin

"God Who gave us life also gave us liberty. And are the liberties of a nation secure when we remove their only firm basis—a conviction that these liberties are the gift of God? That they can be violated without incurring His wrath? Indeed, I tremble for my country when I reflect that God is just, and that His justice cannot sleep forever."

Thomas Jefferson

"Posterity—you will never know how much it has cost my generation to preserve your freedom. I hope you will make good use of it."

John Quincy Adams

AN INTRODUCTION

Unveiling the Truth:

Shedding the Blindfold

I N AN AGE marked by conflicting accounts and complex ideologies, the truth is often obscured beneath
layers of political controversy. As curious and determined individuals, we find ourselves navigating through
a maze of perspectives, each vying for our attention and
allegiance. Our attempts to interpret these multifaceted
narratives can unveil hidden truths, especially when we
confront deceptive tales spun by influential figures such as
our college professors who wield their authority to shape
our perceptions. My own experience reflects the profound
impact of questioning, learning, and seeking truth amidst
a sea of half-truths and distortions.

At the heart of my exploration lies the realization that
the narratives presented to us are seldom straightforward.
Growing up in a politically charged environment, I ab-
sorbed countless creeds, each one claiming to hold the key
to social justice and change. Yet, as I delved deeper into
my studies, I noticed inconsistencies and omissions in the
teachings of my professors. Their perspectives, while valuable to a degree, often failed to address the complexity of
the issues at hand, leaning instead on simplified narratives
that are easily consumed. This observation ignited a spark
of curiosity in me—a desire to peel back the layers and ex-

amine the realities that lie beneath the surface.

As I embarked on my quest for understanding, I discovered that embracing a variety of viewpoints was essential. Conversations with peers who possessed different backgrounds and philosophies expanded my horizon, challenging me to re-evaluate my beliefs. These discussions often highlighted the importance of context in assembling narratives. I learned that history is rarely painted in black and white; rather, it's a tapestry woven with diverse threads that require careful examination. It became clear that openness—to understand opposing views and to change one's mind—was a critical component in my journey toward unveiling the truth.

I also found that personal reflection and critical thinking were indispensable allies in unraveling complex narratives. Engaging in self-assessment allowed me to identify biases and preconceived notions that clouded my judgment. At times, this meant confronting disturbing truths about my own beliefs, as well as acknowledging the role my environment played in shaping them. The more I scrutinized my own perspective, the more equipped I became to approach the narratives presented by my professors with a healthy level of skepticism. Their interpretations, though educated and informed, were still merely one part of a much larger story.

The experience of questioning so-called "truths," engaging with diverse viewpoints, and challenging deceptive narratives has enriched my understanding of the intricate relationship between ideology and reality. As I continue to navigate this landscape, I'm reminded of the power that education holds—not just to enlighten but also to deceive. By remaining vigilant and committed to seeking clarity amidst confusion, I contribute to a more nuanced understanding of the narratives that shape our world.

Ultimately, this journey has led me to appreciate the many nuances inherent in political discourse. I began to recognize that the narratives we consume are often curated to evoke specific responses that may benefit those in power but don't necessarily reflect the broader scope of the real world. Understanding this dynamic has triggered a sense of responsibility in me—one that urges me to challenge dominant narratives. And it's this awareness that solidified my determination to become an advocate for truth in a world where lies so easily prevail.

> *"He who permits himself to tell a lie once, finds it much easier to do so a second and third time, till at length it becomes habitual; soon he speaks lies without realizing it, and truths without the world believing him. This falsehood of the tongue, then, leads to that of the heart, and in time corrupts all its good intentions."*
>
> *Thomas Jefferson*

LIE #1: *The Separation of Church and State Means Removing The Bible and What It Teaches From American Culture...*

In recent years, there has been a heated debate about the separation of church and state in American culture. Many argue this separation means completely removing *The Bible* and what it teaches from society. However, this is a gross misconception that requires clarification. Far from erasing religion from public life, the separation of church and state was established to protect the rights of everyone by preventing the state from establishing or promoting any specific religion, or the church from exerting its power over anyone who practices the faith of their choice. In Chapter One, *Inherited Ignorance: Lies From the Past*, we'll debunk this lie and provide a deeper understanding of what America's Founders really intended when they enshrined the principle of separating church from state.

LIE #2: *You Don't Have to Mention The Bible and Its Principles When You Talk About Politics in America...*
In today's political landscape, the influence of religion is often downplayed or disregarded entirely. As such, there is a prevailing notion that *The Bible* and its principles have no place in discussions about American politics. However, this is a blatant lie that has deeply corrupted our country. The values and principles that once defined the American political system, such as transparency and the power of the people, have been overshadowed by partisan politics and the pursuit of personal gain. But amidst the chaos, there is a fundamental truth that must be acknowledged: *The Bible* and its teachings have played a significant role in shaping American culture. In Chapter 2, *The Broken Machine: A Corrupted Body Politic*, we'll explore how *The Bible* has influenced the political landscape of America and why it's important to discuss biblical principles when talking about American politics.

LIE #3: *America was Founded on the Principle of Pure Democracies Like That of Ancient Greece...*
It is a common misconception that the United States of America is a democracy in the same vein as ancient Greece. In reality, the U.S. functions as a constitutional republic in which the rights of individuals are protected from the tyranny of the majority. While ancient democracies, in places like Athens, embodied a system where citizen participation was direct and palpable, they were nevertheless marked by an underlying oppression of dissenting voices. This critical difference sets our constitutional republic apart from classical pure democracies, and embracing this truth is vital if we hope to understand America's genuine political origins. In Chapter 3, *The Myth of Pure Democracy: The Real Story of American Governance*, we'll examine the historical and constitutional foundations of American government and delve into why this distinction between a pure democracy and a constitutional republic is so essential.

LIE #4: *The Founding Fathers Laid Out a Plan of Government Based on the Assumption that Humans are Innately Good and Honest...*

In today's media-rich landscape, it can be difficult to discern the truth from the headlines. This is particularly true when it comes to understanding the principles and intentions of America's Founding Fathers. One common myth is that they believed humans are innately good and honest, and thus designed a government based on this assumption. However, a closer look at history reveals a far different story. In Chapter 4, *The Media Mirage: The Truth Behind the Headlines*, we'll embark on a journey to decipher the misleading information propagated by mainstream media and explore the reality of the Founding Fathers' plan of government, shedding light on the complexities and nuances of their beliefs.

LIE #5: *Politicians Who are Not Perfect Should be Removed From Office...*

In today's political climate, division and polarization are at an all-time high. Identity Politics, the practice of aligning oneself with a particular group based on shared characteristics, has become a powerful tool for political manipulation. Politicians and pundits alike use this tactic to sway public opinion and gain support for their agendas. More and more, politicians are wielding the sword of Identity Politics to divide and conquer. By focusing on individual identities and exploiting differences, they manipulate public opinion and deflect attention from their own flaws and shortcomings. One common lie propagated by these politicians is that anyone who isn't perfect should be immediately removed from office. This lie not only undermines the democratic process but also ignores the complexities of human nature and the potential for growth and improvement. In Chapter 5, *Divide and Conquer: The Weaponization of Identity Politics*, we'll examine this powerful tool of manipulation and disarm this insidious tactic.

LIE #6: *The Highest Good of Government is to Care for the Poor and Needy...*

In a world where trust in government is eroding and skepticism is on the rise, it's essential to question the narratives we're fed. One of the biggest lies we're told is that the highest good of government is that it should care for the poor and needy. This illusion of benevolence has been used to justify countless policies and actions, but the reality is far from what it seems. The actions of governments have actually shown that their true priorities lie elsewhere; this illusion, in fact, masks a darker truth. In Chapter 6, *The Puppet Masters: Unveiling Hidden Persuaders*, we'll unveil the truth behind this lie and expose the illusion of government's highest good.

LIE #7: *Raising Taxes on the Rich Will Benefit the Average American and Bring Much-needed Relief to the Poor...*

The notion that increasing taxes on the wealthy will result in tangible benefits for the average American and those in poverty is an alluring one, frequently touted by politicians with a populist agenda. However, this promise obscures a more complex economic reality. The truth is that when taxes rise on the so-called "rich," what is often overlooked is that most of their wealth is tied up not in savings or stocks but in the businesses they own. Consequently, raising taxes on these individuals ultimately leads to dire consequences for the very people that these policies intend to uplift. In Chapter 7, *Taking From the Rich: An Economic Ripple Effect*, we'll unpack the fallacies behind this claim and explore the broader implications of higher taxation on wealth.

LIE #8: *In Geopolitics, as in Our Personal Relationships, Americans Must Live by the Golden Rule, and Always Treat Others as We'd Like to be Treated...*

In today's increasingly interconnected world, it's crucial to understand the global consequences of our actions.

Geopolitics, the study of how geography and power relationships influence international affairs, plays a significant role in shaping the world as we know it today. From international trade agreements to diplomatic relations, the decisions made by political leaders have far-reaching consequences, which naturally involve countries that have different worldviews and cultural histories all their own. Despite this, there is a prevailing belief that Americans should approach foreign affairs with the singular mindset of the Golden Rule, which demands that we always treat other countries the way we'd like to be treated. However, because most other countries we deal with have no intention of returning the favor, this kind of one-size-fits-all diplomacy inevitably brings great risk to us by way of undermining our national security, economic stability, and global influence. In Chapter 8, *Foreign Affairs: The Global Consequences*, we'll explore this misguided belief and delve into why Americans need to have a more nuanced understanding of the complexities of international affairs.

LIE #9: *From Israel to America, Being the "Chosen of God" Means Being Special Without any Need for Personal Responsibility...*

In a world full of noise and distractions, we often find ourselves stumbling down a path that leads us further away from our true purpose. But deep down, we yearn for redemption and truth; we yearn for a chance to reclaim our personal responsibility. And when misinformation and lies are so prevalent, it's more important than ever to seek the truth, especially when it comes to matters of faith. One such belief that has been widely debated is the concept of being the "Chosen of God." From ancient Israel to modern-day America, the idea of "chosenness" has been a source of both pride and prejudice. However, it's time to confront the truth concerning this idea and how easy it is to misconstrue what being chosen really entails. That's because being the "Chosen of God" doesn't exempt us from personal responsibility or justify our mistreatment of others. In Chapter 9, *The Road to Redemption: Awakening to the Truth*, we'll explore the arduous path to redemption and the importance of unveiling the truth about this complicated concept.

THE ULTIMATE LIE: *Because Human Governments Will All Be Swept Away Someday, in Favor of Our Real Destiny in Heaven, Politics Have No Purpose in God's Plan...*
In today's tumultuous political climate, many people find solace in the belief that human governments are temporary institutions, destined to be replaced by a divine governance. This idealistic vision of a utopian future can evoke hope and offer a sense of comfort. However, it's important to consider the potential consequences of this perspective. By placing faith in divine intervention, there is a risk of undermining critical thinking and civic engagement—two essential components for a healthy and functioning body politic. While the promise of a higher power may bring comfort, it also poses the danger of complacency and a diminished sense of responsibility among citizens. In The Conclusion, *Refuting the Ultimate Lie: God's True Purpose for the Earth*, we'll delve into the complexities of this perspective, exploring its potential implications and the importance of maintaining active citizenship in our current world.

In conclusion, the exploration of American politics unveils a sobering reality marked by deception and manipulation. Leaders, media, and hidden persuaders weave an intricate web that obscures the truth, culminating in a political landscape fraught with challenges. But through sincere questioning and active engagement, citizens can shine a light on these darker facets, pushing for a more transparent and authentic political discourse. Only then can the American political landscape evolve into one that reflects the true will of the people it serves.

CHAPTER ONE

Inherited Ignorance:

Lies From the Past

LIE #1:

The Separation of Church and State Means Removing The Bible and What It Teaches From American Culture...

O NE DAY after class, I asked my professor about the current state of public affairs, so stained as they were with political division, hatred, and backbiting. I asked him: "What do you think is the root cause of the problem, and how can we fix things?"

This is what he told me, with absolute conviction: "The root cause? Why, of course, the root cause stems from our failure as a society to remove *The Bible* and what it teaches from American culture, as was clearly proscribed by the American founders."

Trying not to sound too confused, I replied, quizzically, "The American founders?"

"Certainly, certainly," sputtered my professor. "Certainly, my boy. You *have* heard of the doctrine of the separation of church and state, haven't you?"

"Why, yes," I replied, still trying my best to conceal my confusion, and then I nodded. "Certainly."

My professor eyed me suspiciously from behind his

9

huge wooden desk. "I can see you're not entirely con-vinced," he continued. "Is that it?"

"Pardon me for saying so, Professor. But I don't quite see how removing *The Bible* from the political landscape would help matters any. I mean, as far as healing the wounds of such a divided nation."

"I understand, my boy. Try to think of it this way, then... If division is what threatens to destroy a nation, then sim-ply eliminate what most inflames that division. This is the driving principle behind removing what is undoubtedly the most inflammatory text in the history of humanity."

Squinting my eyes, I considered his words carefully.

"Now do you see what I'm telling you?" he asked.

"Hmmm," was all I could muster in response, much to the chagrin of the stern old man sitting across from me.

It was at this point that I determined to begin my own investigation into what, exactly, my professor had meant that day and the extent to which he was either correct or incorrect in his thinking. What proceeds, in the following work, represents what I've discovered over the years in my pursuit to ferret out the real truth of the matter.

> *"The highest glory of the American Revolution was this; it connected in one indestructible bond the principles of civil government with the principles of Christianity."*
>
> *John Quincy Adams*

Debunking the Demand to Erase Our Religious Values

ONE OF THE first things I discovered was how often the concept of the separation of church and state is complete-ly misinterpreted, leading to innumerable misconceptions about the role of religious teachings in public life. After many years of being swayed to believe otherwise, as a result of my professor's influence, I eventually realized that when people insist on erasing religious values from public life, they're not only misrepresenting the original vision of the Founding Fathers of America, but they're also diminishing the rich cultural tapestry that *The Bible* has woven into the fabric of the whole history of our country.[1]

At its core, the separation of church and state wasn't designed to remove religion from the realm of the state; it was designed to protect religious freedom, ensuring that individuals could freely worship—or not worship, for that matter—without interference from either the state or a state-sponsored church. Thomas Paine warned us about such interference when he said, "Of all the tyrannies that affect mankind, tyranny in religion is the worst."

The Founding Fathers therefore sought to prevent the establishment of a state-sponsored religion, allowing all faiths, including Christianity, to coexist. Sadly, the perception that this principle demands that we erase biblical teachings from public discourse has manifested in a culture that often sidelines essential moral foundations rooted in Scripture.

What's more, the diminishing presence of *The Bible* in public matters only leads to greater cultural erosion. Values

---

1 *The Founding Fathers of America*: The men who, in 1776, forged a new nation out of 13 original colonies are known as the Founding Fathers of America—a term coined by the 29th U.S. President Warren G. Harding who began using it in many of his speeches in the late 1910s. The Founding Fathers played key roles in securing political independence from Great Britain, and devising the first government apparatus of the United States of America.

The term can refer to: members of the Constitutional Convention, signers of the Declaration of Independence, and Framers of the Constitution. While many contributed to America's founding, the best-known are: John and Samuel Adams, Benjamin Franklin, Alexander Hamilton, Patrick Henry, Thomas Jefferson, James Madison, James Monroe, Thomas Paine, and George Washington.

The Founding Fathers are best known for winning the war for colonial independence, establishing the principle of the separation of church and state, and founding the first large-scale constitutional republic in the modern world.

such as compassion, integrity, and love, often encapsulated in biblical teachings, provide moral grounding that informs the decisions of individuals and leaders alike. When these values are stripped from the public domain, society risks losing sight of empathy and the collective well-being that bind us together. The painful irony is that while promoting a secular government, proponents of complete separation unwittingly advocate for a vacuum of values, which actually leads to an increase in societal discord not a decrease.

In educational institutions, the debate surrounding the presence of *The Bible* and its teachings has become particularly pronounced. Schools often shy away from discussing biblical principles, fearing repercussions in a climate that prioritizes secularism. This results in an educational environment that neglects the rich historical context *The Bible* provides. Students miss out on understanding the profound impact of these teachings on art, literature, and the principles that underlie representational democracy in America. Such a loss of context is sad, as it limits the intellectual growth and moral ethos of future generations.

The cultural implications extend far beyond the educational sphere. Public spaces—once adorned with biblical references and themes—have slowly transitioned towards a secular approach, rendering the moral compass of many silent. Many individuals no longer feel empowered to express their beliefs or consult the teachings of *The Bible* when engaging in meaningful discussions about morality and ethics. This withdrawal inevitably leads to a sense of isolation, causing many who find solace and guidance in biblical teachings to feel marginalized in conversations that shape cultural norms.

The Deep Historical Roots of the Separation of Church and State

THE IDEA OF separating church and state originated in the intellectual activity of 17th- and 18th-century Western

Europe and the experiences of early American colonists. Many sought to escape religious persecution, and as a result, the First Amendment of the Constitution was enacted.[2] It states: "Congress shall make no law respecting an establishment of religion, or prohibiting the free exercise thereof." This simple but explicit clause ensures that government remains neutral in religious matters while simultaneously protecting everyone's rights to practice their own beliefs freely.

The concept of the separation of church and state is deeply rooted in modern society, but understanding its historical foundations reveals a fascinating and complex journey. At its core, this principle insists that religious institutions and government operate independently of one another, in order to, as George Washington put it, "establish effectual barriers against the horrors of spiritual tyranny, and every species of religious persecution."

However, this idea of the separation of church and state wasn't always a given; it evolved through many centuries of philosophical debate, conflict, and cultural shifts that reflected society's changing views on religion, governance, and individual rights. To trace the roots of this concept, we need to look to a pivotal period of intellectual activity in

---

2   *The First Amendment of the Constitution*: Ratified in 1791 as part of the Bill of Rights, the First Amendment of the Constitution protects the following freedoms from government interference:

Freedom of Speech affords every American the right to express their opinion without government restraint. This includes our right to decide what to say and what not to say.

Freedom of the Press affords us the right of the media to report on government activities as a third party. This prevents the government from controlling the media.

Freedom of Religion affords us the right to practice or exercise our religion without government interference. This includes our right to not have a national religion established or one religion favored over another.

Freedom of Assembly affords us the right to peacefully assemble to advocate for our causes, beliefs, movements, or protests.

Freedom of Petition affords us the right to officially bring our concerns to the government by collecting signatures from others.

Western Europe, when thinkers like John Locke, Voltaire, and Montesquieu began to champion the idea of religious freedom.

Locke argued that faith should be a personal choice, wholly separate from governmental influence, and that coercing individuals in matters of belief was unjust. At the time, this was a radical departure from the prevailing view where church and state were typically intertwined, with rulers vigorously enforcing religious conformity.

Voltaire argued that when governments imposed religious conformity upon their population this inevitably led to conflict and religious wars. Such societies were rampant with corruption and stagnation because dissent was suppressed. This led Voltaire to conclude that rather than impose conformity and control, only freedom and diversity would create vibrant, peaceful societies.

Montesquieu famously advocated for civil liberty that could only be assured through a separation of governmental powers, the right to fair trials, the presumption of innocence, and the freedom of thought, speech, and assembly.

In this way, such thinking—which formed the backbone of what came to be known as the Age of the Enlightenment—paved the way for people to question the traditional authority of monarchs and religious leaders, and set the stage for later developments in the United States.[3]

---

3   *The Age of Enlightenment*: A European intellectual movement of the 17th and 18th centuries, the Age of Enlightenment marked a phase in history when ideas about God, reason, nature, and humanity were integrated into a worldview that triggered radical changes in philosophy, art, and politics. Central to the Enlightenment was the celebration of reason, and the way that humans understand the Universe and their place in it. It was nothing less than a philosophical revolution in which a uniquely original pursuit of knowledge, freedom, and happiness was implemented to improve the overall condition of humanity.

Key figures of the Enlightenment were John Locke, Montesquieu, Voltaire, Jean-Jacques Rousseau, Rene Descartes, and Immanuel Kant, all of whom led the way in criticizing the authoritarian state and expressing their ideas about a more just social order, based on the principles of natural rights, the rule of law, and representational democracy. The impact of their ideas ultimately triggered social reform in England and political revolution in America and France.

Fast forward to the late 18th century in America where the Founding Fathers were influenced by these Enlightenment ideas. Many of them, like James Madison and Thomas Jefferson, held a vision of a new nation where government wouldn't interfere with personal beliefs. As Madison described it: "The accumulation of all powers, legislative, executive, and judiciary, in the same hands, whether of one, a few, or many, and whether hereditary, self-appointed, or elective, may justly be pronounced the very definition of tyranny." Jefferson famously spoke of a "wall of separation" between church and state, a phrase that encapsulates the idea that no one should impose their beliefs on someone else. It was a revolutionary vision that helped shape the First Amendment of the Constitution, which guarantees freedom of religion.

Today, the separation of church and state is often a hot topic, especially when arguing about the presence of religious symbols in public spaces or the role of faith in American politics. On one hand, many argue that this principle protects individual freedom of expression, ensuring that no one is censored when professing their religious beliefs. On the other hand, some see it as a call to completely eradicate any and all expressions of religious faith in public or political life. As such, this ongoing debate shows that while the idea of separating church and state was truly revolutionary, the question of how to apply it is still something that remains firmly at the heart of American cultural life.

Separation Doesn't Demand an Erasure of Religious Values

IN A WORLD where conversations about values and morality often intersect with religion, the notion that secularism requires the erasure of religious teaching from public discourse is deeply troubling. This idea suggests that faith and spirituality should retreat into the shadows, as if it were incapable of informing the public sphere where decisions are made and lives are shaped. However, such a separation not only diminishes the richness of our societal dialogue, but it also negates the profound influence that diverse belief systems have on creating a compassionate and understanding community.

The idea that religion must be expelled from the public arena strips away the voices of countless individuals and groups who derive their ethical values from spiritual teachings. For many, faith is a cornerstone of identity and a guide to compassionate living. To dismiss these moral perspectives as irrelevant in discussions about justice, equality, and human dignity is to overlook a vital part of humanity's quest for meaning. This erasure promotes a dangerous narrative that secular thought is the only legitimate framework for addressing important cultural questions. By insisting that religious individuals keep their beliefs private, we risk losing out on the depth of insight that comes from genuine dialogue between diverse worldviews.

What's more, the idea of "separation" doesn't demand an erasure of religious values but, rather, encourages a more profound engagement with them in a pluralistic society. Religious traditions offer rich ethical frameworks that complement secular reasoning. For instance, principles like empathy, charity, and forgiveness can guide discussions on social justice and human rights. The beauty of a democratic discourse is its ability to weave together various perspectives, allowing for a more holistic understanding of complex issues. By erasing religious values, we not only diminish our collective wisdom, but we also contribute to a chilling atmosphere where individuals feel their beliefs are unwelcome.

Additionally, the emotional landscape of society is often painted with strokes of faith and spirituality. The sadness that accompanies the marginalization of these values is palpable, as it reflects a disconnection from the very essence that many people hold dear. Such separation leads to a sense of isolation among those whose values and beliefs are tied intricately to their faith. Communities become fractured as individuals who feel compelled to silence their beliefs withdraw from public participation. This creates an environment where a significant portion of the population may feel misunderstood or invalidated, leading to a loss of connection and community cohesion.

Faith Acting as a Compass

THE SEPARATION of church and state is a foundational principle in America, designed to ensure that religious institutions don't wield political power and that government remains neutral in matters of faith. However, this separation doesn't diminish the significant role that religious communities play in shaping our society. These communities often influence the ethical frameworks within which individuals and groups operate, impacting a wide array of social issues and behaviors that resonate deeply within the pluralistic fabric of American life.

Religious communities serve as crucial sources of moral guidance, helping individuals to navigate complex ethical dilemmas. For many, the teachings of their faith act as a compass, guiding them in their decisions and interactions with others. This moral framework isn't merely theoretical; it also manifests in practical ways, influencing behaviors such as honesty, compassion, and forgiveness. What's more, the values espoused by various religions often promote ideals that transcend individual communities, fostering a broader understanding of ethics and morality.

The charitable works undertaken by religious organizations also underscore their impact on society. From providing food and shelter to the homeless, to financing schools and hospitals, these organizations address critical social needs that governments may struggle to fulfill. The influence of religious groups in charity is particularly significant in times of crisis, such as natural disasters or pandemics, where their mobilization efforts can provide essential services and support to affected populations. By engaging in these acts of service, religious communities not only reinforce their ethical teachings, but they also cultivate a sense of community and belonging among their members and beyond.

However, the intersection of religious and cultural values can present challenges, especially in a pluralistic society where multiple belief systems coexist. While religious beliefs provide a strong foundation for personal morality, they also lead to differing perspectives on social issues, such as marriage, voting, and immigration. These differences create tension and debate within the public sphere, as individuals advocate for their views based on their religious principles. As a result, navigating these complex dynamics requires a careful balance, ensuring that the moral voices of religious communities are heard while also respecting the diverse beliefs of others.

Contributing to the Moral Fabric of the Country

THE INFLUENCE OF *The Bible* on various aspects of American society—literature, law, and ethics—demonstrates its profound power and reach, shaping the nation's values and cultural identity. This sacred text transcends mere religious boundaries, and as such it remains a vital cornerstone that contributes to the moral fabric of the country. By examining its impact in these areas, we can appreciate how the Scriptures still inspire hope and provide guidance in contemporary America.

In American literature, *The Bible* has served as a rich source of inspiration for countless authors. From the allegorical works of Nathaniel Hawthorne to the fiery prose of Mark Twain, biblical references often underpin the narratives, offering profound insights into the human condition. For instance, the themes of redemption and transformation resonate deeply within American storytelling. Writers frequently evoke biblical imagery to explore complex characters and their moral struggles, allowing readers to reflect on their own lives and choices. This literary connection not only enriches the art form, but it also instills a sense of hope, emphasizing the possibility of grace and forgiveness, echoed throughout the biblical narrative.

The influence of *The Bible* on American law is also significant, informing many principles that underpin the legal system. Legal concepts like justice and equality, which are grounded in an objective moral law, find their roots in biblical teachings. The Ten Commandments, for instance, have served as a foundational ethical guide that shapes societal standards of right and wrong. In contemporary discussions on moral legislation, biblical precepts continue to inform debates on issues like human rights and social justice. This intertwining of Scripture and law emphasizes a hopeful vision of a just society, advocating for policies that align with the ethical teachings found in the pages of *The Bible*.

Ethics and morality in America are also deeply affected by biblical principles, framing the nation's collective conscience. The teachings of love, compassion, and forgiveness, central to biblical doctrine, encourage citizens to foster a culture of empathy and understanding. Social reform efforts throughout history, such as the abolition of slavery and the women's rights movement, have all drawn heavily on biblical narratives that champion the worth of everyone. This moral compass, rooted in Scripture, inspires hope for a society that values justice and equality, promoting a future where everyone can thrive.

Literature as a Window into the Human Condition

THE IMPACT OF biblical themes on American literature is immense, echoing through the works of notable authors such as Nathaniel Hawthorne, John Milton, and William

Faulkner. Their narratives, often steeped in moral quandaries and spiritual reflections, reveal a persistent yearning for meaning amid human suffering. In Hawthorne's tales, for instance, the shadows of sin and redemption weave a complex tapestry that reflects the biblical narrative, compelling readers to confront their own inner conflicts.

Delving deep into the themes of free will, obedience, and the consequences of humanity's choices, Milton uses the *Genesis* narrative as a springboard in *Paradise Lost*. The epic poem not only retells the story of Adam and Eve but also invites readers to reflect on the nature of sin and redemption. Through vivid language and rich imagery, Milton encourages a sense of hope and the possibility of salvation, illustrating how biblical narratives can inspire optimism even amid humanity's fallibility.

Using biblical themes as a backdrop for exploring human emotions and relationships, Faulkner creates a tapestry of experiences that resonate with audiences. In his *As I Lay Dying*, the burial of the Bundren family's matriarch echoes the sacrificial undertones of biblical narratives. As the family members navigate their own trials, Faulkner presents a story of commitment and humanity's inherent flaws, emphasizing the importance of love and perseverance in the face of adversity. This optimistic portrayal encourages readers to reflect on their own lives, revealing the potential for growth and understanding in difficult times.

Within such explorations lie an undeniable sadness, as the authors grapple with human imperfections and the seemingly insurmountable distance between divine ideals and earthly realities. The richness of these stories not only provides a foundation for moral and ethical discussions but also opens a window into the human experience. By tapping into these timeless tales, authors explore themes of redemption, love, sacrifice, and the struggle between good and evil, ultimately reflecting the complexities of life in a way that resonates across cultures and generations.

Law as a Foundation for Social Reform

THROUGHOUT history, the interplay between biblical principles and American law has shaped a legal framework that is deeply rooted in religious ethics. This relationship reflects an aspiration for justice and moral order, and its implications resonate through various aspects of the legal system. By examining the foundations of American law, we discern the enduring influence of biblical teachings on concepts such as justice, equality, and the rights of individuals.

At the core of American law lies the principle of justice, a fundamental tenet echoed in biblical teachings. The Scriptures emphasize the importance of fairness and impartiality, as seen in passages like *Proverbs* 21:15, which states, "When justice is done, it brings joy to the righteous." This sentiment is mirrored in the American legal system, particularly through the establishment of courts and the rule of law, which aim to ensure that justice is served without prejudice. The legal system aspires to create an environment where individuals are treated equally, further reinforcing the biblical notion that all people are created in the image of God and deserving of dignity and respect.

Not only that, but the concept of moral order, drawn from biblical ethics, also underpins many statutes and legal principles in the United States. The Ten Commandments, for instance, provide a timeless guideline for ethical behavior, influencing societal norms and legal standards. Laws pertaining to theft, murder, and perjury can be traced back to these commandments, demonstrating how religious ethics have permeated American legislation. This connection underscores the belief that a society grounded in moral principles is better equipped to establish a harmonious community, as articulated in *Micah* 6:8, which calls individuals "to act justly, to love mercy, and to walk humbly with your God."

In addition to these principles, the aspiration for justice

and moral order is exemplified through the work of men like Martin Luther King Jr. who drew heavily from biblical thought to advocate for equality and justice. His emphasis on love and respect for all individuals, as found in Jesus' teachings, galvanized a movement that sought to rectify the moral failings of society and law. This illustrates how biblical principles serve as a foundation for social reform aimed at achieving equality and justice for marginalized groups, reinforcing the idea that American law isn't just a collection of rules; it is also a reflection of a moral vision.

Ethics as a Path to Empathy and Understanding

BIBLICAL teachings have also played a crucial role in shaping America in the realm of ethics. Concepts like charity, forgiveness, and humility echo through social values, offering a path to empathy and understanding. However, the once-clear dichotomy of good versus evil has become blurred in modern discourse, leading to a pervasive sense of moral ambiguity and confusion. This moral dissonance evokes a deep sadness as people struggle to reconcile ancient doctrines with current realities, often feeling lost amid conflicting interpretations and cultural expectations.

From the foundation of the nation to contemporary debates on social issues, *The Bible* has served as a guiding force for ethical discussions. Biblical teachings promote core values such as love, justice, and compassion, which resonate deeply within American life. The emphasis on loving one's neighbor as oneself, as described in *Mark* 12:31, has been a cornerstone for advocacy in social justice movements, inspiring countless individuals to fight against inequality and promote human dignity. These principles encourage a sense of responsibility towards others, shaping how communities interact and support one another.

What's more, American political discourse has often drawn from biblical texts to justify and navigate moral dilemmas. The rhetoric surrounding issues such as abortion, marriage, and healthcare often invokes Scripture, illustrating the profound relationship between faith and legislative decisions. For example, the opposition to abortion frequently cites the sanctity of life as articulated in *The Bible*, arguing that all human life is inherently valuable. This intertwining of biblical ethics with public policy raises important questions about the role of religious values in a pluralistic society and the challenge of balancing these perspectives with secular beliefs.

Of course, the influence of biblical teachings isn't limited to individuals but also extends to communities. Churches and religious organizations have historically been at the forefront of charitable efforts, driven by the biblical mandate to care for the less fortunate, as we see in *Isaiah* 58:5-7: "True worship is to care for the poor and oppressed, and work for justice." This religious motivation has mobilized volunteers and resources, facilitating a culture of giving that is integral to our American identity. The ethical teachings of *The Bible* thus serve to unify individuals in altruistic pursuits, reinforcing the moral fabric of society.

However, the integration of biblical ethics into American moral discourse isn't without tension. Different interpretations and applications of Scripture leads to polarized views on various issues, challenging the notion of a singular moral compass. As society evolves, the relevance of certain biblical teachings is scrutinized, prompting debates over their applicability to modern ethical dilemmas. These discussions, in turn, highlight the need for an ongoing dialogue that respects diverse perspectives while seeking common ground rooted in shared values.

Values That Build Bridges Across Divides

IN MANY PARTS of America, communities flourish under the guidance of shared values and principles that foster unity, compassion, and service. A significant number of these communities derive their moral frameworks and service initiatives from biblical teachings, which promote a sense of purpose and direction in tackling social challenges. This optimistic view highlights the positive impact that such values can have on societal development, illustrating how biblical principles can inspire individuals and communities alike to engage in acts of kindness and support.

One of the core biblical principles that resonates with community values is the concept of love and compassion. The teachings of Jesus, which emphasize loving one's neighbor, lay the groundwork for community service initiatives. For instance, many churches organize food drives, clothing donations, and volunteer efforts to assist the less fortunate. These actions stem from a genuine desire to reflect the love described in Scripture, proving that such spiritual teachings can translate into meaningful community efforts. When individuals internalize the principle of caring for others, it transforms not just their personal lives but also enriches the entire community, contributing to a culture of generosity.

Another important aspect of biblical teachings is the idea of stewardship and accountability. The belief that individuals are entrusted with resources and responsibilities encourages proactive engagement in community welfare. This principle drives many local initiatives, such as environmental clean-ups and efforts to create sustainable living spaces. When community members view themselves as stewards of their surroundings and the well-being of their neighbors, they're more likely to take action that reflects these values. This proactive mindset leads to enhanced community bonding, as people collaborate and support one another in pursuit of common goals.

It is also important to consider how the biblical emphasis on forgiveness and reconciliation plays a significant role in strengthening community ties. In many neighborhoods, conflicts and misunderstandings create divisions; however, the principles of forgiveness encourage healing and understanding. Programs that focus on conflict resolution and restorative justice go a long way toward building bridges across divides, which, in turn, leads to more harmonious and cohesive communities.

Faith-Based Advocacy

IN OUR INCREASINGLY interconnected world, public discourse serves as a vital platform for individuals to express their beliefs and advocate for social issues. Among the many voices that shape these conversations, religious individuals often bring unique perspectives that enrich and invigorate cultural debates. By engaging in public discourse through the lens of their faith, these individuals not only share their moral convictions but also inspire hope and drive positive change in their communities.

One of the most significant ways religious individuals contribute to public discourse is by framing pressing social issues within a moral context. For instance, many faith traditions emphasize the importance of compassion, justice, and love for one's neighbor. When religious individuals speak out about issues such as poverty, inequality, and ecological stewardship, they do so from a place of deep ethical conviction that resonates with people from various backgrounds. Their perspective can galvanize support, encouraging others to recognize the shared humanity that underpins social challenges. This moral framing has the potential to strengthen the sense of collective responsibility, inviting everyone to join in the quest for solutions.

The beliefs of religious people also provide a common ground, helping to mitigate divisions that often arise in societal debates. For instance, interfaith discussions create opportunities for followers of different traditions to unite under shared values, such as peace and reconciliation. These conversations foster understanding and respect, illustrating that advocacy for social issues transcends individual beliefs. When religious individuals advocate for inclusion and collaboration, they model a hopeful vision for society where differences are celebrated rather than feared.

Additionally, the personal stories of faith-driven advocates often serve as powerful narratives that resonate with audiences. When individuals share their journeys of faith and how it informs their commitment to social justice, they humanize complex issues and create emotional connections. Such stories inspire others to act, whether through volunteering, advocacy, or simply educating themselves about important issues. The hope that springs from these narratives is infectious; it compels others to reflect on their own values and to consider how they can make a difference in the world around them. By sharing these efforts publicly, religious advocates not only raise awareness but also inspire meaningful action both within and beyond their communities. This ripple effect of hope demonstrates the potential for faith-based advocacy to effect real change in the world.

A Framework of Love and Unity

THE ONGOING debate on social justice is profoundly influenced by faith-based arguments advocating for equality and truth. These discussions are vibrant and hopeful, reflecting a deep-rooted belief in the inherent dignity of every individual. Faith communities significantly contribute to shaping public policy by championing the idea that every person deserves respect and opportunity, regardless of their background.

At the heart of many faith traditions is the principle of compassion. This ethos encourages adherents to support the marginalized and the oppressed, recognizing that social justice isn't just a political issue; it is also a moral imperative. For example, many religious groups emphasize the importance of advocating for the disenfranchised. This commitment isn't mere rhetoric; it also manifests in actions such as legislative change and grassroots movements. By aligning their beliefs with social justice efforts, faith communities not only amplify their voices but also instill hope that policies can evolve to create a more equitable society.

Not only that, but faith-based arguments also invoke a framework of love and unity, which is essential for fostering dialogue and understanding. These principles transcend cultural and ideological divides, inviting individuals of various backgrounds to engage in meaningful discussions. For instance, interfaith initiatives have been successful in bringing together diverse communities to address common social issues, demonstrating that collective action rooted in shared values leads to positive change. Such collaborations exemplify the potential of united efforts to shape public policy that prioritizes justice.

The influence of faith-based arguments on policy isn't just evident in advocacy; it is also in the moral critiques of existing laws and practices. Religious leaders often call attention to injustices within legal systems, providing a counter-narrative to status quo policies. Their criticism serves as a catalyst for reform, encouraging lawmakers to reconsider measures that may be harmful or discriminatory. The hopeful vision here lies in the belief that policies can be reformed and improved, guided by ethical principles that prioritize love and dignity for all.

The Dangers of Mischaracterizing the Separation of Church and State

THE DIALOGUE surrounding the separation of church and state often highlights a fundamental misunderstanding of the intentions of the Founding Fathers, particularly regarding the role of religion in public life. As such, those who seek to abolish *The Bible*'s influence are mischaracterizing the original intent behind the separation of church and state, leading to a disheartening divide in society and a profound loss of cultural heritage.

The Framers of the Constitution, to a man, all championed the idea of religious freedom rooted in the belief that everyone should be able to practice their faith without government interference.[4] However, contrary to the "learned"

---

4   *The Framers of the Constitution*: The 55 men who drafted the U.S. Constitution are known as the Framers of the Constitution. The Framers were delegates from 12 states who met in Philadelphia, to revise the Articles of Confederation, some 10 years after its creation. But rather than simply revise the outdated Articles, they chose to create a completely new document—the U.S. Constitution—which was approved on September 17, 1787.

The 55 delegates who attended the Constitutional Convention were a distinguished body of men who represented a cross section of 18th-century American leadership. In addition to Benjamin Franklin, notable delegates included George Washington, James Madison, Alexander Hamilton, James Wilson, Gouverneur Morris, Edmond Randolph, and Roger Sherman.

Almost all of the Founding Fathers were well-educated men of means who were dominant in their communities and states, and many were also prominent in national affairs. Virtually every one had taken part in the Revolution; at least 29 had served in the Continental forces, most of them in positions of command. Many were born into prominent families, while others came from more humble beginnings. Many were lawyers, but others were merchants, manufacturers, shippers, land speculators, bankers, physicians, small farmers, and a minister. Some were largely self-taught, while others attended colonial colleges or academies. In terms of religious affiliation, the men mirrored the overwhelmingly Protestant character of American religious life at the time and were members of a wide variety of denominations. Only two were Roman Catholics.

Ironically, there were several key Founders who, for various reasons, didn't attend the Constitutional Convention, most notably, Thomas Jefferson who was serving as the ambassador to France at the time. He did, however, stay in touch with the progress of the convention by way of his close friend James Madison who is considered the "Father of the Constitution." Other notable absentees included John Adams who didn't attend because he was in London, serving as the American ambassador to Great Britain at the time.

While both Jefferson and Adams were staunch Anti-Federalists who generally opposed any strengthening of the federal government, and as such might not have attended even if they weren't overseas, there were others who clearly didn't attend the convention for political reasons: Patrick Henry didn't attend because he feared the convention would create a stronger central government, which he believed would undermine individual liberties and state power, famously saying that he "smelled a rat." Then there was Samuel Adams who didn't attend because he opposed a strong central government, aligning himself with other prominent "Anti-Federalists," like John Hancock and James Monroe, who

opinion of many like my professor, this doesn't equate to the total exclusion of religious principles from public discourse. In their quest to create a secular state, so-called "separation" advocates overlook the reality that religion played a significant role in America's founding and in the lives of its citizens. By disregarding this historical fact, they're not only trying to rewrite history, but they're also eroding a vital aspect of the American identity that once promoted a sense of unity and shared moral values.

For a great many people, *The Bible* isn't just a book; it also embodies countless lessons, cultural narratives, and ethical frameworks that shape personal and collective experiences. The attempt to minimize its presence in discussions about morality or law signifies a broader disconnection from the spiritual heritage that has guided American culture for centuries.

This distortion of the idea of separation also contributes to a chilling atmosphere for those who hold religious beliefs, leading to feelings of alienation and exclusion. An approach that dismisses *The Bible*'s influence neglects the diverse fabric of American society, where individuals from various faiths find strength, hope, and community in their traditions. The erosion of this inclusive approach leaves many feeling as if their beliefs have no place in a nation that once flourished on the principles of tolerance, mutual respect, and unity.

As these core values are increasingly supplanted by exclusion, distrust, and division, a significant dialogue emerges around the implications of removing *The Bible* from public life. This exclusion not only reflects a broader societal trend, but it also symbolizes a disconnect from a shared moral framework that has historically fostered community and cooperation.

---

also chose to not attend. Although he initially opposed the Constitution, Adams eventually did support its ratification after Framers included a Bill of Rights.

Such absences go a long way in highlighting the diversity of the Founding Fathers' opinions during these critical formative years of the U.S. government.

At the heart of this transformation is a growing alienation among diverse groups within society. As individuals increasingly isolate themselves within ideological silos, the ability to engage with differing perspectives diminishes. This alienation is evident in various social spheres, including politics, education, and even within families. The absence of shared values, often grounded in biblical teachings, has led to a fragmentation of the social fabric. When people no longer share common moral standards, the paths to understanding and unity become obscured.

Further complicating this landscape is the increasing exclusion of religious perspectives from public discourse. In many institutions, particularly educational and governmental, *The Bible* and its teachings have been sidelined as evidence of the growing secularization of American life. This exclusion not only alienates those who find value and guidance in biblical texts, but it also erodes the potential for meaningful dialogue that bridges divides. When religious perspectives are dismissed, an opportunity for mutual respect and understanding is lost, further entrenching division among communities.

This division is aggravated by a prevailing culture that often emphasizes individualism over community. The focus on personal rights overshadows collective responsibility, leading to a society where individuals feel disconnected from one another. This detachment is particularly evident in the contentious political climate, where opposing sides increasingly view one another with suspicion and disdain. In such an environment, the biblical call for love, compassion, and unity is overshadowed by a mentality that emphasizes conflict over reconciliation.

Instead of Sowing Seeds of Division and Ignorance

IN TODAY'S increasingly polarized society, discussions around the role of religion in public life can't help but spark intense debate. A significant claim, made by many educators like my professor, is that *The Bible* should be removed from public discourse to promote a more harmonious world. However, this perspective overlooks the true essence of social unity and the positive contributions that the Scriptures bring to divided communities. It is therefore essential to adopt a correct view of Christian unity—one that promotes understanding and collaboration across diverse backgrounds.

The notion that *The Bible* must be removed from public life stems from a misunderstanding of religious coexistence. It is often claimed that excluding biblical teachings will create a more unified society. However, this perspective fails to recognize the fundamental principles of love, compassion, and reconciliation that are deeply rooted in Christian teachings. By embracing the vital lessons found in Scripture, we cultivate a sense of common ground that unites us rather than divides us.

What's more, the idea of removing the biblical influence from American culture disregards the positive impact that Christian unity has on addressing social issues. Many challenges facing our communities, such as poverty, injustice, and inequality, can only be effectively tackled when seen through the lens of Christian principles. When individuals come together in pursuit of a common cause, inspired by the message of Scripture, they create a powerful force for change. Collaboration among diverse groups, motivated by shared values, helps to foster understanding and respect, thereby healing the divides that currently exist.

What a shame, then, that so many of our so-called "higher institutions of learning" could serve as platforms for respectful conversations. So sad that they could honor viewpoints that celebrate the universal themes of hope and love found in biblical teachings. But so often they do not; instead of sowing seeds that encourage mutual respect and common ground, they're busy promoting a different kind of conversation, preferring instead to sow seeds of division and ignorance.

On the other hand, when we promote a correct under-standing of Christian unity, we emphasize the importance of dialogue and mutual respect. Rather than viewing *The Bible* as a divisive text, we can approach it as a resource for building bridges between differing beliefs. Encouraging such interactions can transform public life, allowing indi-viduals to engage in meaningful and respectful ways.

Ultimately, any effort to remove the Scriptures from public discourse, in the name of promoting cultural har-mony, turns out to be a misguided attempt. Instead, a cor-rect view of social unity reveals that *The Bible* is a guiding light for inspiring hope in a darkened world. By embracing the transforming power of its teachings, individuals can work together to overcome barriers and enrich public life. In nurturing these connections, we lay the groundwork for a more equitable and compassionate society—one where the strengths of all beliefs are recognized and valued.

In conclusion, while the perspective that *The Bible* should be excluded from public life is prevalent, it's crucial to champion a hopeful vision that recognizes the impor-tance of genuine Christian unity. By encouraging discus-sions that include biblical teachings, we open the door to collaboration, understanding, and positive change. This hopeful approach taps into the rich potential of our diverse communities, paving the way for a future where unity and harmony triumph over division and ignorance.

CHAPTER TWO

The Broken Machine:

A Corrupted Body Politic

THE NEXT time I visited my professor after class, he didn't hesitate to ask me, "Well, have you given any more thought about our last conversation?"

"I have, sir, yes," I replied.

"And what have you concluded?"

"You mean about why the current state of affairs are so rife with division and anger?"

"That's right, my boy. Do you see how America would be better off if we followed the advice of the Founding Fathers when they sought to separate church from state? Just imagine if we moderns could simply learn from their foresight; no more religious fanaticism, no more bigotry or hate. Do you see that now?"

And having considered his words for several moments, I replied, "Well, sir, pardon me for saying so, but from what I can tell, looking at American history, the Founders never intended for us to remove all traces of *The Bible* and its teachings from our political life. They were just trying to limit the power of either institution, through a wall of separation, as Roger Williams of Rhode Island, first described it."

The old man, again, eyed me suspiciously. Did he think me impertinent, I wondered, for daring to question his position? His authority?

"You mean Thomas Jefferson, don't you?" he asked.

"Sir?" I replied.

"Don't you mean Jefferson, when you cite the beginnings of the American understanding of the separation of church and state?"

"No, sir. Thomas Jefferson wrote about the wall of separation in the eighteenth century, more than a hundred years *after* Roger Williams originated the idea in a 1644 letter he wrote to a fellow pastor."

"Hmmm, you don't say." Suddenly, the old man smiled at me, and said, "Marvelous. I admit, I do admire your confidence. You know, I believe I underestimated you; not that I didn't think you were an intelligent young man. No, sir. In fact, I do believe you're *too* intelligent."

Puzzled by this, I said, "*Too* intelligent, sir?"

"You heard me."

"I did, Professor. But I'm not sure what you're trying to say."

He then leaned forward across his huge desk to get a closer look at me. "What I'm saying, son, is that anyone as smart as you shouldn't be wasting his time with *The Bible*." Then he paused, as if giving me time to consider his words. "Mark my words, my boy, if you ever want to make your mark in this crazy world of politics, you'll put that infernal book back on the shelf and stop warping your mind with its contents."

"But ... Professor," I muttered.

"Oh, don't take it so hard, son. Just give it time; someday you'll grow out of this adolescent nonsense of yours. But for now just take my advice. In matters of your political science studies, avoid any mention of that *Bible* of yours.

I'm telling you, superstition and diplomacy simply don't mix."

And as my professor left off speaking, he leaned back in his chair and eyed me, quite content with himself and his appraisal of the situation. And again, in that same moment, I determined within myself to find out the truth for myself.

"Never forget the religious character of our origin. Our fathers were brought here by their high veneration for the Christian religion. They journeyed by its light, and labored in its hope. They sought to incorporate its principles into every aspect of American society, and to diffuse its influence through all their institutions—civil, political, and literary."

Daniel Webster

When Public Discourse is Deprived of Discussing The Bible

THE INTERSECTION of faith and politics has long been a contentious topic in American society. But if history has taught us anything it's that when public discourse is deprived of any discussion of *The Bible* and its principles, we're not strengthening our nation's political life, as many academics like my professor claimed; rather, we're undermining the very foundation on which our American republic was built. What's more, this isn't merely an academic argument, but it also speaks to the very essence of moral and ethical governance. When biblical principles are marginalized, the result is a society rife with moral decay, disillusionment, and cynicism.

To begin with, biblical principles have historically offered a moral compass that has guided social values and legislative decisions. Concepts such as truth, justice, and compassion are deeply rooted in the Judeo-Christian tradition.[5] When these vital principles are excluded from public discourse, as seen in debates about welfare, poverty, and social justice, the discussions often devolve into mere political maneuvering, devoid of moral grounding. Consequently, this lack of ethical oversight leads to rampant corruption, as decisions are made based primarily on self-interest rather than the common good.

Removing these principles also aids and abets anyone eager to manipulate the political system. In a constitutional republic like America, the integrity of the electoral process is paramount. However, when political rhetoric is stripped of moral underpinnings, it becomes easier for unscrupulous actors to twist narratives to serve their own agendas. Misinformation proliferates, and citizens become targets for propaganda that preys on their fears and biases. This manipulation not only jeopardizes the electoral pro-

---

5   *The Judeo-Christian Tradition*: The idea that Judaism and Christianity share many cultural and religious traits, despite their historical differences, is known as the Judeo-Christian tradition. These shared traits include the fact that Christianity has its cultural and religious roots in Judaism, as well as the fact that much of Jewish Scripture, *The Old Testament*, comprises the first half of *The Christian Bible*. Virtually every Christian moral principle derives from *The Hebrew Bible*, such as: "Love your neighbor as yourself." (*Leviticus* 19:18)

By most accounts, the term was originally coined in the first decades of the 1800s, in describing any Christian church that clung to certain Jewish traditions, hoping to convert Jews to the faith. It wasn't until the 1930s, though, according to historian K. Healan Gaston, that the term came to be used in the context of America itself, at a time when the country sought to forge a unified cultural identity to distinguish itself from European fascism and communism. Then, in 1939, George Orwell spoke, for the first time, of Judeo-Christian values in an ethical—rather than a theological—sense, along with the phrase the "Judeo-Christian scheme of morals." And by the mid-20th century, the term became shorthand for biblical ethics in general, such as the dignity of human life, common decency, and support for traditional family values.

Some have even gone so far as to say that this commingling of Judeo-Christian cultural traits has formed the basis of Western civilization, citing the shared values and connected fates of these two faiths.

cess, but it also erodes public trust in institutions, which is the bedrock of any free and open society.

Is it any wonder, then, that disillusionment and cynicism are natural extensions of a self-interested, self-centered culture? When citizens perceive that their leaders are acting without ethical consideration, they lose faith in the system. A society thrives when its citizens engage and believe in the efficacy of their participation. However, a continuous cycle of disappointment, driven by corruption and manipulation, just fuels an already cynical populace. This disillusionment further disengages individuals from political processes, leading to lower voter turnout and a general sense of disenfranchisement.

Additionally, the moral decay resulting from the absence of biblical principles is palpable in contemporary culture. Ethical frameworks traditionally rooted in religious teachings are in danger of being replaced by relativism, where the concept of right and wrong becomes subject to individual whims. This moral ambiguity leads to a society where the shared values that once unified citizens are abandoned, paving the way for behaviors that contribute to cultural decay. The breakdown of these communal values manifests in increased crime rates, substance abuse, and deterioration of social relationships, all of which erode the fabric of civil society.

Foundational Values That Shape the Nation's Identity

THIS IS WHY the role of biblical principles in American governance is so significant, as it intertwines the foundational values that have shaped the nation's identity and its approach to justice, integrity, and individual dignity. A hopeful examination of this relationship reveals that these principles serve as a moral compass, guiding political discourse and fostering a framework where justice and the inherent value of human life can flourish.

At the heart of American governance is the value of justice, a principle often echoed throughout *The Bible*. The concept of justice isn't just a legal institution; it's also a divine command, urging people to act fairly and protect the rights of everyone. Biblical texts like *Zechariah* 7:9 tell us: "This is what the Lord of Hosts says: 'Administer true justice. Show loving devotion and compassion to one another,'" reminding leaders that justice should be pursued with both righteousness and compassion. This ethical foundation encourages lawmakers to strive for equitable systems that reflect both moral integrity and societal well-being, ensuring that every citizen is treated with fairness.

Integrity, another cornerstone of effective governance, is emphasized in numerous biblical passages. *Proverbs* 11:3 asserts, "The integrity of the upright guides them," encapsulating the importance of honesty and ethical conduct in leadership. In a political arena often marred by scandals and deception, these principles call upon public officials to pursue transparency and accountability, nurturing trust within communities. By upholding integrity, leaders reinforce a culture where truth prevails and corruption is challenged, thus enhancing the relationship between citizens and their government.

What's more, the value of individual lives is a fundamental concept derived from biblical teachings, underscoring the belief, as stated in *Genesis* 1:27, that every person is created in the image of God. This belief instills a profound respect for human dignity and rights, shaping policies that prioritize the welfare of individuals. In a diverse nation, acknowledging the sanctity of life translates into advocacy for social justice, health and human services, and educational resources that uphold the worth of every citizen. By embedding this value into governance, society is empowered to uplift and protect the most vulnerable, nourishing a sense of community and mutual respect.

As we navigate the complexities of modern political discourse, the infusion of biblical principles offers a hopeful vision for American governance. As William Penn described it: "If you would rule well, you must rule for God, and to do that, you must be ruled by Him. Those who will not be governed by God will be ruled by tyrants."

Sentiments like this encourage honesty, sincerity, and self-awareness, urging political figures to engage with empathy and humility. In a time marked by division, a return to these foundational teachings can inspire leaders to seek common ground, putting aside differences to promote the common good. By doing so, they cultivate a political landscape characterized by dialogue and collaboration, ultimately leading to more effective governance.

A Divine Call for Justice

A FUNDAMENTAL theme woven throughout the fabric of Scripture—justice—advocates for the fair treatment of all individuals and emphasizes the need for laws that protect every citizen equally. The principle of justice not only serves as a moral compass for believers, but it also acts as a reminder of the responsibilities that come with governance and community. Throughout *The Bible*, passages illustrate the importance of treating others with fairness and integrity, crafting a narrative that underscores a divine call for justice in society.

One of the foundational elements of biblical justice is the inherent dignity of every person. *Leviticus* 19:15 provides us with a clear mandate against discrimination: "You shouldn't judge your neighbor in a way that unjustly favors the poor or unfairly oppresses the rich." In no uncertain terms, then, this verse urges those in authority to act in a way that respects the rights of every individual, regardless of their socio-economic status. As such, the call for impartiality isn't merely a suggestion; it is also presented as a divine command that requires adherence from those who seek to live righteously.

In addition to promoting equal justice under the law,

The Bible highlights the importance of advocating for the vulnerable and marginalized. *Proverbs* 31:8-9 challenges us to "speak up for those who can't speak for themselves, for the rights of all who are destitute." This prime directive compels us to not only recognize the injustices present in our communities but to also actively work towards rectifying them. The act of speaking out is presented as a moral obligation; it emphasizes that true justice involves a proactive approach to safeguarding the rights of those who don't have a voice. This is a powerful reminder that justice isn't a passive stance but, rather, an active pursuit that demands engagement and commitment.

The New Testament also reinforces these central themes, particularly through the teachings of Jesus Christ, Who consistently emphasized compassion and fairness. In *Luke* 10:25-37, Jesus illustrated, in the Parable of the Good Samaritan, that true neighborliness transcends cultural and social boundaries. The Samaritan's actions—helping a wounded traveler despite his background—serve as a model for how individuals should treat one another. This story urges us to extend justice and kindness to everyone, challenging societal norms that needlessly incite division and prejudice.

Integrity as the Cornerstone of Leadership

ONE OF THE cornerstones of leadership is integrity, a concept deeply rooted in scriptural teachings. The call for honesty and accountability in leadership not only shapes the actions of leaders but also influences the trust and faith of those they lead. As leaders navigate their responsibilities, they are implored to fulfill their promises and act selflessly, reflecting values espoused in sacred texts.

At the heart of integrity lies honesty, which *The Bible* frequently emphasizes. *Proverbs* 10:9 states, "Whoever walks in integrity walks securely, but whoever takes crooked paths will be found out." This passage underscores the importance of truthfulness as a guiding principle for leaders. When leaders are honest, they cultivate a culture of transparency and trust within their organizations. This environment allows community members to feel safe in their roles, knowing that their leaders will uphold their commitments. Consequently, honesty fosters loyalty and encourages a collaborative spirit essential for any successful endeavor.

Accountability is another crucial element of integrity in leadership. A leader's ability to own their decisions and actions not only reflects their character but also sets a powerful example for others. In *James* 3:1, it is noted: "Not many of you should become teachers, my fellow believers, because you know that we who teach will be judged more strictly." This passage serves as a reminder that with leadership comes responsibility. Leaders must be prepared to answer for the consequences of their actions, reinforcing the need for accountability. When leaders accept responsibility, they inspire others to do the same, thus creating a culture where everyone values their commitments and contributions.

Integrity also calls for leaders to act selflessly. This selflessness aligns with the biblical principle of servanthood, as demonstrated by Jesus in *Mark* 10:45, where He stated, "For even the Son of Man didn't come to be served but to serve." A selfless leader prioritizes the welfare of their team over personal gain. By putting others first, they not only gain respect but also enhance community morale and productivity. In such an environment, fellow citizens are more likely to emulate these selfless behaviors, fostering a supportive community driven by shared goals.

The Inherent Worth of the Individual

A FUNDAMENTAL principle—the inherent worth of the individual—resonates deeply throughout American history, particularly within the context of the early *Federalist* and constitutional debates. These documents not only served to outline the framework of governance but also highlighted a profound respect for human life, echoing the moral and ethical teachings found in biblical beliefs. This intertwining of faith and governance is essential in understanding the philosophical foundations of the United States, demonstrating how the reverence for life has shaped the nation's values and legal principles.

One of the most influential works printed in Revolutionary America—written under the collective name of *The Federalist Papers*—is one in which the most prominent theme is the protection of individual rights, which inherently underscores the dignity of each and every human life.[6] In *Federalist* No. 10, written by James Madison, he argued that the rights of individuals are paramount and must be safeguarded against the potential tyranny of the majority. Ironically, Madison did this by drawing a distinction between a democracy and a republic. In his view: "Pure democracies," as he called them, "have always been spectacles of turbulence and contention; have always been found incompatible with personal security, or the rights of

---

6   *The Federalist Papers*: Published between October 1787 and May 1788, a collection of 85 essays, written under the pen name "Publius," *The Federalist Papers* were written to promote the ratification of the Constitution of the United States. We now know the 3 men who anonymously wrote the papers—originally known as simply *The Federalist*—were Alexander Hamilton, John Jay, and James Madison. Their purpose in writing the essays was to build political support to ratify the newly constructed U.S. Constitution, in the hope of replacing the Articles of Confederation that were seen as insufficient to meet the needs of the fledgling nation. And even though *The Federalist Papers* were hastily written and published, they were widely read and had a tremendous impact in shaping subsequent American political institutions. Perhaps the greatest advocate of *The Federalist Papers* was none other than George Washington, who secretly transmitted several of the first published essays to family members in Virginia so the essays could be more widely read. And while no one can say for sure how much *The Papers* affected the ratification of the Constitution, they are to this day considered some of the finest presentations of political thinking ever put in print.

property; and have, in general, been as short in their lives as they have been violent in their deaths." He said this because, in his view "pure democracies" are teeming with "men of factious tempers, of local prejudices, or of sinister designs," who "by intrigue, by corruption, or by other means, first obtain the necessary votes, and then betray the interests of the people." His remedy for this: "A republic, by which I mean a government in which the scheme of representation takes place," which "opens a different prospect, and promises the cure for which we are seeking."

In other words, in a "pure democracy," the rights of the minority are always at risk of being overwhelmed by majority, or "mob," rule—a risk that can only be safeguarded by way of a representational government. So, in this way, Madison further explained, "the influence of factious leaders may kindle a flame within their own particular states, but will be unable to spread a general conflagration throughout the other states."

This is, of course, why the Founding Fathers determined to establish American civil liberties on the firm foundation of a constitutional republic, as opposed to a pure democracy; it also explains why our Founders established foundational institutions like the Electoral College.[7]

---

7 *The Electoral College*: Created by the Framers of the U.S. Constitution, the Electoral College was designed to provide a method of election that was both feasible and consistent with a republican form of government. As such, this group of presidential electors is formed every 4 years to decide who will be the American president and vice president. It does this through a process described in Article 2 of the Constitution: a majority of electoral votes (270 or more) is required to elect the president and vice president. If no candidate achieves a majority, a contingent election is held by the House of Representatives, to elect the president, and by the Senate, to elect the vice president. The number of electoral votes exercised by each state is equal to that state's congressional delegation, which equals 2 senators for each state, plus the number of representatives for that state based on it size and population. Each state appoints electors using legal procedures determined by its legislature. Federal office holders, including senators and representatives, can't be electors.

Once the Electoral College was established, several delegates, including George Mason and Robert Morris, acknowledged its ability to protect the elec-

This perspective, which upholds the importance of every individual as distinct from the collective, thus mirrors biblical principles that advocate for the intrinsic value of each and every person, demonstrating that the Founding Fathers were influenced by these moral imperatives. As such, *The Federalist Papers* serve as a testament to the notion that respect for every human life must be enshrined into the very fabric of American governance.

All this further illustrates the extent to which early constitutional debates reflected a deep-seated commitment to protecting the rights, freedoms, and lives of individuals. The First Amendment, for example, establishes the freedom of speech, religion, and assembly, all of which stem from a belief in the inherent worth of the individual. By securing these crucial freedoms, once and for all, the Framers of the Constitution aimed to create a society where life is valued and individuals can thrive. This direct correlation between constitutional thought and biblical teachings emphasizes the belief that every life possesses divine significance, warranting protection and respect.

This also shows how biblical teachings and *Federalist* principles have influenced American legal and ethical standards. The principle that all humans are created in the image of God (*Genesis* 1:27) forms the backbone of many social justice movements. This belief has led to a broader interpretation of the right to life as not merely the absence of violence but the presence of opportunities for growth,

---

tion process from cabal, corruption, intrigue, and faction. Alexander Hamilton, in *Federalist* No. 68, laid out the advantages to the Electoral College: the electors come directly from the people and them alone, for that purpose only, and for that time only. This avoided a party-run legislature or a permanent body that could be influenced by foreign interests before each election. Hamilton explained that the election was to take place among all the states, so no corruption in any individual state could taint the "great body of the people" in their selection. Hamilton also argued that electors meeting in the state capitals were able to have information unavailable to the general public, and since no federal officeholder could be an elector, none of the electors would be beholden to any presidential candidate.

education, and prosperity. In all of this, then, we see how the philosophical threads connecting *Federalist*, constitutional, and biblical thinking reflect a comprehensive view of human life that transcends mere existence.

Not merely nostalgic ideals, these principles are critical in examining and evaluating the conduct of politicians and the policies they implement. Or as John Witherspoon put it: "It is in the man of piety and inward principle that we may expect to find the uncorrupted patriot, the useful citizen, and the invincible soldier. May God grant that in America, true religion and civil liberty may be inseparable."

The Consequences of Neglecting Biblical Principles

IN THE CONTEXT of political governance, ignoring biblical principles leads to significant political disillusionment and erodes the trust necessary for a vibrant society. As campaigns become increasingly driven by self-interest and false promises, citizens feel alienated from the political process, further aggravating societal divides and undermining civic engagement.

At the heart of this issue is the role of integrity in political leadership. Biblical principles often emphasize honesty, accountability, and service to others, which are crucial for fostering trust between leaders and citizens. When politicians prioritize their personal agendas over these ethical standards, they can manipulate public sentiment through misleading rhetoric. This manipulation not only disillusions voters but also creates a culture where dishonesty becomes normalized, further deteriorating public faith in government. As a result, campaigns that focus solely on gaining power rather than addressing the genuine needs of the electorate contribute to a cycle of disappointment and cynicism, where voters feel they have no true representatives.

The neglect of biblical principles also leads to a deep-seated alienation among citizens. As individuals become disillusioned by a political system that appears unresponsive to their concerns, their willingness to engage in the political process diminishes. The feeling that their voices are disregarded results in voter apathy, where individuals choose to not participate in elections or civic activities. This disengagement creates a vicious cycle, as low voter turnout further shifts power towards those already entrenched in the system, often leading to policies that reflect the interests of a select few rather than the community as a whole.

Not only that, but self-interest in political campaigns also creates an environment where divisive rhetoric prevails. When candidates prioritize winning over uniting, they exploit societal fears and divisions for electoral gain. This approach not only distorts political discourse but also undermines cultural cohesion. Citizens are led to believe that their only identity lies in political affiliation, alienating them even further from their community. And as biblical principles that advocate for love, unity, and mutual respect are omitted from political discussions, an atmosphere of hostility inevitably arises, where collaboration is seen as weakness and discord as strength.

An Atmosphere of Distrust

WHEN LEADERS, who are meant to guide and inspire, disregard ethical standards rooted in these principles, the fallout isn't just immediate but also deep and lasting. Citizens who rely on their leaders for honesty and integrity are often left feeling betrayed and wary, leading to a pervasive atmosphere of distrust.

The role of leaders extends beyond mere authority; they are also seen as moral compasses in society. When such figures choose to overlook ethics, it sends a chilling message: that integrity is negotiable and that the ends justify the means. This stark reality becomes painfully evident as leaders prioritize personal gain over the welfare of their constituents. For instance, political scandals and financial fraud create a landscape filled with skepticism. Voters begin to question not only the actions of individuals but the entire system that allows such behavior to flourish. In this environment, fear and suspicion take root, watering the seeds of discontent among the populace.

The spiritual implications of this disregard for biblical principles can't be understated. Many people turn to their faith for guidance in navigating life's complexities. When leaders fail to uphold these values, they inadvertently lead others away from the ethical paths that provide clarity and direction. The erosion of trust becomes a cyclical problem; as leaders stray further from integrity, citizens not only lose faith in them but also begin to question their own moral foundations. This downward spiral fuels an environment where ethical ambiguity reigns, and the gap between personal beliefs and collective values widens, leaving communities fragmented and searching for a semblance of stability.

This loss of trust not only affects relationships between leaders and citizens but also hampers cooperation within communities. A society built on mutual respect and shared values can often withstand challenges, but when trust is shattered, collaboration diminishes. People become less willing to support initiatives or engage in communal responsibilities out of fear that their efforts may be exploited. The sadness lies in witnessing a community's decline from a united force into a collection of isolated individuals, each wary of the other.

A Re-Engagement With Justice, Integrity, and the Common Good

AS CULTURAL values drift away from a foundation anchored in ethics and accountability, the electorate finds itself trapped in a disheartening perception of politics as little more than a game devoid of genuine responsibility. This erosion of trust not only diminishes voter participation, but it also exacerbates the sense of alienation from society.

When biblical principles of honesty, integrity, and service are sidelined, political engagement suffers. Without these moral guidelines, individuals interpret political actions through a lens of skepticism, believing that motives are self-serving rather than community-oriented. This shift inevitably breeds cynicism, which, in turn, undermines any motivation on the part of citizens to participate in the political process. When people perceive politicians as lacking accountability, they can't help but question the power of their vote, leading to lower turnout rates and apathy towards issues that require urgent attention.

The impact of this moral vacuum can be seen in the increasing number of disenchanted voters who choose to disengage rather than participate. When core values that once guided leaders and citizens alike are ignored, the electorate becomes disillusioned, feeling that their choices are irrelevant. The decline in voter engagement is a testament to this disconnect, as fewer and fewer people view elections as an opportunity for meaningful change. Instead, they see them as futile exercises, reinforcing a sense of helplessness in the face of a political system they perceive as corrupt and illegitimate.

What's more, the absence of a moral foundation in political discourse leads to divisive strategies that prioritize personal gain over the common good. This not only alienates voters but also fuels an environment where misinformation thrives. In a cultural environment where truth is malleable and accountability is hollow, the electorate is further pushed away from civic engagement. The consequences are dire, resulting in a society fragmented by distrust, as citizens become more and more convinced that their participation in the democratic process is useless.

In conclusion, in a political landscape marred by corruption and manipulation, it's vital to acknowledge the foundational role that biblical principles play in American culture. The notion that *The Bible* should remain unmentioned in political discourse detracts from the very essence of governance that seeks justice, integrity, and the common good. As we navigate the complexities of contemporary politics, a re-engagement with these principles is the only antidote to widespread disillusionment and cynicism. Ignoring these biblical teachings merely perpetuates a broken machine—one that, without its moral imperative, risks losing its original essence. It is not just another option to include these discussions; it is absolutely necessary if we ever hope to restore our faith in the American political system our Founders first envisioned so long ago.

CHAPTER THREE

The Myth of Pure Democracy:

The Real Story of American Governance

LIE #3:

America was Founded on the Principle of Pure Democracies Like That of Ancient Greece...

MY PROFESSOR looked at me thoughtfully across his desk and asked me with all earnestness, "So, have you decided what you'd like to write about for your extra credit essay this year?"

"I haven't, Professor, no," I replied respectfully. "I just can't seem to make up my mind."

"Don't you think it's about time that you do? Time is running out, you know."

I nodded affirmatively, and said, "I realize that. But I'm afraid it can't be helped."

"Really," the old man replied with an inquisitive tilt of his head. "What's holding you up, if you don't mind me asking?"

"Well, for one thing, the list you provided us to choose from is ... how do I say this?" I paused momentarily, not sure how my answer would be received.

The professor leaned forward in anticipation. "The list?

What about the list? If anything, I would have thought providing you with a list to choose from would have helped you narrow down the field. Did I miscalculate in that assumption?"

I shrugged, apologetically, not wanting to upset the man.

"Please, my friend," he continued, "you don't have to worry. I can see by your reaction that you feel I'll be offended with your answer. Is that it?"

Again, I nodded, and said, "I do believe so, Professor, yes. And while I appreciate the spirit with which you offered your choices, in my opinion, I feel like you injected a hidden bias without meaning to do so."

The old man's eyebrows rose up like furry caterpillars startled by a predator. "A hidden bias? How did I do that?"

I opened my mouth for just a moment, about to respond, but then thought better of it, and closed it with a nervous sigh. But this only seemed to further agitate the caterpillars as they squirmed above his ever-widening eyes.

"Please, son, I won't be offended. I promise. What is it about the list that seems to express a bias, as you call it?"

"Well, take the first subject you provided, the one about the founding principles on which America's founders looked to in 1776."

"Okay, let's do that," the professor muttered, trying hard to suppress his growing anxiety. "What is it about it that speaks to you of a hidden bias?"

"Well, as you'll recall, you asked the question, specifically, and I quote: In what way was America founded on the principles of those ancient democracies like the one in ancient Greece?"

The old man nodded eagerly, almost relieved at finally hearing what was on my mind, "Yes, of course, I do recall, I do recall. Thank Heaven that is all I asked," he said with a nervous laugh that made me laugh, too. "You had me worried for a moment."

"No worries, sir." I replied, still unsure as to how to

continue.

"But pardon me for saying so, son," the professor continued, "I still don't think I fully understand your objection. How does my question reveal a hidden bias?"

"It does so, sir, in that I believe America's founders never intended to formulate their new government based on the Grecian model but, rather, they sought to build it in terms of what would more properly be called a constitutional republic. Because as the Founders saw it, government based on purely democratic rule was just a step away from 'tyranny of the majority.'"

With that, my professor calmly leaned back in his high-backed chair, and as he did, I was glad to see that the anxious caterpillars also melted away, transforming back into the quiet eyebrows of my professor. "I see," he said. "Then it appears that I had you all wrong, after all."

Tilting my head, I wondered what the old man meant by that. "Sir?"

"All wrong," he repeated quietly. "All wrong. This whole time I thought you had no idea what you were going to write about for your extra credit essay." Then he smiled. "But now I see you do know what you want to write about."

I smiled, too, and said, "Yes, sir, I believe I do; if you think it proper."

Then he nodded, and replied, "Indeed, I do think it proper. I look forward to reading it."

"I'd better get to work, then," I said, rising to my feet and turning to leave. "Good day, sir."

"Good day, young man, good day."

"Democracy is like when two wolves and one sheep vote on what they will eat for dinner. Liberty is a well-armed lamb contesting the vote."

Benjamin Franklin

Misconceptions about American Democracy

IN A WORLD increasingly enamored with the idea of democracy, America stands at a crossroads of understanding its own political identity. Contrary to popular belief, the United States was never intended to be a pure democracy akin to that of ancient Greece. Rather, it was designed as a constitutional republic, a system that offers vital protections for individuals against the tyranny of the majority. Despite a growing call for direct democracy in American politics, it's essential to reflect on why the Founding Fathers shunned this model, to uncover the implications of such a misconception in contemporary discourse.

As recent discussions about the nature of democracy and governance have intensified, it's crucial to clarify the distinction between the kind of democracies found in classical times and that of a constitutional republic currently found in the United States. While the term "democracy" suggests a government directly by the people, America's Founding Fathers established a constitutional republic to mitigate the potential dangers of mob rule. Alexander Hamilton described it this way: "It has been observed by an honorable gentleman that a pure democracy, if it were practicable, would be the most perfect government. Experience has proved that no position in politics is more false than this. The ancient democracies, in which the people themselves deliberated, never possessed one feature of good government. Their very character was tyranny; their figure deformity." Harsh words indeed, and words that naturally fly in the face of what most have been taught, and so think, about the origins of American "democracy."

At the heart of the American political system, then, is the Constitution, designed specifically to protect individual rights and limit governmental power.[8] Unlike pure

---

8   *The United States Constitution*: The primary political document of America, created on September 17, 1787, the United States Constitution was ratified

democratic systems, where the majority can impose its will on the minority, a constitutional republic incorporates numerous checks and balances intended to uphold justice and

---

on June 21, 1788. It was the product of 55 men who had originally gathered to modify the Articles of Confederation at the Constitutional Convention at Independence Hall in Philadelphia. But before long, they realized they needed to replace it with something entirely new: that brand-new document was the U.S. Constitution.

The main purpose of the Constitution was to outline the responsibilities, as well as the restrictions, of the federal government. Its first 3 articles explain the all-important doctrine of the separation of powers, which divides the federal government into 3 branches: the legislative, the executive, and the judiciary. The legislative branch comprises the bicameral Congress, consisting of the Senate and the House of Representatives (Article I); the executive branch, consisting of the president and subordinate officers (Article II); and the judiciary branch, consisting of the Supreme Court and other federal courts (Article III). Articles IV, V, and VI explain the nature of federalism, which outlines the rights and responsibilities of state governments, the states in relationship to the federal government, and the shared process of constitutional amendment. Article VII established the procedure subsequently used by the 13 states to ratify it.

At the time of its creation, the Constitution was unprecedented in its scope and intent. Of course, it was never something that was created out of thin air. Centuries of English political debates about natural rights, political absolutism, republicanism, and religious freedom influenced its creation. In writing the Constitution, the Framers were greatly indebted to documents like *Magna Carta*, the English Bill of Rights, the Virginia Declaration of Rights, The Virginia Statute for Religious Freedom, and the Declaration of Independence. In addition to ideas from English Enlightenment writers like John Locke, Montesquieu, Edward Coke, and William Blackstone, there was the Scottish Enlightenment that brought them the ideas of writers like Thomas Reid, Adam Smith, Francis Hutcheson, and Lord Kames.

In his 1774 book, *Sketches of the History of Man*, Kames prophetically observed: "The colonists have the spirit of a free people, and are inflamed with patriotism. Their population will equal that of Britain and Ireland in less than a century; and they will then be a match for the mother-country if they choose to be independent: every advantage will be on their side, as the attack must be by sea from a very great distance. Being thus delivered from a foreign yoke, their first care will be the choice of a proper government; and it is not difficult to foresee what government will be chosen. A people animated with the new blessings of liberty and independence will not incline to a kingly government … each colony will choose for itself a republican government."

Presently, the U.S. Constitution stands firmly as the oldest codified national constitution still in force in the world today.

prevent the oppression of individual freedoms. This structure includes separating powers among various branches of government, thus ensuring that no single entity can wield unchecked power. The Framers of the Constitution recognized the risk posed by majority rule—namely, that it could lead to the marginalization or outright violation of minority rights.

To that end, the First Amendment of the Constitution plays a key role in safeguarding individual liberties by outlining protections that are independent of popular vote. As such, the freedom to speak, to worship, and to assemble doesn't exist because it's popular but because it's fundamental to the dignity and autonomy of everyone. In this way, the tenets of a constitutional republic stand as a bulwark against the whims of the majority, ensuring that essential rights are preserved even when they are unpopular.

The Tyranny of the Majority

THROUGHOUT HISTORY, democracies have taken various forms, leading to diverse outcomes regarding citizens' participation, the protection of minority rights, and the implications of majority rule. Ancient democracies, particularly in places like Athens, embodied a system where citizen participation was direct and palpable, yet they were often marked by an underlying oppression of dissenting voices. In contrast, a modern political system like that of the United States, despite its flaws, is built on principles that strive to safeguard the rights of all citizens, particularly those of minority groups. Nevertheless, a pessimistic view unveils a darker reality: the struggles against the tyranny of the majority remain prevalent, often threatening the foundational principles of liberty and equality.

In ancient democracies, the populace was encouraged to engage directly in governance, fostering a sense of ownership over political processes. However, this direct participation was strictly limited to a select group of citizens—excluding women, slaves, and the poor. As such, the reality of majority rule led to the suppression of dissenting voices, as the whims of the majority could easily override the rights and perspectives of minority populations. For example, in Athens, the majority could dictate the political landscape, pushing forward decisions that marginalized those who weren't part of the dominant demographic. So, even while the ideal of democratic participation flourished, it simultaneously laid the groundwork for systemic oppression, revealing a paradox where more voices could lead to greater silencing.

In contrast, the United States was founded on ideals that explicitly sought to protect minority rights within the framework of governance. Thus, the Bill of Rights was enacted to guarantee that fundamental freedoms could never be overridden by the majority.[9] However, this promise

---

9   *The Bill of Rights*: Ratified on December 15, 1791, the Bill of Rights consists of the first 10 amendments to the Constitution, which define the rights of Americans in relation to their government. The Bill of Rights guarantees civil liberties, such as freedom of religion, speech, press, and assembly, the right to keep and bear guns, the prohibiting of military personnel to live in your home without your permission, freedom from unreasonable searches and seizures, freedom from prosecution without due process of law, the right to a speedy trial by a jury according to the rule of the law, and prohibiting excessive bail or cruel and unusual punishment.

James Madison authored the Bill of Rights in response to the negative response of Anti-Federalists like Patrick Henry, Samuel Adams, John Hancock, and James Monroe who initially refused to endorse the Constitution because it gave too much power to the federal government and not enough to the states or individuals. Anti-Federalists, as a rule, were small farmers, landowners, shopkeepers, and laborers, so when it came to national politics, they favored strong state governments and individual liberties, and a weak central government. As it turned out, their opposition was the critical factor in why the Bill of Rights was added to Constitution.

According to the National Archives, "The Constitution might never have been ratified if the Framers had not promised to add a Bill of Rights. The first 10 amendments to the Constitution gave citizens more confidence in the new government." And from The American Presidency Project, "With three simple words—'We the People'—the United States Constitution set in motion the most extraordinary experiment in self-governance that the world has ever known. The Bill of Rights made this possible, ensuring ratification by every state then

is often undermined in practice; the nation continuously grapples with the consequences of majority rule, where legislative decisions try to marginalize disenfranchised groups. The legislative and electoral processes, designed to ensure representation for all, frequently become battle-grounds where the rights of the few are trampled by the desires of the many.

Despite the framework intended to uphold individual rights, the American political system illustrates how the delicate balance of power is always in danger of being ma-nipulated for all the wrong reasons. As such, the cyclical nature of political power remains skewed, often favoring those already in dominant positions. As a result, the voices of dissent face ongoing challenges in gaining recognition within the prevailing majority narrative. This persistent tug of war raises questions about the effectiveness of dem-ocratic systems in safeguarding against the oppressive ten-dencies of collective governance, revealing that progress is neither linear nor guaranteed.

Enlightenment Influences and the Framers of the Constitution

THE ENLIGHTENMENT was a pivotal era that shaped modern political thought, significantly influencing the Framers of the Constitution. Enlightenment thinkers such as Montesquieu and John Locke advocated for principles centered around individual rights, liberty, and the necessi-ty of government structures that prevent the abuse of pow-

---

in our new nation. By codifying fundamental freedoms, it won over states skep-tical of a federal government at the time of our founding and proved our Con-stitution to be a living document, capable of evolving to perfect our Union. The basic rights it guarantees—to religion, speech, press, privacy, and more—have come to define our nation. And in the over two centuries since their enumera-tion, 17 other amendments have been ratified—ending slavery, ensuring equal protection under the law, giving women the right to vote, and more—opening the door of opportunity a little wider with each generation."

er. These ideas directly contrast with the Athenian model of democracy, where the majority ruled without sufficient mechanisms to restrain their authority. As such, the checks and balances embedded in the U.S. Constitution serve as unique safeguards against the "tyranny of the majority," a variation from the classical democratic models.

One of the central tenets of Enlightenment philosophy is the idea of separation of powers, a concept championed by Montesquieu, in which he argued that political power shouldn't rest in the hands of a single entity. While Roger Williams, of 17th-century Rhode Island, is cited as being the first to propose the idea of the separation of church and state, it was Montesquieu who would elaborate this idea when he proposed that the power of the state should be divided among different branches of government, to ensure that no single group could dominate. This notion became foundational for the Framers of the Constitution, leading to the establishment of the legislative, executive, and judicial branches. Each branch was designed to have distinct responsibilities and the ability to check the power of the others.

By contrast, in the ancient Athenian model, citizens participated directly in governance, allowing majority rule to prevail in decision-making. While this system fostered a sense of community and collective action, it also left room for the oppression of minority viewpoints. In times of passion or crisis, majority decisions led to impulsive policies that could harm minority rights or lead to tyrannical governance. Because the Framers of the Constitution were keenly aware of this vulnerability, they sought to craft a new system where mechanisms such as veto powers, judicial review, and bicameral legislation would keep the whims of the majority under control. By implementing these checks and balances, the Framers ensured that legislation would require broader consensus, thereby protecting against rash decisions driven by temporary popular sentiment. According to Thomas Jefferson: "The republican is the only form of government which is not eternally at open or secret war with the rights of mankind."

Enlightenment thinkers like Locke also influenced the thinking of the Founders by proposing what they described as a "social contract," positing that government derives its authority from "the consent of the governed," and should exist to protect the rights of all individuals. For Locke, as long as the civil government did its part to promote the common good and to protect the natural rights of individuals—who were all, in his view, equal in God's eyes—those individuals were obligated to obey the government under this social contract. However, if any government failed to uphold its "end of the bargain," so to speak, then the citizens have the right, if not the obligation, to check that government's power, even to the point of social revolution. In today's world, the notion of a social contract that binds the actions of governments as much as it does of its citizens doesn't sound like a radical concept, but it certainly was in the 17th century.

Locke was also known to have stated that, based on his notions about the natural rights of man, all men are universally entitled to "life, liberty, and the pursuit of property." In all this, naturally, it doesn't take much to see the extent to which these ideas influenced Jefferson when he penned the Declaration of Independence, in that he only changed the last word in its preamble: "We hold these truths to be self-evident, that all men are created equal, that they are endowed by their Creator with certain unalienable rights, that among these are life, liberty, and the pursuit of happiness."[10]

---

10   *The Declaration of Independence*: The document that declared the 13 colonies of America were "free and independent" of Great Britain, and so established the United States as a sovereign nation—the Declaration of Independence—is perhaps the most famous political document in the history of the world. Adopted by the Continental Congress on July 4, 1776, the Declaration of Independence was written by a committee of five, including Thomas Jefferson, Benjamin Franklin, John Adams, Roger Sherman, and Robert R. Livingston.
The first of 3 of America's foundational documents—along with the Con-

Locke's philosophy was echoed in the Bill of Rights, too, which guarantees fundamental liberties and protects against government overreach. In contrast, Athenian democracy lacked such protections, relying heavily on the commitment of its citizens to uphold justice and fairness.

Majority Rule With Minority Rights

IN ANY democratic society, the balance between majority rule and minority rights is a fundamental issue that shapes

---

stitution and the Bill of Rights—the Declaration of Independence contains 3 sections: first, a statement about the natural rights of man, and the purpose of government; second, a list of grievances against the British King, and third, the declaration of independence from England. Tasked with the actual writing of the document, in cooperation with the committee of five, Jefferson was heavily influence by previous works such as George Mason's *Virginia Declaration of Rights* and John Locke's *Two Treatises of Government.*

What began as a list of grievances against King George III not only set into motion America's state of independence, it also enabled the colonist to form an alliance with France. Without their aid, America would have almost certainly lost the Revolutionary War. Ironically, what began as one country's call to freedom and independence was soon to create a ripple effect across the globe and throughout subsequent decades. As such, no American document has had a greater global or social impact than the Declaration of Independence. Countries such as France, Venezuela, Hungary, Czechoslovakia, Liberia, and even the Republic of Texas, all looked to it in their push to become free and independent.

Not only these but there are many whom the Founders may not have had in mind, directly, nevertheless the language of their declaration did embrace them, prophetically. In that minority activists like Martin Luther King looked to it when he insisted, "When the architects of our Republic wrote the magnificent words of the Declaration of Independence, they were signing a promissory note to which every American was to fall heir." And in that women activists like Elizabeth Cady Stanton also looked to it when she presented her famous *Declaration of Sentiments,* and said, "We hold these truths to be self-evident; that all men and women are created equal."

In all of these instances, then, it can be safely said that if not for America's original declaration none that followed could have ever hoped to succeed, such that, "when a long train of abuses and usurpations, pursuing invariably the same object, evinces a design to reduce them under absolute despotism, it is their right, it is their duty, to throw off such government, and to provide new guards for their future security."

governance and justice. While the principle of majority rule is essential for decision-making and reflects the will of the greater population, it's equally important to recognize and protect the voices and rights of minority groups. The Founding Fathers of America understood this dynamic deeply, believing that true justice requires a broader approach that includes minority perspectives.

Majority rule serves as a cornerstone of democratic governance, allowing societies to function effectively by reaching decisions that reflect the preferences of the majority. This principle is evident in electoral processes, where candidates or policies that receive the most votes are endorsed. However, the challenge arises when the interests and rights of minorities are overshadowed or completely disregarded. Historically, there have been instances where majority decisions led to the marginalization of certain ethnic, religious, or social groups, highlighting the potential danger of unchecked majority power. The Founders recognized that the voice of the majority shouldn't silence minority rights and that a just society must safeguard against such tyranny.

The concept of minority rights is thus crucial in maintaining the integrity of a truly democratic system. It encompasses the protection of individual freedoms, cultural identities, and specific needs that might be overlooked in a purely majority-driven context. By ensuring that certain fundamental rights are upheld, regardless of popular opinion, the framework of governance remains robust and equitable. According to John Marshall: "Between a balanced republic and a democracy, the difference is like that between order and chaos."

When minority groups are given the opportunity to voice their concerns—be they ethnic, religious, or social— the result is a more comprehensive understanding of societal issues. This inclusion promotes collaborative solutions that benefit everyone, diverging from a one-size-fits-all approach that may alienate many segments of the population.

The Founding Fathers' vision of justice indeed extends beyond mere majority opinion; it emphasizes the importance of dialogue and mutual respect among all citizens.

The Rising Demand for Direct Democracy

IN RECENT years, the United States has witnessed a notable shift in public sentiment, with an increasing number of citizens advocating for a more direct democratic model of governance. This change reflects a growing desire for transparency, accountability, and greater citizen involvement in the political process. However, while the move toward direct democracy can empower the electorate and enhance democratic engagement, it also raises significant implications that must be carefully considered.

One of the most compelling reasons for the shift toward direct democracy is the disenchantment many citizens feel toward traditional political institutions. As trust in elected officials has waned, fueled by perceptions of corruption and inefficiency, there is a palpable appetite for a system that allows for more grassroots participation. Initiatives such as ballot measures, referendums, and citizen assemblies empower individuals to have a direct impact on legislation and public policy. In turn, this participatory approach enhances civic engagement and makes the political process more reflective of the populace's needs and desires.

The accessibility of digital technology has also facilitated this shift, enabling citizens to organize, debate, and advocate for issues with unprecedented ease. Social media platforms amplify voices that have otherwise gone unheard, creating a fertile ground for grassroots movements. This technological revolution fuels a culture of accountability where politicians are more directly answerable to their constituents. By advocating for policies through direct means, citizens can enact changes that align more closely with their values, bypassing entrenched political mechanisms that don't represent their interests.

That said, though, in any system that prioritizes the voice of the majority, it's more important than ever to balance the desire for direct involvement with the need for critical examination of the issues at hand. Complex problems, such as those involving public health, ecological policies, and national security, often demand solutions that require specialized knowledge that the general electorate may lack. A direct democratic model risks undermining the value of informed decision-making, potentially leading to poor outcomes driven by populist impulses rather than by expert consensus.

An Illusion of Freedom

THE IDEA OF direct democracy is often heralded as the pinnacle of freedom in modern governance, where everyone's voice is believed to be integral to the decision-making process. Proponents argue that when citizens are granted a direct say in every policy and law, society becomes more liberated and just. Unfortunately, upon further review, this perspective turns out to be inherently flawed, primarily because it overlooks the complexities of human decision-making and the potential chaos that ensues when everyone is empowered to dictate the course of governance. As such, direct democracy doesn't lead to freedom but, rather, to fragmentation and confusion.

To begin with, the assumption that greater participation equates to enhanced liberty disregards the reality of social dynamics. A society made up of individuals, each holding differing opinions, is always in danger of descending into a cacophony of voices. This fragmentation, in turn, inhibits the decision-making process, making it cumbersome and inefficient. In moments of crisis or when swift action is needed, the drawn-out debates and diverse opinions inherent in a direct democracy become a hindrance rather than a help, leading to paralysis, not progress. This situation suggests that greater individual involvement doesn't necessarily foster a framework for true freedom; rather, it creates an environment ripe for indecision and conflict.

Not only that, but the idea that a direct democracy allows for greater control and representation for the electorate is also flawed. That's because, in such scenarios, the loudest voices often drown out those with nuanced perspectives, leading to a situation that creates an illusion of freedom but one that, sadly, winds up undermining the values of liberty and justice that direct democracy purports to represent.

Even more troubling: the idea of individual empowerment in direct democracy paradoxically leads to increased divisions within society. That's because the greatest strength of a representational democracy is its ability to come to a compromise between differing viewpoints; however, when everyone is encouraged to indiscriminately voice their own opinion, the lines between groups become blurred. This, in turn, contributes to an environment where societal cohesion is sacrificed for individual expression, and rather than a united society striving toward a common good, direct democracy fuels an atmosphere of hostility and competition, further complicating the pursuit of liberty and justice.

The Risks of Reverting to a Direct Democracy

AT THE HEART of the issue is the fundamental challenge of informed decision-making. In a society inundated with information, much of it conflicting or confusing, expecting a significant proportion of the population to make sound judgments on complex issues is optimistic at best. Advocacy groups tend to underestimate the biases that often sway public opinion, as well as the role of misinformation campaigns that are designed to distort the truth. In cases where critical issues are put to a vote, the risk of an electorate swayed by emotional appeals rather than rational discourse becomes alarmingly high. This leads to enacting policies that aren't just ill-conceived but potentially detrimental to the social fabric of the community.

The direct involvement of citizens in decision-making also carries the inherent risk of populism—a political approach that seeks to appeal to the interests and sentiments of the populace. While populism appears democratic on the surface, it often oversimplifies complex issues into digestible narratives that don't adequately reflect the intricacies of governance. This reductionist view creates an environment where simplistic solutions are favored over comprehensive policymaking, potentially leading to hasty decisions that overlook significant long-term consequences.

The instability that arises from direct democracy further complicates matters. When policies are decided through referendums or initiatives, the potential for frequent, radical shifts in governance increases. This fluctuation creates an unpredictable political landscape, undermining the continuity that is essential for effective governance. For instance, a hastily enacted policy may be repealed or altered in subsequent elections, leading to a lack of consistency in laws and regulations that confuse both citizens and businesses alike. Such volatility discourages long-term investments and planning, as stakeholders are left uncertain about the future direction of governance.

Another often-overlooked risk is the impact of voter fatigue. As citizens are called upon to engage in frequent referendums or votes on various issues, the novelty of participation eventually wears off, leading to apathy and disillusionment. Over time, this results in lower voter turnout or a disengaged populace, contradicting the initial intention of empowering citizens. The enthusiasm that advocates promote ultimately gives way to a cynical view of the political process, where citizens feel their participation has little actual impact or value.

Pure Democracies and the
Mob Mentality

THROUGHOUT HISTORY, governments that lack institutional checks have often led to conflict and turmoil. While pure democracy is hailed for its promise of unfiltered representation, its historical precedents reveal a dangerous susceptibility to chaos. In contrast, republicanism—despite it being criticized for its complexities and supposed disconnect from the populace—provides mechanisms that increase stability. Ultimately, societies must choose between a model that engages everyone yet invites upheaval or one that, while less direct, maintains a balance of power essential for enduring governance.

So, while pure democracy sounds ideal in theory, history shows that when every decision rests in the hands of the masses, the result is often mob mentality and the trampling of minority rights. The Athenian experience serves as a testament to this; although it allowed unprecedented participation, it also led to rapid shifts in public opinion that precipitated disastrous military campaigns and led to the city-state's eventual decline. Isn't it ironic that a system meant to empower the people can so easily devolve into instability and anarchy? As such, while the notion that everyone should be able to influence policies may warmly resonate in our hearts, let's never forget how prone such systems are to being undermined by emotional fervor and transient public whims.

In contrast, republicanism, while sometimes perceived as elitist, provides a structure that withstands the test of time. By incorporating checks and balances, a republic curbs the excesses of direct democracy. This ensures that governance isn't just about serving the will of the majority; it is also about respecting the needs of minorities. The Founding Fathers of America understood this well when they rejected pure democracy in favor of a representative system. As Alexander Hamilton put it: "Real liberty is neither found in despotism or the extremes of democracy, but in moderate governments." In other words, instead of succumbing to the volatility of fleeting majority sentiments, republicanism offers a shield against such instability.

Engaging with the underlying principles of governance, then, reveals the undeniable value of institutional checks. Those who champion direct democracy dismiss republicanism as outdated and irrelevant, yet they conveniently overlook the lessons of history. In modern times, we observe many nations teetering on the brink of collapse, undermined by movements that exploit direct democratic ideals. Countries rife with civil strife often exhibit a lack of stable governance structures—the very checks that republics provide. As such, the very advocates of unfettered democracy may actually be nurturing the soil for future conflicts. Said John Adams: "Remember, democracy never lasts long. It soon wastes, exhausts, and murders itself. There never was a democracy yet that did not commit suicide."

Dissent and Discord

WHILE A PURE democracy is often heralded as the pinnacle of citizen empowerment, we're seeing, upon closer inspection, the extent to which this system is fundamentally flawed. Ultimately, this idealized vision of democracy reveals a darker reality marked by fragmentation and confusion. While a pure democracy seems so appealing, the reality is that such a framework fuels an environment ripe for conflict. The diverse and often conflicting interests of the populace inevitably lead to the emergence of factions, each vying for their own agendas and priorities. These competing interests don't just create lively debate; they also trigger intense polarization, making it difficult to achieve consensus. Dissent turns into discord, and vital governance slips through the cracks as the political landscape becomes a battleground of self-interest rather than a collaborative pursuit of the common good.

Worse still, the mechanics of pure democracy amplify this divisive factionalism. With issues subject to popular vote, there is a pervasive risk of majority tyranny, where the rights and needs of minority groups are disregarded. Legislative decisions become pawns in the hands of the most vocal or organized factions, leading to policies that don't reflect the nuanced needs of the entire populace. The lack of mediating institutions, such as a deliberative assembly or a robust judiciary, further exacerbates this problem, allowing passions to dictate policy instead of reasoned discourse. The end result is a governance structure that is reactionary rather than proactive, with the populace frequently shifting from one extreme to another without the stability that comes from a more measured approach.

In stark contrast stands constitutional republicanism, a system designed to diminish the excesses of direct democracy by distancing governance from the whims of public sentiment. Elected representatives, tasked with deliberating on behalf of their constituents, play a crucial role in tempering the effects of factionalism. While constitutional republics certainly face challenges—such as potential corruption and disconnection from the electorate—they provide structures that can withstand the volatile fluctuations of popular opinion. Here lie the benefits of a more deliberative approach: a focus on long-term policy implications rather than short-lived partisan victories.

Cultivating Balanced Representation

THE U.S. Constitution embodies a profound commitment to balanced representation, particularly through the structure of the Electoral College, which plays a pivotal role in the election of the President. This unique mechanism is designed to not only reflect the diversity of all the states but also to protect the interests of smaller states, ensuring that every voice in the nation has an impact. By examining how the Electoral College balances these sometimes conflicting needs, we can better appreciate the intricate architecture of our uniquely American political system.

At its core, the Electoral College serves to maintain a balance between more populous and less populous states in the presidential election process. By allocating electors based on both the total number of senators and representatives a state has, the system provides smaller states with a slightly greater share of influence relative to their population size. For instance, smaller states with a minimum of three electoral votes—regardless of their population—are afforded a voice that is amplified beyond mere population metrics. This design is deliberate, reflecting the Framers' intent to prevent more populous regions from overwhelming the voices of smaller states, thereby promoting a balanced approach to national governance.

The Electoral College also demonstrates a commitment to state sovereignty, recognizing the individuality and rights of each state within the union. The idea that all states should have a role in electing the President stems from the acknowledgment of their distinct interests and agendas. By requiring candidates to garner support across a variety of states rather than just focusing on populous urban areas, the system encourages them to campaign in a way that addresses the unique challenges and concerns of every region in the country. This approach, then, uniquely nurtures a sense of unity among all states, cultivating a national conversation that would otherwise be narrowed by a purely popular vote.

Despite all this, though, there are still those who criticize the Electoral College, arguing that it can lead to an imbalance in representation, where the votes of individuals in less populous states carry more weight than those in larger states. However, this perspective overlooks the original purpose of the system, which was to ensure that leaders consider the nation as a whole rather than catering to just densely populated areas. The Electoral College underscores the principle that every state, regardless of its size or population, has a role in shaping the direction of the country. Such a federal structure forces candidates to think beyond locales and demographics, fostering broader national agendas that encompass a variety of interests.

Federalism and the Dividing of Power

AS A SYSTEM of governance, federalism plays a crucial role in dividing powers between national and state governments, ensuring that local interests are addressed while preventing any single entity from wielding excessive power. This structural arrangement is fundamental in maintaining a republican framework that both promotes democratic principles and protects individual freedoms. The essence of federalism lies in its ability to balance authority, decentralizing governance in a way that encourages local representation and participation.

At the heart of federalism is the principle of shared governance. By distributing powers across different levels of government, federalism allows for a more tailored approach to local issues. For instance, state governments are often more attuned to the unique needs of their residents, which may vary significantly from those of other regions. This decentralization of power enables states to implement policies that are more reflective of their constituents' values and needs. One state may choose to prioritize ecological sustainability, while another might focus on economic development, thereby fostering innovative solutions that a centralized government might overlook.

Not only that, but in federalism, the division of powers also guards against the concentration of authority, not just at the federal level but at the state level as well. The Framers of the Constitution recognized the dangers of tyranny, leading them to create a system that checks any single entity's power. Again, as Madison saw it: "The influence of factious leaders may kindle a flame within their own particular states, but will be unable to spread a general conflagration through the other states." In a well-structured federal system, then, state governments act as counterbalances over against every other state, protecting the rights of individual states and their citizens. As such, these multiple layers of government serve as conduits for accountability, as state officials remain answerable to their constituents, thus promoting responsive governance.

What's more, federalism inspires a spirit of experimentation in policymaking. States often function as "laboratories of democracy," as it were, where various approaches to governance and public policy can be tested. Successful initiatives at the state level can inform national policies, allowing for an adaptive and responsive governmental structure. Conversely, if a particular policy proves unsuccessful, it can be reevaluated without detrimental effects on the entire nation. This flexibility is integral to a vast and sprawling republic like America, which thrives on the ideas and feedback from its diverse and widespread populace.

The Modern Misinterpretation of Republicanism

IN CONTEMPORARY political discourse, the term "republicanism" is frequently misinterpreted, often confusing it with mere democratic principles. This misunderstanding undermines the foundational elements that distinguish republicanism as a distinct form of governance. By exploring the historical context, core tenets, and the modern misinterpretation of republicanism, it's evident that a clearer understanding of this ideology is needed for the healthy functioning of our American political system.

At its core, republicanism is founded on the idea of a representative government operating within the bounds of law and promoting the common good. Unlike pure democracy, which can sometimes succumb to the tyranny of the majority, republicanism emphasizes the protection of individual rights and the establishment of a government that is accountable to the populace but separate from direct popular will. The Founding Fathers, particularly figures like James Madison and Alexander Hamilton, understood republicanism as a way to balance the need for popular sovereignty with safeguards against potential majority overreach. This distinction is pivotal because it sets republicanism apart from the more simplistic notion of democracy, which often prioritizes the immediate desires of the majority over the rights of the minority.

Not only that, but equating republicanism with a purely democratic ethos also has significant implications for contemporary governance. Today, many Americans interpret republicanism through the lens of electoral politics, viewing it as synonymous with party loyalty and majority support. This perspective inevitably leads to a misunderstanding of the responsibilities inherent to citizenship, where the concept of civic virtue—an essential aspect of republicanism—is overlooked. Civic virtue requires citizens to not just participate in elections but to engage thoughtfully in public discourse, consider the long-term implications of policies, and hold elected representatives accountable for their actions. As Thomas Jefferson saw it: "The people are the ultimate guardians of their own liberties. In every government on Earth, there is some trace of human weakness, some germ of corruption and degeneracy... Every government degenerates when trusted to the rulers of the people alone." A reductionist view of republicanism, then, diminishes the emphasis on these civic responsibilities, contributing to division and complacency rather than constructive civic engagement.

Then add to that how the current political climate, characterized by partisan polarization, further complicates the understanding of republicanism. The result: a hyper-partisan alignment that often leads to the portrayal of political opponents as "threats to democracy itself," rather than as fellow citizens engaged in a legitimate, albeit contentious, debate. This perspective risks prioritizing party ideology over the common good and can result in legislative grid-lock, where governance becomes an exercise in partisan conflict rather than a pursuit of collaborative solutions for the benefit of all citizens. That's because without the principles of republicanism guiding political engagement, the ideals of compromise, dialogue, and mutual respect are sacrificed at the altar of party loyalty.

Educational Failures

NOT TO BE overlooked in all this is the extent to which the civics curricula across America's educational institutions often fail to emphasize: 1) the rationale behind a constitutional republic; 2) the principles of federalism, with its emphasis on balanced representation, and 3) the complexities of the Electoral College. This shortfall results in citizens lacking a comprehensive understanding of the significance of republicanism, which is essential for a healthy body politic. A deeper focus on these foundational elements is crucial for cultivating informed citizens who can effectively engage in the American political process.

First and foremost, the importance of minority rights in a constitutional republic must be emphasized within civics education. The protection of minority rights is a cornerstone of republican governance, ensuring that all voices, particularly those of marginalized groups, are heard and respected. A curriculum that neglects this aspect perpetuates the narrow view of direct democracy that favors majority opinion at the expense of inclusion. By highlighting significant historical events, such as the Civil Rights Movement, students can better appreciate the ongoing struggle for equality and the role that minority rights play in safeguarding the health of a constitutional republic.[11]

---

11   *The Civil Rights Movement*: A social and political campaign in the U.S., from 1954 to 1968, the Civil Rights Movement sought to end racial discrimination against African-Americans. The movement took numerous approaches in an effort to communicate their demands, including sit-ins, boycotts, protest

Another integral concept that merits greater attention within civics courses is federalism, with its emphasis on balanced representation. The structure of the United

---

marches, freedom rides, and lobbying government officials for legislative action. They faced fierce opposition from all sides; there were bombings, beatings, arrests, and assassinations.

After the American Civil War and the abolition of slavery, three Reconstruction Amendments to the U.S. Constitution, in 1865, had granted freedom and citizenship for all African-Americans. For a short time, African-American men voted and held political office, but before long, southern Blacks were increasingly deprived of their rights under a system known as Jim Crow laws. The status quo of excluding African-Americans from the political system lasted in the South until national civil rights legislation was passed in the mid-1960s, which provided federal enforcement of constitutional voting rights.

There were numerous pivotal events that marked the Civil Rights Movement but perhaps none was more important than the events surrounding the lynching of Emmett Till. After Emmett's mother, Mamie Till, came to identify her son's remains, she decided she wanted to "let the people see what I have seen," insisting that his body be displayed in an open casket where thousands of visitors came to show their respects. A later publication of an image at the funeral in *Jet* is credited as a crucial moment in the Civil Rights Era, as historian Tim Tyson described it: "Emmett's murder would never have become a watershed historical moment without Mamie finding the strength to make her private grief a public matter." The visceral response to his mother's decision to have an open-casket funeral galvanized the Black community throughout the U.S.

Despite the murderous opposition directed against the movement, leaders like Martin Luther King Jr. managed to restrain the natural urge to counter violence with violence, advocating for nonviolent responses that included Rosa Parks' famous refusal to give up her bus seat to a white person. Then there was the Little Rock Nine, a group of students who were part of a move to desegregate a high school in Mississippi, in a decision that has also been hailed as a landmark event in the Civil Rights Movement.

Eventually, public sympathy for the movement led John F. Kennedy's administration to order the Interstate Commerce Commission (ICC) to issue a new desegregation order. When the new ICC rule took effect on November 1, 1961, passengers were permitted to sit wherever they chose on buses; "white" and "colored" signs were removed from terminals, separate drinking fountains, toilets, and waiting rooms were combined, and lunch counters began serving people regardless of their skin color.

By the end of the 1960s, the Civil Rights Movement managed to bring about significant changes in both the law and in public practice; and more importantly, it brought lasting effects that secured legal protections, rights, and freedoms for African-Americans that would shape American life for years to come.

States government, including its bicameral legislature and the mechanisms ensuring representation at both the state and federal levels, should be thoroughly explored. This discussion would illuminate how balanced representation not only reflects the diversity of American society but also contributes to the legitimacy of government institutions. When students understand the importance of equitable representation, they are more likely to recognize their stake in the political process and the impact of their participation.

Unfortunately, though, the principle of federalism is often glossed over in civics education, despite the vital role it plays in delineating the powers between the national and state governments. A robust understanding of federalism could inspire students to appreciate the complexities of governance in a diverse nation. It could also foster an awareness of how local and national policies can affect their daily lives and encourage active engagement in both state and federal issues. Educators should provide students with case studies and examples that illustrate the practical implications of federalism, thereby enhancing their analytical skills and civic knowledge.

The Electoral College is another area where civics education frequently falls short. This institution, designed to balance the influence of populous states with that of smaller ones, often remains a point of contention and confusion among students. A comprehensive curriculum could explain the rationale behind the Electoral College, its implications for presidential elections, and the ongoing debates surrounding its effectiveness. Understanding this system is essential for students to engage in discussions about electoral reform and to critically assess the political processes that govern our country.

Hope for Future Generations

IN A WORLD where individual rights are increasingly challenged, America stands as a beacon of hope, committed to the principles that safeguard freedoms and ensure that all voices are heard. The foundational elements of American society—protecting individual rights, limiting government power, and promoting balanced representation—aren't just historical concepts but are vital frameworks that continue to shape the nation's identity. Our steadfast commitment to these principles remains crucial as America strives to create a more republican society where every citizen feels valued and represented.

At the heart of America's political system, standing like twin pillars of our republic, are the Constitution and the Bill of Rights, which together provide a powerful safeguard against government overreach and tyranny. This framework empowers citizens to express their opinions, practice their beliefs, and pursue their aspirations freely. It is a reminder that each person has inherent worth and that their rights must be respected and upheld. In a hopeful vision for the future, this recognition of individual rights inspires ongoing movements advocating for marginalized communities and individuals, reminding us that protecting these rights is an ongoing journey rather than a completed task.

Appreciating American Uniqueness

THE DISTINCTIONS between pure democracies and constitutional republics, then, hold significant relevance in appreciating the unique qualities of our American political framework. Understanding these differences is crucial, especially as the nation navigates the challenges posed by a society that is growing ever more complex and diverse.

A pure democracy, with its insistence on direct voting on policy issues by the populace, is always in danger of succumbing to the "tyranny of the majority." This form of governance, while seemingly democratic, doesn't preserve the essential liberty of all citizens, particularly those in the minority. The potential for the majority to overrule the voice of smaller groups lays the groundwork for instability and division, especially in a nation as diverse as America.

In contrast, a constitutional republic provides a framework designed to protect individual rights and maintain a balance between majority rule and minority rights. The U.S. Constitution establishes a system of checks and balances, and it delineates authority among the three branches of government, which is a hallmark of our constitutional republic. This structure ensures that no single entity can gain excessive power, while the Bill of Rights safeguards the freedoms of all citizens, regardless of popular sentiment. The interplay of these elements is vital for effective governance, especially in addressing the complexities of different cultures, beliefs, and backgrounds within the American populace.

The American political system also encourages civic engagement and deliberation. Within this constitutional framework, citizens participate in elections not merely as voters but also as active contributors in the political process through discussion, debate, and representation. Elected officials are accountable to their constituents, which, in turn, cultivates a sense of responsibility and engagement among the citizenry. As such, the ability to vote for representatives who reflect the diverse values and interests of the populace further distinguishes this system from pure democracies, reinforcing the idea that liberty is maintained only through balanced representation.

Upholding the Values of a Constitutional Republic

IN THE LANDSCAPE of governance, the contrast between pure democracies and constitutional republics reveals significant insights into how societies can effectively balance majority rule with the rights of minority groups. America's Founding Fathers recognized that while democracy is vital for expressing the will of the majority, a stable governance framework is essential to ensure that the diverse interests of all citizens are represented. As such, republicanism not only upholds freedom and justice but also nurtures a culture of public debate that enriches the political discourse and strengthens societal bonds.

At the heart of republicanism is the principle that governance is grounded in the rule of law rather than the whims of the majority. This is why the framework established by the Founding Fathers incorporated checks and balances that protect minority rights while allowing for majority influence in decision-making processes. This equilibrium helps to sustain an environment where diverse opinions can coexist, creating a more balanced and representative governance structure.

The encouragement of public debates is also a critical element of republicanism that enhances the political landscape. In a republic, citizens aren't simply passive participants but are active stakeholders in the governing process. Open discussions allow individuals from various backgrounds and beliefs to voice their opinions, challenge the status quo, and advocate for their interests. As these debates intensify, they catalyze civic engagement and help forge a sense of community. When citizens are involved in discussions about policies that affect their lives, the resulting dialogue not only promotes understanding but also fosters a sense of responsibility toward one another and the collective future.

Republicanism, therefore, enables mechanisms that promote freedom and justice while ensuring that every voice has the potential to be heard. This commitment to balanced representation is particularly important in a diverse society, where differing perspectives can lead to more nuanced policy outcomes. As stakeholders engage in debates about pressing issues, they contribute to feelings of empathy that encompass not only the desires and needs of the majority but also those of various minority groups.

In conclusion, by establishing a framework that effectively balances majority and minority rights, the Founding

Fathers succeeded in creating a stable governance environment that not only upholds the principles of freedom and justice but also allows for a multiplicity of interests to thrive. And by continuing to embrace this kind of republicanism, we help to sustain an increasingly diverse political culture that recognizes the importance of every citizen's voice, ultimately leading us all toward a more hopeful and humane future.

The Media Mirage:

The Truth Behind the Headlines

LIE #4:

*The Founding Fathers Laid Out a Plan of Government Based on
the Assumption that Humans are Innately Good and Honest...*

M Y PROFESSOR and I were enjoying another after-school discussion when the old man asked
me, pointedly, "So, what did you think of my main
thesis in today's lecture?"

"You mean the part about the philosophy of the Founding Fathers being more in line with classical Renaissance
thinkers than with those of the biblically inspired Reform-
ers?"

"That's right," he said, almost with an arrogant grunt.

"Well, I have to admit, it goes against some of what I
grew up believing."

"Why? Because you believe the Pilgrims came here
seeking religious liberty in the name of the Christian God?"

"That, yes, among other things," I replied confidently.

"That's understandable. That's what your parents
taught you. No shame in that. But you're a young man
now; you're your own man now. Time to put away childish
things, as it were. Wouldn't you agree?"

"Yes, sir; I suppose you're right."

"So think about it. What do you remember about the views of men like Jefferson, Franklin, and Paine?"

"I guess you'd have to describe them as humanists."

"That's correct, yes. And humanism was born in Renaissance Italy, right?"

"Right," I echoed my professor, with a nod.

"Right, then," said my professor. "And while the Old World viewed humans as irrevocably flawed and sinful, the Renaissance gave rise to a new view of man, in which he was seen as innately good and honest."

"I suppose so, yes, sir. But..." I hesitated, not exactly sure how to respond.

"But what?" asked the old man. "Look, I know it's not easy to hear things that contradict ways of thinking you've grown up with. But isn't that why you entered university? To learn the ways of this great, big world of ours? Not just to confirm the world of your parents?"

"Of course," I replied, thoughtfully.

"Think, then; use that wonderful brain of yours. What does it tell you? The American colonists of the seventeenth century were all by and large Puritans. Isn't that what your history books tell you?

I nodded affirmatively.

"Which means they were steeped in a pessimistic view of humanity. Why? How did they come to that conclusion? They got it from your *Holy Bible*. But the Founding Fathers? Absolutely not; no, sir. They were different. They rejected all that. They rejected it in favor of optimism—an optimism that was borne of the spirit of the Renaissance. Am I right?"

As I carefully considered my professor's words, I reviewed in my mind what I already knew about men like Thomas Jefferson, Benjamin Franklin, and Thomas Paine, who I had to admit did reject all the major tenets of Christianity: original sin, the Trinity, the deity of Christ, His resurrection, all of it.

But was my professor's argument really so cut-and-dry? In that moment I also had to admit that I had my suspicion that it was not. So rather than immediately respond, I set about, once again, to learn more about the subject before answering.

"Human nature is the same on both sides of the Atlantic, and will be influenced by all the same causes. The time to guard against corruption and tyranny is before they have gotten hold of us. It is better to keep the wolf out of the fold than to try withdrawing his teeth and claws after he has got you."

Thomas Jefferson

The Myth of Optimism

THROUGHOUT history, the narrative surrounding America's Founding Fathers has often been painted in warm hues of optimism and unwavering faith in human potential. However, this appealing portrayal frequently glosses over complex realities, leading to a deeply flawed understanding of both the intellectual underpinnings of the American Revolution and the true nature of humanity. The distortion of these ideas is compounded by mainstream media, which propagates misleading information that caters to a superficial sense of optimism. It is therefore essential to examine these misconceptions critically, as they not only misrepresent historical figures but also fuel unrealistic expectations about societal progress.

The Founding Fathers of the United States, figures such as Thomas Jefferson and Benjamin Franklin, are often seen as idealists who believed wholly in the goodness of humanity and the nation's inevitable march toward greatness. However, the writings and speeches of these men reveal a much more nuanced perspective. Jefferson, for instance, was acutely aware of the flaws inherent in human nature; he advocated for checks and balances within government precisely because he understood that power could corrupt even the noblest of intentions. Similarly, Franklin remarked that "the only thing more expensive than education is ignorance," implying a recognition of humanity's propensity toward folly that required constant vigilance and learning. This pragmatic acknowledgment challenges the overly simplistic narrative of boundless optimism that has become prevalent in contemporary discourse.

Not only that, but the contemporary media landscape also reinforces a distorted version of the Founding Fathers' legacy, favoring narratives that often highlight progress and prosperity while downplaying conflict and compromise. News outlets, in an insatiable quest for more viewers, tend to sensationalize success stories, creating the illusion that society is moving forward on an unbroken trajectory of improvement and enlightenment. Such portrayals neglect to address the persistent societal issues, such as inequality and injustice, reminding us that human nature, with all its potential for greatness, is equally fraught with selfishness and error. By promoting a false sense of optimism, the media encourages complacency and undermines a much-needed engagement with our past and present.

This misconception of optimism also extends to how citizens perceive their role in political processes. Many view participation in governance as either futile or unimportant, mirroring the simplistic idea that society will somehow improve on its own. The belief that positive change is inevitable can lead to indifference and disengagement, inhibiting meaningful dialogue and activism. If we fail to embrace the more complex, often challenging realities of human nature and our historical foundations, we risk the erosion of the republican principles that underpin society.

The Founders' Realist Approach to Governance

THE FOUNDING Fathers of America approached governance with a distinctly realist perspective, deeply shaped by the Enlightenment and an awareness of humanity's inherent flaws. Their experiences with political tyranny and social chaos informed the foundational principles of the American republic, leading them to craft a system designed to mitigate the abuse of power and promote social stability. As such, the Founders' realist approach to governance serves as a testament to their understanding of human nature, the historical context of their time, and the lasting implications of their decisions.

Acutely aware of the history of tyranny, especially British colonial rule, the Founders recognized the axiom that power tends to corrupt—a sentiment echoed in the writings of Lord Acton—and so created our political system of checks and balances. Our arrangement, then, of dividing power amongst the legislative, executive, and judicial branches, was in fact a direct response to their concerns about human fallibility.

What's more, the Founders' experiences with the chaos of the Articles of Confederation further solidified their realist approach.[12] The inability of the central government

---

12   The Articles of Confederation: Adopted by the Continental Congress on November 15, 1777, the Articles of Confederation was a document that served as the United States' first Constitution, and which outlined the functions of the fledgling national government after it declared independence from Great Britain. It was in force from 1781 to 1789, when the present-day Constitution went into effect. Establishing a loose political union between the 13 states, the Articles of Confederation established a weak central government—a "league of friendship"—one that largely preserved state power and independence. This is because when the Articles were written, the colonists did so in response to their fear of powerful central governments like that of Great Britain.

The Articles created a national government centered on the legislative branch, which was comprised of a single house. As of yet, there was still no separate executive branch or judicial branch. As best they could, the Articles detailed the powers of Congress, such as regulating foreign affairs, war, and

to effectively govern in those first few decades of our country's existence highlighted the dangers of overly decentralized power. They understood that social chaos could arise from disunity and a lack of authority, leading to anarchy or tyranny of the majority. In this, we see just how the crafting of the Constitution reflected their understanding that only through a strong but limited central government could we preserve liberty and maintain order at the same time. This duality represents a striking acknowledgment of humanity's flaws—the need for governance to enforce laws, while simultaneously safeguarding individual freedoms.

The complexities of governance often reflect the inherent imperfections of human nature, a perspective articulated by James Madison in his discussions on checks and balances within the framework of the U.S. Constitution. As Madison saw it: "What is government itself but the greatest of all reflections on human nature? If men were angels, government would be unnecessary. And if angels governed men, no external or internal controls on government would be needed." In other words, because human beings are flawed, governance must acknowledge and address these imperfections to ensure stability and justice. As such, a sincere understanding of human nature guides the creation of a governance system that balances power and ensures accountability.

Madison's insights stem from a pragmatic view that acknowledges the realities of human behavior. He believed

---

the postal service; appointing military officers, controlling Indian affairs, borrowing money, determining the value of coin, and issuing bills of credit. Over time, though, the weaknesses in the Articles of Confederation became more and more apparent. Congress commanded little respect or support from state governments who were still anxious to maintain their own power. Not only that, but Congress also couldn't raise funds, regulate trade, or conduct foreign policy without the voluntary agreement of the states. As a result, the Union was continually in danger of collapsing, until finally, in 1786, states like New York were calling for alterations to the Articles, which eventually culminated in the Philadelphia Convention of 1787 and the creation of the Constitution as we know it today.

that individuals, driven by their ambitions and desires, could act against the public good. Therefore, the structure of government was designed not only to empower but also to restrain those in positions of authority. The concept of checks and balances—where different branches of government limit and oversee one another—serves as a safeguard against the potential for abuse of power. By operating from a realistic perspective rather than an idealistic one, Madison advocated for a system that addressed the flaws inherent to humanity.

The Founders' commitment to realism is also evident in their willingness to compromise on contentious issues in pursuit of a functional government. The debates surrounding the Constitution, including the Great Compromise, the Origination Clause, and the Three-Fifths Compromise, illustrate their pragmatic approach.[13] Rather than

---

13   *The Great Compromise*: Established during the Constitutional Convention of 1787, the Great Compromise was the name given to the agreement that created the Legislative Branch. According to the compromise—also known as the Connecticut Compromise—Congress would be made up of two separate and distinct houses: the Senate and the House of Representatives. The Senate, or upper house, would provide equal amounts of senators, affording equal representation for each state; and the House of Representatives, or lower house, would provide a proportional number of representatives based on the population of each state.

The Great Compromise was proposed by delegates from Connecticut, including Roger Sherman and Oliver Ellsworth, and adopted by the Constitutional Convention on July 16, 1787. The compromise resolved disputes between larger and smaller states. It also included: a census every 10 years, which would allow reapportionment based on census results; the Origination Clause, which gave the House of Representatives the power to originate all legislation dealing with the federal budget and revenues/taxation; and the Three-Fifths Compromise, an agreement that counted three-fifths of enslaved people when determining a state's population.

The Origination Clause, also known as the Revenue Clause, was instituted to ensure that the legislative body most responsive to the people had the power of the purse. As such, the House of Representatives would be the place where all bills for raising revenue must be initiated, but the Senate may propose or concur with amendments, as in the case of other bills. The Origination Clause stemmed from a British parliamentary practice that all money bills must have their first reading in the House of Commons before being sent to the House of Lords.

stubbornly cling to ideological purity, they prioritized the establishment of a governing framework that could garner widespread support and effectively function. This willingness to engage in compromise reveals a profound understanding that perfect ideals often falter in the face of practical realities.

The Framers of the Constitution also incorporated a series of deliberate mechanisms to ensure that governance reflected a true understanding of human imperfections. The separation of powers is a quintessential example, with each branch being responsible for different aspects of governance. This division prevents any single entity from gaining unchecked authority, reflecting a sincere commitment to limiting the potential for tyranny. In this system, each branch checks the others, reinforcing the idea that governance should be grounded in a recognition of the often self-interested nature of human beings.

Within this finely balanced framework, the role of citizen participation can't be overstated. Madison and his contemporaries understood that a well-informed electorate serves as yet another layer of oversight, holding leaders accountable to the standards of the community. Said Thomas

---

In the final analysis, the Origination Clause was a major selling point for the ratification of the Constitution, primarily because of the way it resonated with a citizenry so opposed to taxation without representation.

The Three-Fifths Compromise gave southern states more representation in the House of Representatives by counting three-fifths of each enslaved person toward their state's total population. It also counted three-fifths of the enslaved population when determining how much money each state would pay in taxes. It was a result of negotiations between the northern and southern states: southern states wanted to count their entire population to determine the number of representatives they could elect. Northern states wanted to exclude the counting of slaves because they had no voting rights.

At the time, the compromise helped build support for the Constitution's ratification in 1789. However, it had lasting impacts that led to the Civil War. In 1868, the 14th Amendment finally put an end to the Three-Fifths Compromise.

According to most historians, the Great Compromise helped save the Constitutional Convention and stimulated efforts to resolve many other important issues that would face the nation in the years to come.

Jefferson: "Whenever the people are well informed, they can be trusted with their own government; that whenever things get so far wrong as to attract their notice, they may be relied on to set them to rights."

Placing citizens at the center of governance, then, creates a dynamic where the imperfections of all individuals are counteracted by collective engagement and scrutiny. This interplay, between those being governed and those in power, acknowledges that human fallibility exists on both sides of the equation, fostering a more resilient and responsive system of governance.

Separation of Powers

IN AN ERA where information flows so abundantly, the role of mainstream media has become increasingly critical yet profoundly troubling. Misinformation disseminated by these outlets not only distorts public perception but also undermines the very fabric of our culture. The separation of powers, a principle designed to prevent any single entity from wielding excessive authority, seems to be an academic exercise rather than a lived reality. As we grapple with the implications of distorted truths, we must confront the somber reality that the unchecked power of media can erode political structures and civic trust.

The presence of misinformation in mainstream media isn't just a fringe issue; it also manifests daily in various forms, from sensationalist headlines to outright inaccuracies. This persistent problem ignites a culture of distrust, where citizens increasingly question the validity of the information they consume. When media outlets focus more on driving sensational narratives than on genuine fact-checking or responsible journalism, they contribute to a landscape where misinformation thrives. This erosion of journalistic integrity is particularly disheartening, as it creates a vicious cycle: the public becomes skeptical of reliable sources, leading to an increased vulnerability to false claims that often spread like wildfire.

The consequences of allowing misinformation to permeate our cultural landscape are dire. When the mainstream media irresponsibly wields power in the name of shaping public opinion, the lines between truth and lies blur. As individuals retreat into echo chambers where their beliefs go unchallenged, political polarization deepens, and the result is a fractured society incapable of meaningful discourse. Instead of serving as a watchdog, the media becomes a relentless instigator of division. In turn, a healthy body politic, which relies on informed citizens, becomes increasingly dysfunctional.

In light of this, we see just how the current cultural landscape reveals a troubling trend: mainstream media has amassed unwarranted power, often eclipsing accountability. In an age where a few corporations dominate the information sphere, the ideal of a balanced power structure is virtually a thing of the past. The very foundation meant to safeguard every other aspect of our republic is suddenly at risk because so often the mainstream media fails to perform its role responsibly, leaving room for despotism masked under the guise of information dissemination.

As we face this somber reality, it's essential to acknowledge the ways in which we can reclaim the narrative. Promoting media literacy is critical; educating the public on discerning credible information can slow the tide of misinformation. Not only that, but advocating for stricter regulations on media conglomerates also helps to diminish their unchecked influence. The hope is that through a collective effort, we can transform the current trajectory, ensuring that the American ideal of the separation of powers isn't merely theoretical but is a concrete reality.

The Growing Epidemic of Fake News

TO UNDERSTAND the relevance of the Founding Fathers' original vision, it's essential to recognize the role that the media plays in America. Just as the Founders aimed to prevent tyranny by creating layers of governance, a similar structure of accountability in the media serves to mitigate the spread of misinformation. The First Amendment protects freedom of the press, which is crucial for an informed society. Said Thomas Jefferson, in no uncertain terms: "Our liberty depends on the freedom of the press, and that cannot be limited without being lost."

However, that freedom also comes with the responsibility to report truthfully. When misinformation is allowed to circulate unchecked, it leads to public distrust and societal division, undermining the very foundations of our culture that the Founders sought to protect. As such, the freedom of the press contains within it the seeds of a peculiar paradox. After all, it's one thing to establish the sacred right to freedom, which the press has every right to claim for itself, but it's quite another thing when that same freedom is so easily corrupted when left uncontested. Certainly Jefferson had this in mind, when he warned us about the dark side of this tendency to abuse that freedom, even in his day: "Nothing can now be believed which is seen in a newspaper. Truth itself becomes suspicious by being put into that polluted vehicle."

Not only that, but the layered governance model established by the Founders can also be analogously applied to modern media systems. Just as state and national authorities are beholden to a hierarchy of accountability, so too should the media be held accountable. For example, local news outlets often have a more direct connection to their communities who are themselves positioned to hold local media accountable for its actions. Therefore, if larger media corporations prioritize sensationalism or profitability over against honesty and accuracy, local journalism should stand as a counterbalance, providing nuanced perspectives and fostering informed public discourse.

The rise of digital media also exacerbates the challenge of misinformation. In an age where information is so accessible, the speed at which stories spread often outpaces the verification processes traditionally employed by journalists. To address this, a multi-layered approach to media accountability could include the establishment of editorial standards and regulatory bodies that hold media companies accountable. Thus, such measures would resemble the Founders' vision of divided governance, where different entities work in tandem to create a more transparent and responsible media landscape.

In today's information-saturated world, the way we perceive significant issues, such as the decentralization of power, is heavily influenced by sensationalism, biases, and the growing epidemic of fake news. As these factors shape our understanding, they obscure the true potential and importance of decentralization in minimizing corruption and abuse of power. Therefore, it's crucial to examine how these elements interconnect and impact our collective vision of a more accountable society.

Sensationalism is a driving force in mainstream media narratives, often prioritizing shocking headlines over nuanced discussions. Instead of recognizing the potential for, say, greater accountability in decentralized systems, news outlets may focus solely on isolated failures or conflicts. This inevitably skews public opinion, ultimately undermining support for public policies that could lead to a more transparent and responsive governance structure.

Then there are the biases inherent in media coverage that complicate and obscure our understanding. News outlets may reflect the interests of their owners, leading to a selective portrayal of events that bolster certain narratives. When discussing decentralization, for example, it's essential to highlight how personal biases can create an incomplete or misleading picture. If a media outlet only reports scandals related to decentralized power structures while ignoring successful initiatives, the public may conclude that such systems are inherently flawed. This selective reporting reinforces existing prejudices and diminishes the legitimacy of decentralization as a corrective mechanism against political corruption and human weakness.

The epidemic of fake news, then, aggravates these challenges, clouding our comprehension of important socio-political issues. Misinformation can proliferate rapidly online, leading to widespread misunderstanding about decentralization and its impacts. For instance, false narratives might claim that decentralization leads to chaos or a lack of law and order, disregarding numerous examples where decentralization has sparked innovation and citizen empowerment. Such pervasive misinformation creates an environment of skepticism, preventing meaningful discussion about how decentralization effectively holds power to account and curbs corruption.

Unchecked Passions

THE CONVERSATION surrounding the efficacy and integrity of the electoral process in the United States is another issue that is increasingly fraught with confusion and disillusionment. As misinformation proliferates, particularly through mainstream media, a tragic narrative emerges: the Electoral College, which was designed by the Founding Fathers precisely to safeguard society, is frequently dismissed as irrelevant in modern-day America. This dismissal is often a reaction to the allure of popular sentiment, yet those passions can be misguided, leading to significant societal consequences.

At the heart of this issue is the troubling reality that many individuals engage with news sources that prioritize sensationalism over nuanced discourse. As such, the portrayal of the Electoral College is typically framed in stark terms: it is either criticized as being an outdated mechanism or derided as an outright obstacle to the will of the people. However, such black-and-white depictions overlook the complexities that originally shaped its creation—a mechanism to temper the volatility of public opinion with a more deliberative approach to governance. Yet, alarming misconceptions abound, suggesting that the Founders were instead seeking to eliminate the voice of the populace altogether, rather than crafting a system designed to harmonize popular will with careful reflection.

In reality, the Founders were acutely aware of the unbridled enthusiasm that could sweep through the populace, and they believed that unchecked passions could lead to detrimental decisions. To counteract this natural human tendency, the Electoral College was created to act as a buffer against impulsive choices made in the heat of the moment. So, rather than dismissing this ingenious framework, we should be mourning the failure of many to recognize its intended purpose. How sad, then, that because of the mainstream media's oversimplified narratives, which reinforce a sense of helplessness among our citizens, many are fooled into believing their voices are being nullified by an antiquated system. And how sad that this sense of helplessness only deepens the disconnect between people and the institutions meant to represent them, further blurring the lines of accountability.

Unfortunately, the consequences of this disconnect extend far beyond mere misunderstanding among voters; they breed apathy—one of the greatest enemies of a healthy body politic. Because when citizens are fed the narrative that their votes are irrelevant or their voices aren't being heard, the likelihood of their engaging in the political process diminishes drastically. This apathy is in fact the true tragedy of misinformation, as it undermines the principles of civic engagement that the Founding Fathers fought so hard to instill.

Influence of Historical Precedents

THE FRAMERS of the United States government didn't just dream of a perfect society built on the principles of liberty and justice for all; they also meticulously studied historical government failures to develop a pragmatic and cautious blueprint for governance. Their insights into human nature and political power were informed by cautionary tales of the past, shaping a framework that emphasized the need for checks and balances, rather than blind faith in humanity's inherent honesty and goodness.

An examination of history reveals numerous failures of governments that devolved into tyranny and chaos, providing valuable lessons for America's Founders. The downfall of the Roman Republic, with its gradual descent into autocracy, is a prime example.[14] The Founders observed how power, when concentrated in the hands of a few, inevitably corrupts and leads to the erosion of liberty. This understanding led them to create a divided government designed to prevent any single entity from gaining dominance. Each branch—the executive, legislative, and judicial—serves as a counterbalance to the others, ensuring accountability and

---

14   *The Downfall of the Roman Republic*: From Renaissance thinkers like Machiavelli, to Enlightenment thinkers like Montesquieu, the West has long speculated about the downfall of the Roman Republic. While Rome's decline is often blamed on a single figure like Julius Caesar, the process was complex and involved many factors. The primary reason that the Roman Republic degenerated into an autocracy was due to internal political turmoil, including growing social inequality, rampant corruption, and civil violence.

Add to that how the Roman Senate, once a body providing checks and balances, became increasingly corrupt due to struggles between factions and political gridlock. Also, as the Roman Empire expanded, military commanders, with their loyal armies, gained tremendous influence, giving them more and more power within the political landscape.

In turn, the gap between the wealthy elite and the common people widened, causing further unrest, and creating fertile ground for populist leaders to exploit. Widespread corruption within the government eroded public trust and allowed powerful individuals to manipulate the system for personal gain. As a result, Julius Caesar, a successful military leader, garnered immense popularity among the people and used his power to manipulate the political system, until eventually he was declared dictator.

Despite his popularity, Caesar's unbridled power alarmed many senators, which then led to his assassination. Following Caesar's death, his adopted heir Augustus used his military might and political cunning to defeat his rivals and establish himself as the first Roman Emperor, effectively ending the Republic.

protecting against the tyranny that so often arises when
authority is unchecked.

Additionally, reflections on the English Civil War further shaped the Founders' perspective.[15] They recognized

---

15   *The English Civil War*: Fought between Royalists and Parliamentarians,
beginning in 1642, the English Civil War was a struggle to determine the future
of England regarding numerous complex issues, including religion, the king's
use of power, and economic policy. Royalists supported King Charles I, convinced he should have absolute power over Parliament and the Church. The
Parliamentarians supported Parliament and opposed the absolute rule of King
Charles I and his supporters.

The role of religion is clearly what sparked the English War, with King
Charles I, on one side, who leaned heavily toward Catholicism. On the other
side was Oliver Cromwell and his Puritans who advocated for Puritanism. Both
sides invoked highly charged religious language to justify their position, framing the struggle as nothing less than a fight for the "true faith."

The king believed he had a divine right to rule, which meant he thought he
was king by the will of God and therefore his decisions couldn't be challenged or
questioned. This was opposed by those who believed that the people and their
representatives in Parliament should have more say in how the nation was governed. Charles also preferred an Anglican form of worship, which emphasized
rituals, lavish ornamentation, and a hierarchy of bishops and priests, especially
alarming for most Protestants because of his unpopular marriage to the prin-
cess Henrietta Maria, the Catholic daughter of the Bourbon king of France.

Economic factors also played a major part. After a costly and humiliating
defeat in a war with Spain, members of Parliament, in 1626, denied the king
any more money in support of the war, so the king resorted to raising money
through forced loans, and imprisoning anyone who refused to cooperate. Then,
in 1628, Parliament created a list of demands to end the king's abuse of the law
and his power to tax. In dire need of the money granted by Parliament, Charles
gave in, but it came at great cost. Once he obtained the money, the king dismissed Parliament, and didn't recall it for the next 11 years.

The English Civil War is arguably the bloodiest conflict in the history of
Britain. The final battle took place in 1644 when the Parliamentarians won the
Battle of Marston Moor. Five years later, Parliamentarians sentenced Charles I
to death, marking the only time in British history that the country was ruled
by a Republic. Oliver Cromwell ruled as Lord Protector of the Commonwealth.

This was the last civil war ever fought on English soil, and it has left an enduring legacy. The war forever altered the relationship between monarch and
Parliament, stimulating ongoing debates about justice, liberty, and democracy.
Ever since this period, the English have had a profound distrust of standing
armies, while ideas first introduced in the 1640s, particularly about religious
toleration and limitations on power, have survived to this day.

that revolutions, while often born from noble intentions, could still lead to instability and oppression if not carefully navigated. By establishing such foundational documents as the Bill of Rights, the Founders sought to institutionalize a respect for individual liberties amidst a political process so often swayed by unbridled human passions.

Distinguishing Fact From Fiction

IN A MEDIA environment deluged by sensationalism, personal biases, and fake news, it remains crucial to reflect on the foundational principles laid down by the Founders of America. While many of these individuals were deeply religious, they approached governance with a tempered understanding of human frailties, recognizing that lofty ideals must be balanced with practical considerations. As such, the Founding Fathers' realistic view of human nature informed their governance structures, helping to guard against the very biases and sensationalism we witness in contemporary society.

The political framework established by the Founders was heavily influenced by their awareness of human weakness and imperfections. Figures such as James Madison and Alexander Hamilton acknowledged that individuals are driven by self-interest and susceptible to passion and error. This is what led them to advocate for our system of checks and balances, to prevent the kind of authoritarian governance that arises from unchecked power. According to Hamilton, in *Federalist* No. 6: "Men are ambitious, vindictive, and rapacious," and should anyone think to dismiss his view, he insisted they'd be in danger of disregarding "the uniform course of human events," and defying "the accumulated experience of the ages." This pragmatic perspective serves as a reminder that, much like today, those in positions of power must navigate the complexities of human behavior, a reality that particularly resonates in our current battles against personally biased news reporting.

What's more, the Founders' commitment to the principle of free speech was born not only from Enlightenment ideals but also from an acute awareness of the dangers of misinformation. They understood that a well-informed citizenry is essential for a healthy body politic; however, they also recognized that the dissemination of lies undermines this goal. In this regard, the First Amendment can be seen as both a protection for free expression and a warning against the potential for that expression to be manipulated or distorted. Today's rampant spread of fake news serves as a stark illustration of how the very freedoms intended to enhance public life can be exploited, echoing the Founders' concerns about the frailty of human judgment in distinguishing fact from fiction.

In addition to governance and free speech, the Founding Fathers established a judicial system designed to mitigate the effects of bias and emotional responses. The courts were envisioned as independent entities capable of providing a fair application of the law, free from the whims of public opinion or political pressure. This foresight demonstrates their commitment to a system where reasoning could prevail over sensationalism. In our contemporary landscape, where media outlets often prioritize sensational content to attract viewers, the need for a just and impartial judiciary becomes even more pronounced. The Founders' realization of human biases in legal contexts underscores the importance of accountability in maintaining the rule of law amid societal distractions.

A Marvelous Interplay

THE U.S. Constitution stands as a testament to the foresight of the Founding Fathers, who understood that governance shouldn't depend solely on the goodwill of those in power. Instead, they embedded accountability mechanisms directly into the fabric of the Constitution, ensuring a system that promotes fairness, balances power, and protects the rights of individuals. This realistic framework lays the groundwork for a sustainable political process, fostering an environment where the rule of law prevails over partisan whims.

At the heart of the Constitution lies the principle of checking political power—a brilliant mechanism born of an acute awareness of human weakness and greed. By distributing authority among the legislative, executive, and judicial branches, the Founders created a structure in which each branch could monitor and challenge the other. This system not only serves to deter the corruption of power but also encourages a collaborative spirit among the branches. For instance, while the President can veto legislation, Congress can override that veto, showcasing a marvelous interplay that ensures no single entity can wield unchecked authority.

Not only that, but the Bill of Rights, added shortly after the original Constitution, also reinforces individual liberties and holds government accountable to the people. By explicitly protecting freedoms such as speech, religion, and assembly, the Founders anticipated that a government too comfortable in its own power might infringe upon the citizens it was meant to serve. This innovation represents a profound commitment to ensuring that governance remains attuned to the needs and rights of the populace—a belief that the voices of ordinary citizens matter immensely and must be safeguarded from potential abuses.

Another cornerstone of accountability embedded in the Constitution is an independent judiciary. The judicial branch acts as the guardian of the Constitution, allowing judges to interpret and apply laws impartially. This independence protects individuals from government overreach and assures that even the most powerful figures are subject to laws that hold them accountable. The optimism inherent in this structure lies in the principle that justice can prevail through reasoned interpretation rather than political favoritism.

Overcoming Cognitive Biases

THE DOMINANT narrative that America's Founding Fathers laid out a plan for government anchored in an idealistic view of humanity oversimplifies a deeper truth: their approach was actually both realistic and pragmatic. The Founders were acutely aware of humanity's myriad shortcomings, and so they sought to build a system that could withstand human failings. However, in a modern age like ours, where information travels faster than ever, the prevalence of media misinformation poses a significant challenge, especially in the context of American government. Understanding the complexities of human behavior is vital in navigating this landscape while upholding individual rights and recognizing inherent human frailty.

At the heart of addressing media misinformation lies a robust understanding of human behavior. Cognitive biases, such as the Confirmation Bias, the Dunning-Kruger Effect, and the Optimism Bias, often lead us to accept and share information that aligns with our pre-existing beliefs, regardless of its accuracy.[16] The American government, by

---

16 *Cognitive Bias*: The tendency to interpret what we see and hear in a way that confirms our pre-existing beliefs, a Cognitive Bias often leads to errors in judgment. Cognitive biases are our brain's way of simplifying the processing of information. Biases often work as shorthand to speed up our attempts to make sense of the world and make important decisions.

The Confirmation Bias describes our tendency to ignore or downplay evidence that contradicts our pre-existing beliefs, while doubling up on everything else that confirms our thinking, essentially creating a filter that only lets in evidence that corresponds with our existing views.

The Dunning-Kruger Effect refers to how we tend to assume we know more than we really know about a particular subject, which leads to a false sense of confidence due to our lack of awareness about our own limitations.

The Optimism Bias leads us to believe that we are less likely to suffer from misfortune and more likely to attain success than our peers. As a result, we focus on things we look forward to rather than negative events, and anticipate bad things that may happen to others but not ourselves.

Together, these tendencies inspire us to seek personal rewards without acknowledging the negative impact they might have on those around us—including ourselves.

acknowledging these behavioral patterns, can tailor its outreach strategies to promote media literacy. By educating citizens about the psychological traps that misinformation exploits, the government can empower us to critically analyze the information that we consume, contributing to a healthier information ecosystem.

Further still, celebrating individual rights within the context of misinformation emphasizes the need for free speech while implementing safeguards against harmful content. Yes, the First Amendment does protect the right to freely express our ideas, but that's not all there is to the story. In the context of the Founders' acute awareness of human failings, it also creates dilemmas in which false information lead to real-world consequences. A sincere approach to this issue, then, requires a delicate balance between protecting free expression and curbing the spread of dangerous misinformation. Strategies such as unbiased fact-checking initiatives could help to uphold this balance, providing the public with resources to discern truth from lies while respecting the press' autonomy.

Recognizing human weakness and failure is equally critical. We don't always act rationally, especially under emotional stress or during crises. Misinformation thrives in times of uncertainty, as fear and anxiety push us toward sensational or misleading narratives. By taking into account these emotional responses, the American government could develop more humane communication strategies that address the emotional undercurrents of misinformation. Crafting messages that resonate emotionally while providing factual clarity could help bridge the gap between individual feelings and objective reality.

What's more, collaboration with social media platforms presents a practical avenue to counter misinformation. The government could work with these platforms to create guidelines that prioritize the dissemination of factual information while still empowering us to express our own views. Such partnerships could facilitate a collective effort to reduce misinformation's impact, emphasizing the importance of shared responsibility in fostering an informed citizenry.

In conclusion, overcoming the bias of media misinformation in America requires a complex understanding of human behavior, a steadfast commitment to individual rights, and an acceptance of human imperfections. The distortions propagated by narratives such as the one that states that America's Founders assumed humans are innately good and honest remind us of the importance of critical thinking. By debunking myths like this, we not only honor the original vision of the Founders, but we also equip ourselves with the knowledge we need to navigate the realities of governance and the nature of humanity. As we reflect on their intentions, we must ask ourselves: are we equally prepared to recognize and confront our own imperfections?

CHAPTER FIVE

Divide and Conquer:

The Weaponization of Identity Politics

LIE #5:

Politicians Who are Not Perfect Should be Removed From Office...

I REMEMBER the day I sat down for another after-school session with my professor, and I noticed the strangest look on the old man's face. At first, I couldn't decide what it meant. Was he looking at me the way my mother looked when she was going to lecture me about one of my character defects? Or was it the way my father looked when as a child he caught me "playing doctor" with the neighbor's young daughter?

Finally, he spoke up and mercifully answered my question. "So ... have you heard the news about your guy running for office?"

Clueless about what he meant, I shrugged. "News? What news?"

"Scandal, my boy, scandal."

And at that point, my professor proceeded to relay the latest story, hot off the press, describing all the sordid details about a political candidate that my professor knew I was planning to vote for. Something about an alleged extramarital affair, and then more about an alleged payoff to keep the story from hitting all the major news outlets. Sadly, it wasn't the first time I had heard such things, which I considered to be nothing more than the basest form of politically motivated gossip designed to sway votes away from this person.

"Pretty despicable stuff, eh?" my professor spouted.

Trying my best to act unaffected, I shrugged again. "Pardon me for saying so, Professor, but are you sure it isn't just more political gamesmanship?"

"Good God, man, how can you say that? You, of all people? I thought you were a Christian. What happened to your scruples? This is a public office we're talking about. If what they're saying is true, this isn't just some minor indiscretion: we're talking cover-up here. You know very well if someone is caught doing stuff like this in their private life, they'll do the same thing in their public life."

After carefully considering his words, I slowly replied, "I noticed you said, 'If what they're saying is true.' Aren't you at all worried the story could turn out to be false?"

"Good luck with that," the old man smugly replied, with an arrogance I had never seen in him before. "This isn't the first time stories like this have circulated, you know."

"I realize that," I said, still unwilling to pile on without any real evidence. "What ever happened to due process? I thought in America, we were innocent until proven guilty."

And at this, that look of his returned: part disapproving mother, part shocked father. He leaned back in his chair, and exhaled deeply. "I don't mind saying so, but I am surprised at you."

"Surprised? You're surprised at me?"

"Why, yes, I expected so much more from you. I mean, we're talking about someone who, if elected, could potentially defile an esteemed position of public trust. Don't you find that troubling?"

"Yes, I do," I quietly replied, which seemed to satisfy my professor, as if he'd changed my mind. However, what really troubled me wasn't so much a politician's alleged misdeeds but how my usually rational professor could become so emotionally charged without his typically scholastic approach to evidence. And as was my typical response, I, in turn, determined to explore the dynamics of such reactionary behavior, hoping to avoid a similar irrationality in myself.

> *"I walk on untrodden ground. There is scarcely an action of mine whose motives is not subject to a double interpretation. There is scarcely any part of my conduct which may not hereafter set a precedent."*
>
> *George Washington*

Prioritizing Survival Over Service

IN TODAY'S polarized political landscape, the atmosphere is rife with accusations, rivalries, and the frequent removal of imperfect political figures from office. This phenomenon not only highlights the fragility of republican institutions, but it also raises questions about the extent to which political rivalries and divisive strategies have dominated our political discourse. The Founding Fathers of the United States envisaged a political system that would guard against such fractious dynamics, understanding that excessive polarization impedes governance and tears at the very fabric of political life in America.

The current political climate is characterized by deep divides along ideological and identity lines. Politicians often exploit these divisions for personal gain, encouraging a culture of antagonism that undermines constructive dialogue. This divisive strategy isn't new, though, as historical precedents demonstrate how effective such tactics are in galvanizing support, leading to a fragmented elec-

torate, making consensus-building increasingly difficult.
While such strategies might yield short-term victories for
political parties, they create an environment that incites
mistrust and hostility among different groups, reminiscent
of the warnings issued by the Founding Fathers regarding
factionalism.

The Founders, in their wisdom, recognized the dangers
posed by partisanship, and although they could have never
known what we know now, they did anticipate and provide
safeguards against what is today known as Identity Politics.[17] In *Federalist* No. 10, James Madison expressed concern that factions could lead to the tyranny of the majority,
undermining the rights of minority groups. Said Madison:
"Complaints are everywhere heard from our most considerate and virtuous citizens, that our governments are too
unstable; that the public good is disregarded in the conflicts of rival parties; and that measures are too often decided, not according to the rules of justice and the rights of
the minor party, but by the superior force of an interested
and over-bearing majority." This foresight was crucial for
shaping a governance framework designed to check the
ambitions of factions through a system of checks and bal-

---

17   *Identity Politics*: Rather than organizing around traditional party affiliations, Identity Politics seeks to mobilize social activism based on a shared
ethnic group, social background, or personal attachment, to form exclusive
political alliances, while moving away from typical broad-based party politics.
As such, members of a particular constituency assert this unique membership
allows them greater opportunity to challenge dominant characterizations,
with the goal of greater self-determination. This identification can also include
membership based on ideological positions such as nationalism, inter-ethnic
relations, or more abstract philosophical themes.

The notion of Identity Politics emerged as a social movement in the 1980s
and 90s when the civil rights and women's movements began to focus more on
cultural identification than on political identification. In cultural terms, Identity Politics can also be described as the belief that identity itself—its elaboration,
expression, or affirmation—is and should be the fundamental focus of political
work. As such, Identity Politics has politicized areas of life never before defined as being political, including "sexuality, interpersonal relations, lifestyle,
and culture."

ances. Yet, the very system put in place to prevent the rise of oppressive factions is being strained under the weight of contemporary political rivalries and the relentless pursuit of power.

What's more, the culture of removing political figures from office based on accusations—often inflamed by partisan media—further complicates the political landscape. While accountability is a cornerstone of American society, the manner and frequency with which officials are dismissed can create an environment of instability and fear. It breeds a cycle where politicians prioritize survival over service, further aligning their actions with their political identity rather than the broader public interest. This shift not only erodes trust in elected officials but also in the American political process itself, leaving citizens feeling disenfranchised and conflicted.

The Flawed Logic of Perfection in Politics

THE FIRES OF political rivalry are often stoked by a singular, damaging narrative: the belief that any public official who demonstrates imperfections is unfit for office. This notion reflects a broader divisive strategy rooted in Identity Politics—a tactic that serves to manipulate voters and create discord based on race, religion, and political affiliation. Upon closer inspection, though, the view that imperfect political figures should be removed from office reveals a deeper, more troubling trend within contemporary politics. This inclination, often fueled by public outrage and an insatiable demand for perfection, reflects a political strategy that is less about promoting qualified leadership traits and more about oversimplifying complex human experiences into binary judgments that only undermine the American political process.

At the heart of this belief is a tendency to view political figures not merely as individuals with their own flaws but as representatives of larger identity groups. In an era characterized by heightened polarization, the expectation for political leaders to embody an idealized version of their constituents leads to unrealistic standards. When these figures inevitably make mistakes or fall short of these exaggerated ideals, the calls for their removal can be intense and immediate. What gets lost in all this, though, is how this reaction completely overlooks the multifaceted nature of governance, where mistakes are often part of a learning process necessary for growth and improvement.

Not only that, but the removal of political figures based on imperfections also distracts from the important issues at stake. Instead of engaging in meaningful dialogue about policies and priorities, discussions devolve into character assassinations rooted in identity-based grievances. This shift not only erodes public trust in leaders but also diminishes the quality of political discourse. It creates an environment where individuals are more willing to engage in personal attacks instead of confronting the challenges in policy that face their communities and the nation.

Adding another layer of complexity, the divisive nature of this belief is often exacerbated by social media, which amplifies outrage and mobilizes identity-based responses. The instantaneous nature of online platforms allows for rapid dissemination of information, often focusing on sensationalized portrayals of political figures. This creates echo chambers where imperfections are magnified, overshadowing the leaders' accomplishments and capabilities. Thomas Jefferson described this tendency to criticize every public figure, no matter how hard they tried to serve their constituents, when he said: "There is no act, however virtuous, for which ingenuity may not find some bad motive." As a result, the public's perception of political figures becomes increasingly skewed, prioritizing their flaws over their potential to effect real social change.

Understanding Identity Politics

WHILE DEFENDERS of Identity Politics argue that it fosters a sense of belonging and representation for marginalized communities, it also raises concerns about divisiveness, contributing to an "us versus them" mentality. This dual nature necessitates a nuanced examination of Identity Politics, highlighting both its potential benefits and its inherent risks.

At its core, Identity Politics aims to empower groups that have historically faced exclusion or discrimination. By prioritizing the perspectives and needs of specific communities, advocates argue that these movements are able to promote social justice and equity. For instance, the feminist movement has historically fought for women's rights, revealing the unique challenges that women face and advocating for social changes. Similarly, movements focused on racial justice bring attention to the social inequalities that affect people of color. In this way, Identity Politics serves as a vehicle for representation, allowing marginalized voices to be heard in political discussions where they have been previously silenced.

In a society that often marginalizes certain identities, the formation of supportive communities can be healing and empowering. These groups provide not just a platform for advocacy but also a network of shared experiences and solidarity. Through shared narratives, individuals find strength and support, which is crucial for psychological well-being and social resilience. This sense of belonging is particularly vital in an era where isolation and alienation are prevalent, giving individuals the opportunity to connect with others who identify with their struggles.

However, the emphasis on group identity can also lead to significant divisiveness. This "us versus them" mentality creates barriers to understanding and communication between different groups. When dialogue is framed in terms of identity categorizations, it reduces the complexity of individual experiences to simplistic binaries. This oversimplification perpetuates stereotypes and provokes resentment, making it difficult for coalitions to form across different identity groups. The potential for conflict intensifies when individuals feel that their group's interests are under threat from others, leading to a climate of competition rather than cooperation.

What's more, Identity Politics can detract from broader issues that affect all members of society, such as economic inequality and social justice. When political discourse becomes centered around group identities, essential intersections of class, geography, and circumstance may be overlooked. This focus inadvertently weakens alliances among those who might otherwise unite in addressing shared societal problems. So, instead of building bridges, Identity Politics often winds up deepening existing divisions, undermining the social cohesion needed to tackle enduring challenges.

The Weaponization of Identity

IN CONTEMPORARY society, Identity Politics has become a double-edged sword, wielded skillfully by politicians seeking to galvanize support while simultaneously demonizing their opponents. This increasingly prevalent tactic not only skews public perception but also fuels an environment rife with conflict and division. As political leaders manipulate various identities—be it race, gender, or socioeconomic status—they guide their narratives in ways that overlook the complexities of human experience in favor of an oversimplified dichotomy of "worthy versus unworthy."

The first element of this troubling dynamic is the exploitation of identity for political gain. Politicians frequently emphasize shared qualities among certain demographic groups, overemphasizing the "us versus them" mentality that so effectively galvanizes their bases. By doing so, they cultivate a sense of belonging and purpose among their supporters, who then become more passionately aligned with a given political agenda. This focus on identity becomes a convenient battle cry, yet it often leads to a dangerous oversimplification of issues that require nuanced understanding.

More and more, the demonization of opponents has become a hallmark of this political strategy. Rivals are framed as lesser beings due to their moral failings, policy missteps, or unfavorable personal beliefs. This relentless pursuit of character assassination has far-reaching implications; it turns political discourse into a battlefield where human flaws are magnified, and the complexities of political thought are reduced to caricatures. As a result, public perception is skewed, contributing to a culture of intolerance that condemns anyone who disagrees. The political arena transforms into a no-win game, where the perceived failure of one side is celebrated as a victory by the other.

The environment of conflict created by this approach isn't just theoretical; it is also manifested in real-world consequences. Political discussions, once rooted in policies, are overshadowed by personal attacks. Civility fades, and constructive dialogue is replaced by shouting matches and social media outrage. This deterioration of discourse ultimately leads to a citizenry that is more polarized and less equipped to engage with complex issues. The relentless cycle of identity exploitation and rival demonization ignites not just hostility but a complete breakdown in trust among different groups, making it exceedingly difficult to find common ground.

The Hypocrisy of Pursuing Perfection

IN CONTEMPORARY political discourse, the accusation of imperfection directed at politicians is often employed as a favored tactic within Identity Politics. However, upon further review, we see just how this strategy, while seemingly grounded in accountability, reveals an inherent hypocrisy: it erects a standard of perfection that no human being can realistically attain. Politicians are routinely subjected to scrutiny over their past actions, statements, or affiliations, creating an unforgiving environment that demands an absurd level of flawlessness. The expectation that these public figures exist devoid of faults not only distorts the criteria for public service but also undermines the nuance necessary for measured political discourse.

Identity Politics thrives on the notion that individuals speak from their own experiences, and thus, they should embody a flawless representation of the constituencies they represent. However, this often translates into an unrealistic expectation that all politicians, especially those from marginalized groups, must exemplify unblemished ideals. Naturally, calling out flaws or missteps does have its proper place, but to declare that such imperfections wholly disqualifies someone breeds an exclusionary atmosphere rather than an inclusive one. In this way, Identity Politics paradoxically attacks the very voices it aims to elevate, reducing political figures to mere symbols rather than complex individuals with a myriad of experiences.

This pursuit of perfection also leads to dismissing capable leaders who don't quite fit the ideal mold. But keep in mind: Politicians, because they are human, will always be flawed; however, this fact doesn't negate their ability to serve effectively or advocate for the interests of their constituents. Yet through the lens of Identity Politics, which prioritizes purity over experience, the bar is set so high that it effectively eliminates those who could otherwise bring diversity of thought and experience to political debates. As such, it's a self-defeating strategy that actually betrays the very principles it claims to uphold.

The hypocrisy of this approach becomes even more apparent upon reflection of the broader implications. If society continues to elevate its demand for flawless politicians, based on an unreasonable expectation of perfection, it perpetuates a cycle where only the most strategically polished candidates thrive, usually at the expense of genuine engagement with complex social issues. The result: a political landscape overrun by individuals who lack the necessary understanding of the diverse experiences they represent, thus contradicting the very aims of Identity Politics.

Promotion of Extremism

IN RECENT years, political narratives have shifted dramatically, favoring extreme viewpoints that are often cloaked in the guise of idealism. This trend poses a significant threat to moderate candidates who seek to engage in thoughtful discourse and compromise. The allure of radical perspectives, which promise sweeping changes and ideal solutions, has captivated a large segment of the electorate. As a result, candidates who advocate for practical, moderate policies are overshadowed and marginalized in a political landscape that rewards hostility over sensibility.

More and more, our current political climate is marked by an intense polarization that feeds on itself. Enthusiastic supporters of extreme viewpoints often view all opposition as not merely different but as "existential threats." Add to that the way this culture of extremism is amplified by social media platforms, and it's no wonder that everywhere you look, you're confronted by echo chambers of radical ideas that drown out any and all moderate voices. In turn, the characterization of moderate stances as timid or lacking conviction further alienates those who might otherwise support pragmatic solutions. Consequently, moderates find it increasingly difficult to compete in an arena that rewards bombastic rhetoric over nuanced policy discussion.

The mainstream media also plays a crucial role in shaping these political narratives. Unfortunately, because coverage tends to gravitate towards sensationalism, only the most extreme positions are spotlighted. This not only skews public perception, but it also rewards politicians who adopt more radical positions to gain attention and support. The mainstream media, in its quest for higher ratings, neglects the subtleties of moderate policymaking, which only further entrenches the belief that the more extreme one's ideas are, the more authentic they are. As a result, moderate candidates often lack the visibility and recognition that is required to mount successful campaigns.

The danger of this shift is manifold. When political discourse is dominated by extreme viewpoints, the space for compromise and bipartisanship diminishes. Issues that are critical to the well-being of society—such as health care, social justice, and economic stability—require collaboration and debate. Yet, the prevailing narrative increasingly frames compromise as weakness, leading to inaction and stagnation. And so, pushed to extremes, the populace becomes more and more cynical, which, in turn, contributes to a culture that is reactive rather than proactive.

The Theater of Politics

IN TODAY'S political landscape, removing imperfect leaders under the guise of moral superiority isn't just prevalent; it is also deeply hypocritical. Politicians and voters often assert that their disdain for leaders' flaws stems from a desire for ethical governance. However, this purported pursuit of moral authority frequently distances these same voters from the practical implications of effective governance. Instead of focusing on meaningful policy-making, a legislative gridlock ensues—one in which officeholders are more concerned about public perception than about enacting laws that actually benefit their constituents.

To begin with, the relentless push to unseat "flawed" leaders calls into question the sincerity of these concerns. Voters demand accountability and high ethical standards, yet they often ignore the complexities of governance that require compromise and negotiation. Instead of selecting leaders who can navigate these challenges, they opt for "ideal" candidates—paragons of virtue who often lack the practical skills required to legislate effectively. This makes for an amusing contradiction; while voters clamor for moral integrity, they simultaneously dismiss those who understand the nuanced reality of governance. Instead of collaboration, we find ourselves in a state of paralysis, as the very leaders who might be capable of enacting change are branded as morally inferior.

What's more, this self-righteous high ground, taken by voters and politicians alike, overshadows the essence of effective governance, which is practical policy-making. When politicians prioritize image management over critical reforms, the public suffers. The theater of politics—focused on an endless cycle of virtue signaling—distracts from the need for compromise and dialogue. Legislative gridlock becomes an all-too-familiar narrative, as elected officials find themselves ensnared in a web of public scrutiny, ever fearful of being labeled as inadequate or immoral. The irony is palpable; by elevating their principles above practicality, both leaders and constituents unwittingly contribute to their own political impotence.

This disturbing trend not only stunts legislative advancement but entrenches a cycle where the perception of morality impedes the execution of policy. Many politicians feel compelled to align their actions with public opinion and in the process sacrifice groundbreaking policies just to maintain an impeccable image. In such an environment, the true spirit of the republic—where elected officials should navigate the complexities of governance for the common good—is cast aside in favor of a facade of righteousness.

A Culture of Black-and-White Judgments

IN TODAY'S politically charged atmosphere, media outlets employ divisive rhetoric that amplifies discontent with political figures, often portraying leaders as irredeemably flawed. This strategy, while effective in attracting viewers, ultimately perpetuates a culture of dissatisfaction and distrust among the public. As the mainstream media serves as a primary source of information, the way it frames political narratives has profound implications for societal morale and engagement with governance.

At the heart of this issue lies the age-old tendency of many media organizations to prioritize sensationalism over meaningful reporting. By focusing on the flaws of political leaders rather than their policies or achievements, these outlets create a distorted image that warps public perception. This portrayal not only positions leaders as irredeemable but also fuels an environment where criticism becomes the default stance. The result is a disillusioned electorate that feels disconnected from a political system perceived to be inherently corrupt and ineffective. This disengagement is aggravated by a media landscape that rewards outrage instead of rational discourse, leading to a cycle of negativity that breeds frustration and apathy.

Not only that, but the use of hyperbole and loaded language also deepens the divide within the political landscape. Media outlets often resort to exaggerated descriptions of political leaders and their actions, contributing to a culture where complex issues are reduced to black-and-white judgments. This oversimplification not only deprives viewers of a nuanced understanding of political dynamics, but it also reinforces their biases, creating echo chambers of discontent. As audiences are bombarded with messages depicting leaders as incompetent or villainous, their trust in these figures diminishes, spawning a pervasive sense of hopelessness about political accountability and reform.

The consequences of this media-driven narrative extend far beyond individual perceptions of leaders; they permeate the broader political discourse. With public trust eroded, civic engagement suffers as citizens become increasingly cynical about their ability to influence meaningful change. This disenchantment inevitably leads to widespread disengagement from the electoral process, as individuals feel that their votes are futile in a system dominated by flawed representatives.

Manipulation That Breeds Contempt

IT IS AMUSING how, in today's political landscape, media manipulation has led voters to align with what they perceive as the "perfect" candidate, effectively isolating themselves from opinions and advice that come from those they deem imperfect. This phenomenon not only highlights the superficiality of such a viewpoint but also underscores the sheer absurdity of how the idealized version of a candidate blinds people to the complexities of real-world politics. The idea that one can find a flawless candidate in a sea of human imperfection is both laughable and dangerously naive.

To begin with, the media plays a pivotal role in shaping voter perceptions. Political narratives are often carefully crafted to amplify the strengths of a candidate while conveniently burying any flaws beneath layers of favorable coverage. Voters, seduced by this manipulation, begin to develop an almost cult-like admiration for these so-called "perfect" candidates. It is comical how these individuals fail to recognize that the very qualities they idolize—pristine records, unwavering stances, charismatic personalities—are often products of strategic media portrayal rather than genuine human traits. The irony, of course, is that by aligning with such a manufactured ideal, they become unwilling to consider alternative perspectives, dismissing any counsel as a direct affront to their chosen candidate.

Rejecting the counsel of those seen as imperfect also further compounds the farcical nature of this phenomenon. It is intriguing how individuals who tout their open-mindedness become strikingly intolerant when faced with dissenting views. The moment a piece of advice or an alternative opinion doesn't align with their image of a perfect candidate, it's summarily dismissed. This behavior isn't just hypocritical; it is also a testament to how dogmatic adherence to a single narrative can stifle healthy discourse. The rejectionist attitude is especially vivid in online platforms, where echo chambers thrive and dissent is routinely silenced. Thus, voters who once championed the idea of "democracy" morph into advocates of a worldview that is vastly different from the one they claim to champion.

Also important to recognize is the role of social media in facilitating this bizarre alignment. Platforms that encourage sensationalism often reward overly simplistic narratives about political candidates, heightening the allure of selecting an "ideal" choice. The cacophony of likes, shares, and comments inflames an environment where the image of the perfect candidate isn't just embraced; it is exalted. How sad to see, then, how easily manipulated these voters are; they grab hold of a carefully curated facade and blindly endorse candidates who, in reality, are just as flawed as everyone else in the political arena. This act of selective blindness speaks volumes about their inability to confront the imperfect nature of humanity, particularly in a political context.

Inducing Hostility

IN A DIGITAL age dominated by instant information, the mainstream media's manipulation of public perception has become a significant force. This manipulation, so often driven by personal bias, has curtailed genuine interaction among diverse groups and has instead fanned the flames of animosity, division, and prejudice. Rather than promoting understanding, this digital environment feeds a frenzy of hostile voices and cultural rifts.

As such, the pervasive nature of biased media can't be overstated, because the constant prioritizing of sensationalism over factual reporting is so pronounced that the result is an environment where individuals are only exposed to viewpoints that reinforce their existing beliefs, further entrenching their mistrust of opposing perspectives.

Worse still, the impact of media manipulation on diverse groups is particularly detrimental. Individuals from different backgrounds, cultures, and political beliefs find themselves increasingly alienated from one another. Instead of seeking common ground, they mindlessly push toward conflict and misunderstanding. Debates that could be rooted in productive discourse are instead marred by hostility, leading to prejudice based on misrepresentation and lack of accurate information. This spiral into divisiveness is alarming, as it undermines the foundational pillars of a cohesive society.

The cultural implications of this strategy of divide and conquer are profound. As animosity grows, so does the potential for violence and unrest. When groups are pitted against one another, the underlying nuances of different perspectives are lost. Rather than working together toward unity and harmony, communities fracture, leading to a landscape littered with distrust and resentment. Long-standing relationships among diverse groups are often irreparably damaged, with members choosing sides instead of embracing diversity.

In a world where understanding and unity could thrive, the current media landscape has instead sown seeds of mistrust and paranoia. The consequences of this manipulation extend beyond individual interactions; they shape societal narratives and directly influence political decision-making. The pessimistic reality we face is that as long as media continues to manipulate biases and reinforce division, the potential for understanding and harmony among diverse groups remains alarmingly out of reach.

Social Media as an Amplifier

IN THE DIGITAL age, social media has transformed from a simple communication tool into a potent platform for Identity Politics, where personal biases are routinely reinforced and dissenting opinions are seldom confronted. This sad reality stems from the very nature of these platforms, designed to connect like-minded individuals while breeding an environment that discourages open dialogue. The consequences are profound, as the voices of those who dare to challenge the dominant narratives are often drowned out, leaving many feeling isolated in their beliefs.

Yes, the great allure of social media lies in its ability to create communities virtually overnight. However, this instant community-building does come at a tremendous cost. That's because so often users can't resist the urge to curate their feeds, surrounding themselves with content that reflects their own views and experiences. Unfortunately, this selective exposure inevitably leads to an amplification of biases, as algorithms prioritize content that aligns with user interests. When faced with contrasting opinions, many users choose to disengage rather than engage, contributing to a culture where dissent is avoided, and polarization flourishes. This division impedes the opportunity for growth and understanding, leaving individuals trapped in silos of thought.

With Identity Politics flavoring discussions in this way, the atmosphere of social media is stifled with ever-increasing levels of hate and hostility rather than empathy and compassion. When disagreements arise, they typically escalate into personal attacks, prompting users to retreat further into their comfort zones. Those who might have entertained differing views may feel a deep sense of sadness at the deterioration of constructive dialogue, recognizing that their own humanity is challenged when others fail to see the nuanced realities that define us all.

As these trends continue, it's disheartening to observe how social media is increasingly shaping our identities in such divisive ways. More than ever, the importance of empathy and openness is overshadowed by the clamor of echo chambers. The pain of this reality is felt by many who long for connection yet find themselves ensnared in tribalism.

A Culture of Instability

THE CALL for the removal of imperfect leaders has gained substantial traction in recent years, more often driven by public outrage than by meaningful civic engagement. This trend signifies a troubling shift in how citizens interact with their political systems, reflecting a broader disillusionment with leadership that many see as failing to meet their expectations. The implications of this vicious cycle poignantly highlight the dangers of replacing leaders based predominantly on emotional reactions rather than informed decision-making.

At the heart of this phenomenon lies a pervasive dissatisfaction with those in power. Many citizens have become increasingly vocal about their grievances, particularly in response to political scandal, economic hardship, or social injustices. While it's vital for a healthy society to hold leaders accountable, the emotional intensity that often accompanies these calls for removal can lead to impulsive decisions. This approach neglects a critical aspect of civic engagement: the thoughtful evaluation of a leader's policies and qualifications. Instead of fostering productive discourse, outrage can create an atmosphere ripe for rash judgments that ultimately disrupts the political process.

Worse still, this cycle feeds on itself, perpetuating a culture of instability. When leaders are removed based on outrage rather than a comprehensive understanding of their policies and performance, the replacements may not bring the necessary foresight or expertise to address the underlying issues. The constant rotation of leadership can hinder long-term planning and policy implementation, leaving communities adrift. For example, in various political contexts, frequent leadership changes—born out of fiery public sentiment—have led to governance that lacks continuity. This instability can exacerbate the very problems that citizens are protesting against, creating a feedback loop of dissatisfaction and leadership turnover.

In addition, the reliance on outrage as a primary motivator for political change can alienate those who seek more constructive avenues for engagement. Civic engagement is grounded in the principles of dialogue, education, and community involvement. When the focus shifts to emotional reactions, it risks marginalizing those who advocate for a more measured approach. This marginalization, in turn, leads to a disconnect between leaders and constituents, further aggravating the public's sense of disenfranchisement. In contrast to a reliance on outrage, a healthy body politic should seek to empower citizens to engage thoughtfully with their leaders, fostering an environment where informed criticism and informed support coexist. As James Madison insisted: "A popular government without popular information, or the means of acquiring it, is but a prologue to a farce or a tragedy, or perhaps both. Knowledge will forever govern ignorance; and a people who mean to be their own governors must arm themselves with the power which knowledge gives."

In Pursuit of Unattainable Perfection

IN THE REALM of political discourse, the pursuit of perfection in governance often overshadows the more realistic and humane understanding of leadership. While the idea of an immaculate political system is tempting, it's essential to recognize that imperfection is an inherent aspect of human experience and governance. The Founding Fathers of the United States, who sought to establish a viable framework for republicanism, appreciated this complexity and designed a system that acknowledges flaws and encourages growth.

Embracing the complexity of governance begins with acknowledging that human nature isn't without its flaws. Leaders are, after all, individuals shaped by their experiences, beliefs, and imperfections. Because the Founders recognized that absolute control or unyielding perfection would lead to tyranny, they chose a system characterized by checks and balances. This framework wasn't merely a safeguard against the concentration of power, but it was also a testament to their understanding of human fallibility. By crafting a government that encourages debate, compromise, and participation, they embraced the messy reality of political life.

Not only that, but striving for political perfection also diverts attention from pressing real-world issues. When leaders and citizens fixate on idealistic goals, they may overlook prevailing inequalities and injustices. In contrast, a governance model that accepts imperfection allows for gradual yet persistent progress, where policies are revisited and revised in light of new evidence and changing circumstances. This flexibility is crucial, especially in an increasingly complex world that demands dynamic responses to multifaceted challenges. The Founders' emphasis on adaptability in the Constitution suggests their foresight into the evolving nature of society.

Recognizing the flaws inherent in leadership also promotes a culture of empathy and understanding among citizens. When leaders openly acknowledge their imperfections, it humanizes the political process and encourages accountability. The public is more likely to engage with and support leaders who convey authenticity and vulnerability rather than those who project an impossible ideal. This sense of connection is vital for the health of any society, as it inspires active participation from the citizenry, transforming the governance process into a collective endeavor rather than a solitary pursuit of unattainable perfection.

Policy Rather Than Personality

UNDERSTANDING the inherent imperfections of leadership in today's complex political landscape can significantly enrich our political dialogue. Rather than fixating solely on the moral integrity of politicians, an approach that encourages us to evaluate their actions and policies fosters a more constructive and insightful discourse. By embracing the inherent flaws that come with leadership, we cultivate a political environment that prioritizes accountability and informed decision-making over idealistic narratives.

One of the key benefits of recognizing imperfection in leadership is that it encourages critical thinking among citizens. When we accept that politicians are, by nature, fallible individuals, we open ourselves to the idea that their decisions and policies are subject to scrutiny. This focus on policy rather than personality allows us to engage in more meaningful discussions about the effectiveness of political decisions and achievements. For instance, rather than decrying a politician for past misdeeds, we can evaluate how their specific policies affect the community. This shift in perspective promotes dialogue based on evidence, rather than on emotional reactions to a politician's character.

Acknowledging imperfection in leadership also leads to more robust accountability mechanisms. Political discourse often becomes polarized when individuals adopt an "us versus them" mentality, idolizing or vilifying leaders based on their perceived morality. By understanding that all leaders make mistakes, we're better able to inspire a culture of constructive critique rather than blind allegiance or disdain. This ultimately leads to a more nuanced understanding of governance, where politicians are expected to learn from errors and grow in their roles. As citizens, we can encourage this growth by advocating for transparent discussions about the impacts of policy instead of attacking the individual behind it.

Most importantly, a focus on policy rather than personality promotes collaboration across ideological lines. When discussions center around the benefits and drawbacks of specific policies, it's easier to find common ground. Instead of engaging in debates that revolve around perceived moral superiority, politicians and citizens alike can work together to develop solutions that benefit the entire community. This cooperative spirit paves the way for innovative ideas and bipartisan collaboration, ultimately leading to more effective governance.

Building Bridges, Not Walls

IN AN INCREASINGLY polarized world, the narratives shaped by Identity Politics often create division rather than unity. To counter these divisive narratives, a concerted effort must be made to build bridges, not walls, between varying groups. This approach not only offers the promise of social cohesion but also enhances our collective ability to engage with one another in meaningful ways.

Building bridges begins with recognizing the shared humanity that exists among all individuals, regardless of their backgrounds. Many people, despite their different experiences, face similar challenges in life—be they economic struggles, emotional hardships, or aspirations for a better future. By focusing on these commonalities, we can initiate conversations that emphasize compassion and understanding rather than perpetuating narratives that underline differences. For instance, community initiatives that bring diverse members together around common goals, such as local community projects or social service endeavors, create shared experiences and foster collaboration.

Add to that the crucial role that education can play in dismantling divisive narratives. Schools and community organizations have the opportunity to cultivate environments where discussion and cooperation are encouraged. Curricula that highlight diverse perspectives teach young people the value of empathy and critical thinking. When students learn to appreciate various viewpoints, they become equipped to engage in constructive conversations that transcend Identity Politics. Programs that promote intergroup dialogue and mutual respect further combat stereotypes, allowing individuals to see each other as allies instead of adversaries.

Another powerful means to build bridges is through storytelling. Sharing personal narratives can humanize complex issues and challenge oversimplified perspectives that contribute to division. When individuals hear the stories of people from different backgrounds, they can't help but develop a deeper understanding of the experiences that shape the world of others. Community storytelling events can serve as platforms for this exchange, enabling individuals to share their journeys and celebrate their unique identities while recognizing the universal threads that bind us all.

Social media, despite its potential for fueling division, can also be harnessed as a tool for connection. Campaigns that encourage positive interactions across cultural and ideological lines can inspire individuals to engage with those they might not typically encounter in their daily lives. By promoting content that uplifts diverse voices and nurtures collaboration, we can reshape the narrative surrounding Identity Politics. Online platforms that prioritize dialogue over diatribe can create a virtual environment where people connect based on shared interests and goals, moving beyond superficial labels.

Stepping Stones to Progress

IN AN ERA marked by polarization and division, the promotion of a political landscape that values diverse opinions, empathy, and understanding is essential for the health of America. Leaders play a crucial role in shaping this landscape, and when they recognize their failures and shortcomings as opportunities for growth, they catalyze a more constructive discourse. Emphasizing the importance of dialogue and mutual respect nurtures a society where varied perspectives aren't just tolerated but are embraced.

But to cultivate a political environment that cherishes diverse opinions, leaders must first model behaviors they wish to see in their constituents. When political figures openly acknowledge their mistakes and demonstrate vulnerability, they lay the groundwork for an atmosphere of accountability and transparency. This approach helps dismantle the barriers of fear that often inhibit honest discussions about differing viewpoints. Instead of perceiving disagreements as threats, leaders and citizens alike can learn to view them as opportunities for collective growth. By creating forums for dialogue, leaders encourage their followers to engage with, rather than shy away from, differing opinions, ultimately enriching the political discourse.

Empathy is another fundamental ingredient in promoting understanding among diverse groups. Empathy allows individuals to step into each other's shoes, recognizing the humanity behind differing beliefs. Leaders who display empathetic engagement inspire their constituents to consider perspectives they might otherwise overlook or dismiss. By actively listening to constituents from all backgrounds and experiences, leaders can bridge divides and contribute to a sense of community. Initiatives that bring together individuals from various political, social, and economic backgrounds further deepens this understanding, showcasing the value of unity in diversity.

One of the most constructive mindsets is viewing leaders' failures as stepping stones to progress. Political leaders, like anyone else, are bound to encounter obstacles and setbacks. However, the ability to frame these moments as learning experiences rather than failures promotes a culture of resilience and growth. When leaders publicly reflect on their shortcomings and articulate lessons learned, they set an example for others to follow. This not only humanizes them but also motivates citizens to take ownership of their own learning journeys. Citizens are inspired to engage more actively in their communities, viewing their political participation as a chance to contribute to a larger narrative of change and progress.

Constructive Engagement

IN AN INCREASINGLY divided world, it's more important than ever to encourage honest discussions about our true selves. Embracing the idea that imperfection is part of the human condition serves as a liberating and unifying antidote to the derision and cynicism so common in contemporary America. Acknowledging our own inherent defects allows us to engage with one another more sincerely, creating spaces where diverse perspectives can coexist, ultimately enriching our collective understanding.

At the heart of all healthy political discourse lies the recognition that no one is without his or her imperfections. By accepting that we're all flawed in some way, shape, or form, we create a foundation for compassionate discourse. This acknowledgment helps dismantle the walls that separate us. Instead of viewing differing opinions or behaviors as disqualifying, we can appreciate them as reflections of our collective experiences, promoting a more engaging dialogue where everyone feels heard.

What's more, listening to others without the immediate goal of retribution enriches our sense of connection, which, in turn, empowers us to rise above ideological divides. As we share our stories, we come to realize that the emotional landscapes we navigate are very much the same—filled with similar doubts, hopes, failures, and frustrations. This shared humanity allows us to bond over our vulnerabilities rather than allowing our shortcomings and disagreements to push us apart.

In this context, engaging in political discussions isn't just about exchanging ideas; it is also about building community. Such gatherings forge a culture of acceptance and respect, where individuals feel empowered to express their thoughts without fear of judgment. This unifying approach to dialogue leads to more effective problem-solving, as collaborative efforts often yield creative solutions that individualistic thinkers may miss.

Acknowledging that all humans are imperfect also offers a refreshing perspective on political engagement. Rather than becoming trapped in a cycle of criticism or contempt, we can choose to elevate our discussions by focusing on learning from one another. By admitting that we're all works in progress, we encourage ourselves and others to continually refine our beliefs and actions. This mindset not only liberates us from the constraints of rigid thinking but also allows us to approach politics as a living, evolving conversation rather than a battleground of absolutes.

In conclusion, we now see how the belief that flawed political rivals should be removed from office is nothing more than a damaging lie that can only disrupt rational discourse and ignite political division. As we navigate the complexities of Identity Politics, then, it's essential to acknowledge the inherent imperfection in all leaders, which, in turn, enables us to prioritize meaningful governance instead of personal attacks. By reframing our expectations and focusing on collaboration, we can work toward creating a more productive political environment that benefits all citizens. Ultimately, the strength of our republic lies not in the pursuit of perfection but in embracing the diverse tapestry of perspectives that contribute to the kind of shared political life first envisioned by our Founding Fathers.

CHAPTER SIX

The Puppet Masters:

Unveiling Hidden Persuaders

LIE #6:

*The Highest Good of Government is to Care
for the Poor and Needy...*

O NE AFTERNOON, I knocked on my professor's open door, and he cordially invited me to take a seat. Despite the adversarial nature of many of our conversations on American politics, I enjoyed our after-school meetings, as did my professor, as far as I could tell.

"So good to see you, my boy; how are you today?"

"I'm doing well, Professor, thank you. And yourself?"

Leaning back in his chair, he sighed with a weary smile, "I'm well, I suppose."

"Pardon me for saying so, but you looked tired. Are you sure everything is okay?"

He eyed me, thoughtfully, for several moments, as was his habit, before answering me. "My, my, you are an exceptional young man. Bright, inquisitive, *and* compassionate. A rare combination indeed."

I smiled awkwardly. Did I even blush slightly, I wondered.

Then, the old man cleared his throat and slowly continued, "Just a trying situation on the home front, that's all. A situation that has me preoccupied, it seems."

"So sorry to hear that," I said. "I hope things work out for you."

"As do I, young man, as do I. Come to think of it, I'd be interested to hear your take on the matter."

"Me? How so, Professor?"

"Well, it just so happens that my wife is an avid philanthropist."

"Really, how interesting."

"Oh, yes," he said, trying to restrain an awkward enthusiasm. Maybe it was enthusiasm, and then again maybe it was irritation; I couldn't quite tell. "And so," he continued, "she's constantly flitting about, from cause, to cause, to cause, you see, in an effort to lend a helping hand wherever she sees the need."

"How nice, sir. She sounds like a fantastic lady. What kinds of causes are we talking about?"

With yet another weary sigh, the professor replied, "Well, therein lies the rub, I'm afraid." Then he chuckled quietly under his breath, and lowered his gaze. "Actually, we're talking about too many causes for me to even remember half of them. One month it's the homeless; the next month, orphans. Then another month, it could be fatherless households or single mothers. No doubt it's most admirable, and no doubt I admire her efforts immensely ... but sometimes, I'm sorry to say..." And then his words trailed off into silence.

"Sometimes," I said, breaking the awkward silence, "I can imagine it takes a toll on even the most resilient of families ... families like yours."

And looking up at me, he smiled again, this time more hopeful than before, as if encouraged by someone who had provided him a psychological shoulder to lean on.

"Yes, that's right," he said. "Which leads me to what I wanted to ask you about."

"Anything, sir. What's on your mind?"

"You see, my wife and I have a kind of running argument—well, she calls them *discussions*," he said with a sheepish grin.

I smiled back. "Of course, I understand completely."

"Yes, well, these *discussions* of ours, you know, they concern her philanthropic endeavors. And she keeps insisting that we provide our maximum effort to all these causes, and while she knows very well that I have my commitment to this university, she still looks to me as her ever ready sounding board in regard to her commitments."

"That sounds like it could be quite a drain on your resourcefulness and energy."

"Exactly, which is why I keep insisting that we—and when I say we, I mean to say, we citizens in general—should not be expected to singlehandedly bear the burden of the poor and needy in American society. In fact it's my firm belief that it's the primary burden of the state to do that. After all, ever since the days of FDR's New Deal and JFK's Civil Rights Movement, it's become obvious that issues like poverty and unemployment can only be solved through decisive government intervention. What do you think?"

For several thoughtful moments, I considered how I might respond to my professor's pronouncement, but suddenly his phone rang, and he reluctantly answered it. "Hello," he said; and with a bittersweet smile, he continued. "Yes, my dear, how nice to hear from you. How are you?" And as he silently gestured to me that he preferred to speak privately, I rose to my feet and waved goodbye, determined as ever to investigate the matter further.

"I am all for doing good to the poor, but I do not think the best way of doing good to them is to make them easy in poverty but to lead or drive them out of it."

Benjamin Franklin

Balancing Freedom and Responsibility

THE INTERPLAY between compassion and governance has long been a cornerstone of American political discourse, particularly as to how the government should care for its most vulnerable citizens. The narrative that emphasizes the moral responsibility of the state to assist the poor and needy resonates deeply within the American psyche, striking a chord with the ideals of compassion and communal responsibility. However, upon closer investigation, this sentiment reveals a much more complex landscape that extends beyond mere altruism, suggesting that the Founding Fathers of America understood the intricacies of such governance better than we often acknowledge.

At the heart of the discourse on government caring for the needy lies the fundamental question of how society defines its moral obligations. Many argue that a compassionate government should actively intervene to support the poor, providing social safety nets and welfare programs that alleviate poverty and promote social mobility. This perspective is rooted in the belief that society is a collective entity responsible for the well-being of all its members. Historically, this view gained traction during the Great Depression era, culminating in President Franklin D. Roosevelt's New Deal initiatives, which reflect a more pronounced belief in government as a vehicle for social equity.[18]

---

18   *The New Deal*: A series of U.S. domestic programs, public work projects, and financial reforms and regulations enacted by President Franklin D. Roosevelt, between 1933 and 1938, The New Deal aimed at addressing the Great Depression, which began in 1929. The term was taken from Roosevelt's speech accepting the Democrat nomination for the presidency in 1932.

Among the many areas the reform effort focused on were industry, agriculture, finance, water power, employment, and housing. At a time when the country was in the throes of the Great Depression, The New Deal's appeal was that it went beyond the traditional approach of *laissez-faire* American governance, and instead embraced the concept of a government-regulated economy aimed at achieving a balance between conflicting economic interests.

The New Deal created a broad range of federal government programs that

Yet, as we delve deeper into the policies advocating for such compassionate government intervention, we may uncover unintended consequences that complicate the narrative. The Founding Fathers envisioned a government that limited its interference in the lives of its citizens, preferring instead to create a framework within which individual initiative could flourish. Alexander Hamilton and Thomas Jefferson, although frequently at odds, both appreciated the dangers of government overreach. Hamilton's advocacy for a strong federal government coexisted with a caution regarding dependency on government assistance, while Jefferson's agrarian ideals prioritized self-sufficiency and personal responsibility.

The complexity increases as we scrutinize the impact of social welfare programs on human behavior and socio-economic outcomes. While such programs are often implemented with the best intentions, they can sometimes foster dependency rather than empowerment. Critics of welfare

---

offered economic relief to the suffering, regulated private industry, and stimulated the economy. The New Deal is often summed up by the "Three Rs": Relief for the unemployed; Recovery of the economy through federal spending and job creation; and Reform of capitalism, by means of regulatory legislation and the creation of new social welfare programs.

To revive economic activity, the National Recovery Administration (NRA) was created to shape industrial codes governing trade practices, wages, hours, child labor, and collective bargaining. The Federal Deposit Insurance Corporation (FDIC) provided government insurance for bank deposits in member banks of the Federal Reserve System. And the Securities and Exchange Commission (SEC) was created to restore investor confidence in the stock market by ending the misleading sales practices and stock manipulations that had led to the Crash of '29.

Key elements in the New Deal remain with us today, including federal regulation of wages, work hours, child labor, collective bargaining rights, and the social security system. As such, the New Deal—for good or for ill—fundamentally changed how the federal government functioned, and more importantly, how the American public sees the role of the federal government in their lives. As one historian, Eric Foner, has put it: "Before the 1930s, national political debate often revolved around the question of whether the federal government should intervene in the economy. After the New Deal, debate rested on how it should intervene."

often argue that prolonged reliance on government assistance both hinders initiative and stifles ambition among recipients. This raises a critical question: How can a government embrace its compassionate role without compromising the values of independence and self-reliance that are quintessential to the American ethos?

Not only that, but the narrative surrounding the government's attempt to alleviate poverty also intersects with broader socio-political dynamics, including race, class, and regional disparities. As such, the bottom line is: compassionate care can't be uniformly applied. The diverse needs of different communities require nuanced and targeted approaches. Urban versus rural poverty, for example, presents unique challenges, so a one-size-fits-all solution is unlikely to yield desirable results. Thus, the task of aiding the poor assumes a complicated dimension that requires thoughtful investigation and informed policymaking, echoing the wisdom of the Founders who understood the fine balance between freedom and responsibility.

The Illusion of Government's Highest Good

IN THE GRAND theater of American politics, a prevalent narrative emerges: that the highest good of government is to care for the poor and needy. While this sentiment strikes a chord with many, particularly when framed as a compassionate responsibility, a deeper investigation reveals a more complex web of influences that steers the policy narrative away from genuine compassion towards a facade of benevolence. While many politicians may proclaim their dedication to alleviating poverty, the underlying motives often remain shrouded in self-interest, power dynamics, and economic considerations.

At the forefront of this illusion is the language of compassion that certain political parties use to garner public support. These partisan politicians regularly engage in rhetoric that paints them as champions of the downtrod-den. This narrative, though, isn't merely about concern for the public but is deftly designed to secure votes and main-tain power. By presenting themselves as saviors of the poor, these officials mask their true intentions and create an emotional distance from the actual struggles faced by those they profess to help.

What's more, the policies enacted to support the poor are frequently shaped by external influences that prioritize economic gain over genuine welfare. Lobbying groups, cor-porate interests, and influential donors play pivotal roles behind the scenes, guiding legislation to serve their own interests. The result is a patchwork of policies that may superficially appear beneficial but ultimately perpetuate a cycle of dependency and failure. More often than not, the need for political capital undermines the effectiveness of these policies, resulting in initiatives that do little to ad-dress the root causes of poverty and instead reinforce ex-isting inequalities.

For instance, while the government might allocate funds for welfare programs, these programs are often rid-dled with inefficiencies or conditions that benefit contrac-tors more than the recipients. Add to that how bureaucratic red tape and a convoluted decision-making process dilute accountability, and we see just how policies emerge from this process that are so disconnected from their intended purpose that they're ultimately counterproductive.

The Divide Between Rhetoric and Reality

THROUGHOUT HISTORY, political leaders have often risen to prominence by championing various causes, par-ticularly those aimed at uplifting the impoverished. Their platforms shine a spotlight on the struggles of the disad-vantaged, while presenting themselves as advocates for change and progress. Yet, beneath the surface of these initiatives lies a question that casts a long shadow over their intentions: Is this advocacy a genuine expression of altruism, or merely a facade designed to garner votes? The skepticism surrounding such motives isn't unfounded and reflects the caution that the Founding Fathers themselves harbored regarding the true nature of human ambition.

The political landscape is rife with examples of leaders who have leveraged the plight of the poor to rally support for their agendas. Often, these leaders make grand promises that resonate with the electorate's emotional and social concerns. For instance, they may advocate for reforms in education, healthcare, and housing, all while painting a vivid picture of a brighter future for those in need. However, once they attain power, the once-vibrant promises often fade into the background, replaced by pragmatic politics that prioritize party interests or personal desires. This pattern raises questions about the authenticity of their commitment to altruism; it appears increasingly possible that their focus is primarily on securing votes rather than on effecting meaningful change.

As the Founders warned, the allure of power can corrupt even the noblest of intentions. They understood that political leaders are extremely prone to succumbing to self-interest—a trait that often overshadows any purported commitments to social welfare. This sentiment is echoed in modern times as citizens observe cycles of empty rhetoric. The refrain of "change" often rings hollow when the policies enacted don't significantly alter the status quo for the impoverished. Instead, what emerges is a disheartening reality where social issues are exploited for political gain, leading to disillusionment among the very populations that politicians claim to champion.

The superficial engagement with societal problems also manifests in the form of symbolic gestures rather than substantial actions. Politicians may stage appearances at community events or make flowery speeches, all while failing to follow through with the necessary legislative changes. The difference between their proclaimed intentions and actual results gives credence to the belief that many leaders prioritize optics over authentic progress—an approach that serves their image and political longevity more than it aids those in distress. The Founding Fathers' concerns about the motivations behind political actions are thus validated in contemporary society, as the divide between rhetoric and reality continues to widen.

Trapped in a State of Reliance

ONE OF THE major culprits in the effort to assist the needy are the many organizations that ostensibly act as compassionate advocates. However, these organizations—known as special interest groups—are typically so heavily funded by corporate donations that their goals don't always align with the best practices for addressing the issues they profess to address. As a result, examining the methods of these special interest groups often reveals a disconnect between their advocacy claims and their actual practices for alleviating poverty. Rather than providing sustainable solutions, these groups may inadvertently perpetuate the very issues they seek to resolve, leading to a cycle of dependency and ineffective assistance.

First, many special interest groups operate within narrow frameworks that prioritize short-term relief over long-term empowerment. While immediate aid, such as food banks or temporary housing, may relieve some pressing issues, it often fails to address the root causes of poverty. For instance, providing meals or shelter without accompanying programs that promote education or job training can keep individuals trapped in a state of reliance rather than facilitating their transition to self-sufficiency. Consequently, while these groups may garner support and sympathy, their approach often lacks the structural changes needed to make a lasting impact.

What's more, the agendas of these special interest

groups can be swayed by funding and political influences, leading to goals that don't align with the most effective ways to alleviate poverty. When resources are tied to specific objectives that don't prioritize the needs of the impoverished, the effectiveness of assistance diminishes. For instance, a group focused primarily on attracting donations might divert attention from comprehensive policy changes or advocacy efforts aimed at societal reform. Instead, the focus becomes narrowed on perpetuating funding cycles rather than addressing the multifaceted nature of poverty.

Additionally, many of these organizations may overlook the voices of those they aim to help. By operating from a top-down perspective, they end up implementing solutions that don't actually reflect the experiences or needs of the recipients. This disconnect, in turn, leads to initiatives that are neither relevant nor productive. We see this happening when, say, a program designed without input from low-income communities simply reinforces damaging stigmas or ignores vital cultural contexts, rendering these initiatives woefully ineffective.

The Bureaucratic Maze

ANOTHER NEGATIVE factor impacting this issue is the way the government spends money on social programs that claim to support the poor and needy. Because these initiatives are so entangled with bureaucratic red tape, they no longer benefit the poor so much as they benefit the system that perpetuates a vicious cycle. As such, the intent of these programs may be laudable, but the execution typically falls short of providing the necessary support to those who need it most.

One of the primary concerns regarding social programs is the complexity so inherent in their bureaucratic structures. As governments expand their social safety nets, layers of administration multiply, leading to confusion, redundancy, and inefficiency. Each layer of bureaucracy then absorbs resources that could otherwise be directed toward direct aid, creating a situation where the very systems put in place to assist the vulnerable become unwieldy and bloated. To this point, studies show that a large percentage of funds allocated to social programs often go toward administrative costs rather than benefiting recipients.

What's more, the bureaucratic maze, which individuals must navigate to access these funds, acts more like a barrier than a bridge, deterring eligible beneficiaries from receiving the assistance they need. Long application processes, complicated eligibility requirements, and varying regulations across agencies create a scenario where the most vulnerable individuals feel overwhelmed or discouraged from seeking help. In many cases, what should be a life-transforming experience becomes an arduous journey marked by frustration and uncertainty, further entrenching the cycle of poverty.

Additionally, the rigid frameworks within which social programs operate inadvertently limit their responsiveness to the needs of the population they are meant to help. Bureaucracy often prioritizes adherence to existing rules and regulations over flexibility and innovation. This rigidity, in turn, results in services that fail to evolve alongside societal changes or shifts in demographics, rendering them less effective over time. For instance, as the nature of poverty evolves and becomes increasingly multifaceted, social programs continue to apply outdated models that fail to address the current realities faced by the poor and needy.

Media Manipulation

THEN THERE is the role that the mainstream media plays in maintaining this illusion of government's supposed highest good. Coverage of government initiatives often lacks depth, focusing instead on sensational headlines that reinforce the narrative of politicians as compassionate caretakers. This often happens because investigative journalism so rarely delves into the complexities of these partisan policies or seeks to expose their inherent short-comings. This then reinforces the public perception that is consistent with certain politician's portrayal of themselves as benevolent, conveniently ignoring the cultural issues that persist despite their best efforts.

In today's interconnected world, raising awareness about poverty is vital for fostering empathy and driving social change. However, it's equally important to thor-oughly evaluate the narratives constructed around pover-ty, as some media outlets may present self-serving agendas rather than the interests of those in need. That's because all too often, sensational images of marginalized groups, suffering in destitute conditions, can generate sympathy, but they also wind up perpetuating negative stereotypes that dehumanize them.

As such, media narratives of victims of poverty often align with the agendas of organizations or individuals who seek to gain from these portrayals, whether through fund-raising or political leverage. Nonprofits and charities may use emotive imagery to encourage donations, presenting poverty as a problem requiring immediate financial inter-vention rather than addressing the need for sustainable change. Sadly, this can't help but create the impression that poverty is a perpetual condition that can only be addressed through donations, rather than tackled through policy re-form. Such an approach inevitably undermines the digni-ty of those experiencing poverty, creating a narrative that they're helpless and in need of being saved rather than ac-tive participants capable of contributing solutions.

Undermining Personal Responsibility

IN THE FACE of social inequality and economic struggles, promises of expanding welfare, free healthcare, and gov-ernment handouts always emerge as soothing balms for the poor. However, these promises, cloaked in the guise of compassion and care, can lead to tragic repercussions. At the heart of this complex issue is the philosophical shift towards neo-socialism—a system that relies heavily on state intervention in the economy and the redistribution of wealth. On the surface, this approach appears to provide immediate relief to those in need. Sadly, though, the implementation of neo-socialism, while seemingly beneficial, often results in unintended consequences that echo throughout society, aggravating issues such as mass immigration and skyrocketing unemployment. Rather than benefiting the poor and needy, the prioritizing of short-term aid over long-term solutions, creates a dependency that stifles individual initiative and undermines the foundational principles of personal responsibility. As more and more citizens turn to the government for assistance, the fabric of society begins to unravel, leading to a stagnation of economic growth and innovation.

Mass immigration to America has increasingly compounded the challenges posed by such systems. As welfare benefits attract individuals from around the globe, communities are often strained under the weight of an increasing populace that may not contribute to the local economy in the same way. This influx leads to cultural clashes, resource scarcity, and heightened tension among citizens, ultimately jeopardizing social cohesion. The narrative of open arms, in turn, ignites an environment where resentment simmers beneath the surface, threatening to erupt into conflict and further divide society.

Then there is the promise of free healthcare, which despite its noble intentions, often becomes a double-edged sword. As the government seeks to provide free healthcare, they only manage to create a system that is unsustainable and overburdened. Long wait times and reduced quality of care are just a few of the frustrating outcomes that arise when the state bears the weight of such expansive programs. This erosion of healthcare quality is especially devastating for the very individuals these programs are designed to help, leading to disappointment and despair.

Skyrocketing unemployment is yet another grim repercussion of these well-meaning policies. On one hand, when people feel entitled to receive government handouts, no one feels the need to go to work any longer. After all, why would anyone work for a living if they can simply draw limitless welfare checks? On the other hand, as businesses grapple with increased regulation and taxes to fund welfare programs, many are forced to reduce their workforce or close their doors. This creates a paradox where those who are meant to benefit from such welfare systems find themselves struggling to make ends meet in a job market that is shrinking rather than flourishing.

A Cycle of Dependency

WELFARE programs have long been designed with noble intentions—to provide a safety net for low-income families and to assist those caught in the relentless grip of poverty. However, while these initiatives are designed to uplift, the reality is: instead of promoting independence, many welfare programs inadvertently create a cycle of dependency. This tragic outcome highlights not only the flaws inherent in these systems but also the broader implications for individuals and families striving for empowerment and a better life.

At the heart of the issue is how welfare programs strip individuals of autonomy. Eligibility requirements, such as work restrictions and income caps, create barriers that prevent recipients from pursuing fulfilling employment. Rather than seeing welfare as a temporary solution, many find themselves relying on it for extended periods, discouraged by the prospect of losing assistance when they do seek to better their circumstances. This dependency breeds a sense of hopelessness, forcing families to settle into life within the confines of limited options instead of daring to dream beyond the confines of welfare.

Even worse, the emotional toll of such financial dependency is profound. Individuals who rely on welfare may experience feelings of shame and inadequacy, further entrenching their struggles. The cultural stigma attached to receiving aid leads to isolation, leaving recipients feeling unworthy and disconnected from the very aspirations that could catapult them out of poverty. In many ways, the very structures designed to help people create an invisible barrier that dooms them to a life of poverty, preventing them from taking the steps necessary to reclaim their identities and futures.

The impact of this dependency extends beyond the individual to the family unit. Children of welfare recipients grow up in an environment where poverty and reliance on financial aid are normalized. This sets a crippling precedent for future generations, perpetuating a cycle that seems insurmountable. When children don't see their parents actively working towards self-sufficiency, it can stifle their own ambitions and aspirations. The loss of hope becomes intergenerational, as the very programs meant to provide a path forward inadvertently lay the groundwork for future dependency.

A Tidal Wave of Immigrants

THE PROMISE of limitless government handouts poses a significant allure for citizens of foreign lands escaping the challenges and instability of their home countries. This phenomenon reveals both the moral implications and practical consequences of welfare programs, especially for nations like the United States with robust social safety nets.

As financial resources become increasingly accessible, a complex interplay of economic and social dynamics emerges, raising questions about sustainability, national identity, and economic responsibility. Nations plagued by poverty, corruption, and violence may find their citizens increasingly tempted to relocate to America. The appeal of a system where basic needs are met—through expanding welfare and free healthcare—is clearly more attractive than the harsh realities faced at home. This, in turn, results in a tidal wave of immigrants that strains the resources of our nation when we so willingly offer such robust programs. The double-edged sword of compassion and consequence becomes apparent: while many foreign nationals seek more favorable living conditions here, their arrival challenges the very systems they are hoping to benefit from.

As many see government handouts as an easy solution to their problems, a culture of dependency develops that inevitably attracts those who aren't motivated by genuine need but by the allure of economic comfort. This, then, leads to abuses of the welfare systems, putting further strain on public finances, which inevitably triggers a backlash, as resentful citizens begin to question the sustainability of these programs and societal tensions escalate.

The Hollow Promise of Free Healthcare for All

THE QUEST for free healthcare for all is another of those worthy causes, yet it's also one that is fraught with complexities that can't help but undermine its success. While government officials strive to implement an initiative like this, with all good intentions, the multifaceted nature of healthcare inevitably renders it less effective than envisioned.

One of the main challenges in providing free healthcare lies in the intricacies of health insurance systems. Many countries struggle with the tension between public and private insurance models. In systems where private insurance operates alongside public initiatives, disparities constantly arise. This duality leads to confusion and frustration among individuals seeking care, as many find themselves caught in bureaucratic red tape or insufficient coverage. The lack of a standardized approach also creates inefficiencies that hinder access to necessary services, ultimately leaving many individuals without adequate care despite the promise of free healthcare.

Affordability stands as another critical barrier in providing so-called "free" healthcare. While the overarching goal is to reduce out-of-pocket expenses for citizens, the reality is that implementing these systems requires considerable funding. After all, nothing is ever truly free in life. No matter how free politicians insist healthcare should be, somebody still has to pay the price. As a result, governments must raise taxes or reallocate funds from other essential services, leading to public resistance and debate.

Additionally, there can be a disconnect between politicians' promises and real-world financial limitations. If funding mechanisms aren't robust enough, the sustainability of free healthcare options becomes questionable. Individuals frequently find themselves in a cycle of underfunded services, inadequate staffing, and insufficient facilities, further perpetuating their struggles for quality care.

Availability is yet another hurdle that complicates the delivery of effective healthcare services. Just because free healthcare options are put in place, that doesn't eliminate the difficulty of accessing those services. In rural areas or impoverished urban neighborhoods, healthcare facilities may be few and far between, making it hard for individuals to receive timely and effective treatment. Long waits for appointments, limited specialists, and inadequate hospital infrastructure lead to frustration and worsening health outcomes. Therefore, simply establishing free healthcare doesn't guarantee accessibility, and until these availability issues are resolved, the promise of free healthcare for all will remain hollow.

A Hammock for the Unmotivated

THE ALARMING rise in unemployment has cast a long shadow over the very foundations of an ever-expanding welfare state. As the job market deteriorates and the prospect of meaningful employment diminishes, a troubling trend emerges: individuals begin to feel less incentive to seek work, which then leads to a greater sense of disillusionment. This phenomenon not only threatens the economic viability of the welfare system, but it also undermines the social fabric that encourages hard work and self-sufficiency.

In the past, the welfare state was designed to support individuals during times of hardship, assisting them in traversing the often challenging path back to work. However, as unemployment continues to climb, more people rely on welfare benefits as a primary source of income rather than as a temporary measure. This shift reveals a stark reality; when jobs become so scarce that the motivation to work fades, the safety net intended to catch the vulnerable transforms into a hammock for the unmotivated. The detrimental impact on society is profound, as the dignity of meaningful work is lost and the spirit of industriousness erodes.

What's more, the psychological implications of sustained unemployment are severe. With fewer individuals engaging in productive labor, communities suffer from diminished social interaction and increased feelings of isolation and hopelessness. Studies have shown that long-term unemployment leads to a decline in mental health, exacerbating feelings of worthlessness and despair. In this way, a welfare state that was once a beacon of hope turns into a breeding ground for apathy and resignation, where people struggle to find a sense of purpose.

Transitioning away from this crippling cycle, then, requires a concerted effort to revitalize the job market and reignite the drive to work. However, the reality is bleak; as unemployment rates remain stubbornly high, the urgency to act diminishes. Instead of fostering an environment where individuals can strive for independence, we risk cultivating a culture where reliance on the welfare state becomes the norm. This transition could have irreversible repercussions, perpetuating a lifelong dependency that robs individuals of their necessary ambition.

The Illusion of Social Equity

MISGUIDED POLICIES intended to assist the poor and needy have ignited a fierce debate concerning the implications these measures carry for the core values of a constitutional republic that the Founding Fathers envisioned. The intention behind such policies often stems from a genuine desire to help those struggling in society; however, the consequences can inadvertently perpetuate dependency and undermine individual initiative.

At the heart of this debate lies the fundamental question of how best to assist those in need without compromising the principles upon which our country was built. The Founding Fathers recognized the importance of individual liberty and personal responsibility as essential components of a thriving society. They believed that prosperity stems not from government handouts or the redistribution of wealth but from the opportunities provided to individuals to pursue their own paths. As Thomas Jefferson described it: "To take from one person because it is thought he has acquired too much from his hard work, to give to others who have not exercised equal industry and skill, is to arbitrarily violate a fundamental guiding principle: that everyone is guaranteed to maintain ownership of the fruits of their own labor."

One example of the kinds of misguided policies that would have alarmed the Founders is the proliferation of welfare programs. Rather than empowering individuals by offering them the tools and skills necessary to improve their circumstances, these programs can instead trap them in a state of reliance. This results in a discouraged populace that finds it increasingly difficult to break free from the shackles of poverty. Debates surrounding welfare reform often highlight the need for a balanced approach that encourages self-sufficiency while still providing support during times of hardship.

The implications of these policies also extend beyond mere economic outcomes; they touch upon social cohesion and the integrity of community structures. When government assistance becomes the primary means of support for a significant portion of the population, it incites resentment among those who feel that they bear the burden of supporting such a system. This divide can't help but lead to animosity and a fragmented society, undermining the shared values that are crucial for a constitutional republic. The Founders envisioned a nation where citizens would work together, not against each other, which is fundamentally at odds with this misguided approach to unbridled social welfare.

What's more, the heated debate over social equity often brings to light the deeper ideological rifts within the nation. Advocates for extensive social programs argue that they are necessary to rectify systemic injustices and provide equal opportunity for all. However, detractors caution against the potential for these policies to infringe upon personal freedoms and elevate the role of the government to an extent that the Founders would undoubtedly find troubling. The challenge, then, lies not just in crafting policies that support the needy but in doing so in a way that respects the underlying principles of individualism and self-governance.

A Legacy of Hope and Liberty

THE FOUNDING Fathers of America envisioned a nation built on the principles of liberty, equality, and self-governance. As we navigate the complexities of modern society, it's essential to reflect on their ideals, particularly when discussing the role of political power and the temptation of systems like socialism that radically undermine these tenets. Rather than exploiting the less fortunate to gain political power, we must strive to uplift and empower all citizens, fostering a society grounded in hope and opportunity.

One of the most significant lessons we can learn from the Founding Fathers is the importance of individual rights and personal responsibility. They believed in the potential of the individual to succeed, emphasizing that a society thrives when citizens are empowered rather than dependent. This philosophy underscores the necessity of creating governmental systems that provide opportunities without stifling personal initiative.

While there are instances where welfare programs have succeeded in providing much-needed support, it's crucial to recognize the broader effects of dependency they can trigger. To genuinely empower individuals and families, there needs to be a paradigm shift—toward initiatives that promote skills training, education, and job placement without the punitive structures that typically accompany welfare aid. By focusing on long-term empowerment rather than immediate survival, the chance to break the cycle of dependency becomes more attainable. Thus by focusing on lifting people up through education, providing access to resources, and creating jobs rather than exploiting their struggles for political gain, we nurture a sense of hope and agency that is vital for a thriving society.

History has also shown us that paths leading to socialism often stem from a desire to redistribute wealth and power under the guise of equity. While the intention to help those in need is admirable, the consequences are extremely detrimental. Systems that prioritize wealth redistribution over empowerment can only lead to economic stagnation, loss of individual freedoms, and decreased motivation for innovation and hard work. As Benjamin Franklin recalled: "In my youth, I traveled much, and I observed in different countries that the more the poor were given public provisions, the less they provided for themselves, and of course they became poorer. And on the contrary, the less that was done for them, the more they did for themselves, and so they became richer."

Upholding the values of entrepreneurship, then, aligns more closely with the original vision expressed by the Founding Fathers. By contributing to a spirit of private initiative, we create a more vibrant and enterprising society. So, while it's true that in contemporary America the increase of political polarization poses a challenge to unity and mutual understanding, the Founders remained confident that a diverse society could come together under shared principles and values. By focusing on building bridges and encouraging dialogue amongst different groups, we can inspire collaboration and resourcefulness, reinforcing the belief that together we can create a sense of belonging and purpose so essential for a healthy body politic.

In conclusion, as we look forward to shaping our society, we must heed the lessons of our Founding Fathers. Rather than exploit others simply to gain political power, we must embrace an energetic vision that empowers individuals and strengthens our communities. By uplifting all citizens and maintaining a commitment to individual rights and responsibilities, we can work towards a future that aligns with the noble ideals upon which this nation was built. Let us therefore strive to create a society where everyone has the opportunity to succeed, ensuring that a legacy of hope and liberty endures without succumbing to the pitfalls of socialism.

CHAPTER SEVEN

Taking From the Rich:

An Economic Ripple Effect

LIE #7:

Raising Taxes on the Rich Will Benefit the Average American and Bring Much-Needed Relief to the Poor...

A S WAS MY professor's habit, he eyed me for several thoughtful moments before breaking the silence: "Good to see you again, my boy; how have you been?"

"I've been well, Professor. How about you? You're looking like your old self again; not like you did when we last spoke about your wife's philanthropy."

He smiled enthusiastically. "Oh, yes, well, fortunately for my sake, we've turned a bit of a corner in regard to that issue."

"Really. How nice. Without sounding nosy, can you share what you did to make that happen?"

"Of course, I'd love to share that with you. And to tell you the truth, I'd be disappointed if you didn't risk being 'nosy,' as you put it. It's the mark of a great political scientist. What great movement or development in politics ever occurred as a result of apathy or indifference? What a failure I'd be if a student of mine lacked the tenacity to get to the bottom of every great question. And I don't mind telling you, my boy, when I think of you I never think of you as being merely nosy. No, sir. I'm proud to say: You, my friend, are nosy with a purpose." Amused with himself, he let out a tremendous laugh.

Laughing along with him, I smiled irresistibly at the thought that my professor was proud of me. Even with our obvious differences, he never made me feel inferior or stupid for holding fast to my own opinions or feelings, and for that reason, I would always admire him. That told me that even while he was a man of firm convictions, he never let that interfere with his ability to communicate respect and appreciation for the views of others, even when they were opposed to his own.

"So tell me, then," I said, as our laughter subsided. "What did you do to turn the corner?"

"Why, of course, what would any good professor of political science do? I challenged my wife to a debate."

"A debate?" I exclaimed. "With your wife?"

"Certainly."

"What were the opposing arguments?"

"Well, my wife, naturally, advocated that the burden of philanthropy should fall primarily on the shoulders of the private sector. And for myself, I insisted that that burden should be shouldered by the state."

"Now when you say the private sector, what was your wife looking to in that area?"

"Well, naturally, churches were her number one choice because of the biblical mandate to care for the impoverished and underprivileged."

"Naturally," I said, trying to not sound condescending.

"Add to that, community action groups, philanthropy societies, that sort of thing."

"How do you think she did? I mean, in stating her case?"

"Very well, actually. But unfortunately, her argument couldn't hold a candle to my position."

"Oh, really?"

"Yes, really," he said, slyly.

"So what is your position? Certainly you can't expect the federal government to shoulder the entire burden—not with the crushing debt they're already responsible for."

"Naturally," the old man said, and pausing for dramatic effect, he eyed me with an impish grin.

"Well?" I asked with baited breath. "What's your magic bullet?"

And after several anxious moments, as if hoping to add even more drama to his response: "Robin Hood," was all he said.

"Excuse me?" I asked wide-eyed.

"Robin Hood—the greatest equalizer of history." Seeing the confused look on my face, the old man leaned forward across the desk. "You have heard of Robin Hood, haven't you?"

"Sure. Medieval English guy. Stole from the rich, gave to the poor. That guy?"

"One and the same," he said, again pausing so I could further consider his intended meaning.

"Hmmm," I muttered, considering his words, unsure of how I should respond.

"Don't you see?" the old man went on with the energy and enthusiasm of a hippie activist. "The only way to empower the state, to enrich their coffers, to enable them to help others in need, is to once and for all do what politicians promise in every election cycle. But instead of letting them off the hook—again—demand that they make good on their promise. Demand to raise taxes on the rich; demand that the wealthy finally pay their fair share. Then and only then will we be able to benefit every American in this country—be they middle class or lower."

"Hmmm," I said again, and then I answered slowly, "And this is the argument that helped you win the debate with your wife?"

"That's right," he said proudly.

"And now you're sleeping better at night?"

"Like a baby."

"Hmmm," I couldn't help muttering again; and clearing my throat, I continued. "Well, Professor, while I do agree with you, in principle, I'm not clear as to how you'd actually make your plan a reality."

"Ah, my wife said the same thing. *Spoil sports.* But I'm telling you: Where there's a will, there *is* a way."

And therein lay the irony of the old man's plan. On the surface, the idea certainly seemed agreeable—in principle, that is. However, in reality, I couldn't help thinking that there might just be a hidden flaw, to be revealed upon further investigation.

"To compel someone to contribute money for the promotion of opinions for which they disbelieve is sinful and tyrannical."

Thomas Jefferson

The Intricate Nature of Wealth

THE ISSUE OF taxation is frequently discussed in terms of fairness and economic equity, but current debates often overlook the complexities of wealth accumulation and the unexpected consequences of raising taxes on the affluent. The Founding Fathers of America understood the implications of taxation on individual prosperity and economic growth, cautioning against policies that stifle ambition and hinder wealth creation. The modern discourse centers on the idea that raising taxes on the wealthy—defined primarily by income from wages—will lead to greater equity and benefit society as a whole. However, this perspective often neglects the intricate nature of wealth, which encompasses not just income but also investments in stocks and businesses, and it can result in dire economic consequences.

To begin with, it's essential to recognize that wealth is multi-faceted. The notion that wealthy individuals are merely hoarding savings leads to an oversimplification. By focusing solely on liquid assets, such as bank savings and immediate cash flow, we ignore the substantial portions of wealth that are tied up in stocks and business equity. These investments not only generate income but also stimulate economic growth by funding innovations and creating jobs. When taxes rise disproportionately on what is perceived as "the rich," it can deter their willingness to invest, thereby stifling entrepreneurship and reducing overall economic dynamism. This risk echoes the warnings from men like Thomas Jefferson, who understood that burdensome taxes could lead to a decline in individual initiative and economic stagnation. Said Jefferson: "A wise and frugal government is one that restrains men from injuring each other, that leaves them free to regulate their own pursuits of industry and improvement, and that does not take from the mouth of labor the bread it has earned. This is the sum of good government, and this is necessary to close the circle of our contentment."

What's more, raising taxes on the wealthy often results in unintended consequences that can't help but undermine economic stability. A stark example can be found in the response of high-income earners to tax increases, as many simply choose to relocate to jurisdictions with more favorable tax environments. This trend isn't merely theoretical; it has also been observed in various regions where tax policies have become overly burdensome. When high-net-worth individuals leave, they take their wealth and potential investments with them, depriving local economies of resources essential for growth and sustainability. This phenomenon contributes to a vicious cycle, where higher taxes lead to lower economic activity, further aggravating the financial challenges faced by governments.

The historical context surrounding taxation also reveals a guiding principle advocated by the Founding Fathers—the importance of balanced tax policies that encourage wealth creation and support government funding without discouraging personal initiative. They recognized that the path to prosperity is often paved with the entrepreneurial spirit and the willingness of individuals to take risks. A pivotal part of maintaining this spirit is ensuring that taxation is perceived as fair, and not punitive. When the wealthy feel targeted by escalated tax rates, they may withdraw investments or, worse, engage in tax avoidance strategies that could deprive governments of necessary revenue altogether.

Taxation as an Incentive Killer

THE IDEA that raising taxes on the wealthy will benefit the average American, as well as those in poverty, is an alluring one, frequently touted by politicians with a populist agenda. However, this promise obscures a more complex economic reality. While many people, like my professor, argue that raising taxes on the rich is justified, this perspective overlooks an essential aspect of wealth: much of what is classified as "wealth" isn't tied up in savings or stocks but is in the businesses owned by the wealthy. Consequently, raising taxes on the rich can lead to dire consequences for the very people that these policies are intended to benefit.

It is crucial to recognize that many wealthy business owners have invested a great deal of their time, energy, and resources into building enterprises that create jobs, drive innovation, and trigger economic development. When taxes on these individuals rise, it diminishes their ability to reinvest in their companies. This reduction in capital stifles growth and leads to fewer job openings. Thus, in an environment where job creation is paramount, hindering the prospects of successful business owners through higher taxes is ultimately counterproductive.

Not only that, but the idea that wealthy individuals will absorb higher taxes also ignores the interconnected nature of the economy. When businesses face increased tax burdens, they often respond by implementing cost-cutting measures. This includes layoffs, reduced employee benefits, and a decrease in wages, all of which negatively affect the same middle-class employees that tax policy proponents seek to support. As such, a tax increase on the wealthy adversely impacts economic stability and employee welfare.

It is also essential to consider the psychological impact of ever-increasing taxation on the entrepreneurial spirit. Taxation is often viewed as an incentive killer to those who take risks. For entrepreneurs, risk-taking is intrinsic to innovation and progress. When the potential rewards of success are severely taxed, individuals may become less inclined to pursue new ventures. This stagnation not only hampers job creation, but it also stifles technological advancements and creativity that drive society forward.

Silos of Discontent

THE RISING tide of tax hikes has become an undeniable burden for business owners, leading to dwindling profit margins that challenge the viability of operations. As the government continues to impose heavier taxation in their quest for revenue, the ripple effects on small and large enterprises alike are stark and alarming. To counteract these fiscal pressures, business owners often resort to measures that have dire consequences on the financial wellness of their employees.

Profit margins—the lifeblood of any enterprise—are critical for sustaining growth and innovation. Yet, as tax increases chip away at these margins, owners find themselves in a precarious position where survival seems to depend on harsh measures. The instinct to protect the bottom line often leads to difficult decisions, including the unfortunate necessity of slashing payroll costs. By reducing wages, employers may see immediate financial relief; however, this relief is a double-edged sword that ultimately severs the bond between employer and employee.

The repercussions of lowering wages extend far beyond the immediate financial metrics of a business. Employees, now facing reduced income, grapple with daily struggles to meet their financial obligations. This added stress leads to a decline in morale, productivity, and job satisfaction. As workers navigate increasingly challenging economic conditions, the once-vibrant workplace degenerates and fragments into silos of discontent. The negative impact on employees creates a vicious cycle that harms the business itself, as disillusioned and disengaged employees are less inclined to contribute positively to the organization's success.

Cutting benefits is another painful and damaging way for business owners to offset tax burdens. Commissions, health insurance, retirement contributions, and other forms of employee support are often the first targets in these austerity measures. The loss of such benefits leaves employees vulnerable and questioning their allegiance to an employer who once touted itself as a caring organization. This erosion of trust, in turn, leads to a talent drain, where skilled workers seek employment elsewhere, placing further strain on businesses already suffering from decreased profit margins.

The Illusion of Protection

THE IMPACT of increased taxes on businesses often filters down to consumers in the form of higher prices for goods and services. This ripple effect, while perhaps not the primary intention of policymakers, ultimately harms the very demographics they aim to protect. As taxes rise, companies find themselves squeezed between the need for profit and their obligation to remain functional within a competitive market. Ironically, then, the intended beneficiaries of tax increases—lower-income households and vulnerable populations—end up being the unsuspecting victims of economic policy designed without foresight.

Yes, increased taxation does seem like a reasonable method for funding social programs or relieving the financial burden on specific demographics. However, the reality is that businesses typically respond to heightened costs by inflating their prices, further straining consumers' already limited budgets. This not only negates the intended benefits of the tax hike but also exacerbates financial difficulties for those most in need.

The narrative constructed by policymakers also neglects the broader economic implications. When businesses are forced to increase prices, it's not just lower-income families that suffer; the middle class—often seen as the buffer zone—also bears the brunt of these decisions. Higher prices lead to a general decrease in consumer spending, which, in turn, stifles economic growth. As purchases decline, businesses may have to lay off more employees or reduce investment even further, resulting in larger and larger swaths of society experiencing economic hardship.

The reality is: this cycle of increased taxation, business costs, and consumer prices strikes at the very heart of economic equity. Rather than supporting vulnerable groups, the outcome tends to be diminished purchasing power and increased poverty levels. At the end of the day, the illusion of protection offered by new tax legislation crumbles under the weight of its unintended consequences, leaving marginalized individuals more vulnerable than ever.

The Hidden Costs of Redistributing Wealth

ALONG WITH a call for raising taxes on the wealthy, there is talk of redistributing wealth, which is framed as a noble endeavor aimed at achieving greater equity and social justice. At first glance, this rhetoric seems appealing; it promises a fairer society where the burden is shared more equally among citizens. However, beneath this seemingly altruistic surface lies a more troubling interpretation of these policies—a shift towards socialism dressed in less alarming terminology. This gradual movement towards wealth redistribution signals a departure from individual freedom and economic responsibility, raising serious questions about the implications for society as a whole.

Politicians who push for this redistribution carefully craft their words to evoke positive sentiments. Terms like "equitable," "fair share," and "equal starting point" resonate with many who yearn for a more just society. Yet this strategic choice of words actually masks a deeper ideological shift. By framing these policies as necessary reforms rather than revealing their socialistic underpinnings, advocates obscure the consequences of such actions. This linguistic sleight of hand not only distracts people from the realities of government intervention but also fosters an acceptance of concepts that undermine personal autonomy and economic freedom.

The historical context of wealth redistribution also reveals a pattern of disillusionment and failure. Throughout history, many countries that have embraced socialist principles have faced significant economic challenges, ranging from stagnation to outright collapse. Politicians often ignore these historical lessons, opting instead to promote optimistic narratives that predict a different outcome this time around. This selective disregard for past failures only serves to cloud judgment, as individuals become enamored with the idea of a utopian society without fully understanding the structural issues that accompany such reforms.

The implications of these proposed policies also extend far beyond mere taxation. Wealth redistribution undermines the incentives that drive innovation and economic growth. While it may appear justifiable, this short-sighted strategy inevitably stifles entrepreneurship and discourages investment. All this to say, that in the end such promises of shared wealth, of equal prosperity, belies the uncomfortable truth that socialism inherently curtails individual ambition and success, leading to societal stagnation rather than the promised improvement.

Entangled in Bureaucratic Red Tape

THE SYSTEM of taxation, while often hailed as a necessary means for redistributing wealth and funding public services, carries with it a heavy burden of bureaucratic complexities and inefficiencies. As the government collects taxes to redistribute wealth, it creates a labyrinth of protocols and regulations that fail to achieve their intended goals. This squandering of resources not only undermines the ideal of equitable distribution but also breeds disillusionment among citizens and hinders economic growth.

First, the sheer complexity of tax codes hinders the effectiveness of the distribution of these taxes. Add to that the way the government tries to adjust taxes to serve multiple purposes, whether in the name of social equity or economic stimulation. In doing so, they create a system that is so convoluted that the average citizen struggles to understand his or her obligations. This complexity then leads to a significant portion of tax revenue being wasted in compliance costs and legal disputes instead of being funneled into meaningful social programs. Consequently, rather than supporting the populace, this bureaucratic maze diverts resources away from where they are most needed.

Then there are the bureaucratic inefficiencies that plague tax collection and redistribution. Collecting taxes incurs substantial administrative costs. So the government has to hire vast armies of bureaucrats to manage the processes, enforce compliance, and audit tax returns. This not only wastes public funds but also sows seeds of distrust and discontent among taxpayers. As such, citizens feel their hard-earned money is being squandered on excessive bureaucracy rather than being utilized for public welfare. In this disheartening cycle, the quest for redistribution falters, as the resources intended to alleviate poverty or enhance public services become entangled in bureaucratic red tape.

Not only that, but this redistribution also fails to target those who often need support the most. With a myriad of exceptions, loopholes, and special provisions, resources can easily flow to unintended recipients. As a result, the misappropriation of funds due to bureaucratic shortcomings winds up perpetuating inequality rather than reducing it, demonstrating an alarming disconnect between the stated aims of taxation and the real-world outcomes.

New Cycles of Dependency

THE INFUSION of additional funds from the wealthy into government programs has become a common practice in many nations, often heralded as a solution to pressing social issues. However, this approach frequently proves to be ineffective and simply creates new cycles of dependency instead of nurturing true independence among those it aims to help. That's because the complexities surrounding financial aid and social support reveal a troubling reality: reliance on the affluent actually undermines the long-term sustainability and individual autonomy that America's Founders were so keen on establishing in the first place.

It does this because the influx of wealthy contributions distorts the effectiveness of government programs. Rather than addressing the root causes of poverty or social disparity, these funds serve as band-aid solutions, enabling programs to operate without necessary reforms. For example, when affluent individuals or corporations donate large sums to supposedly combat homelessness, these donations merely prolong existing systems that fail to create permanent solutions. Instead of prompting a comprehensive evaluation of housing policies, the funding allows superficial programs to persist, ultimately stagnating progress. In this way, a reliance on external wealth just delays any attempts to make the essential structural changes needed to create more robust support systems.

The dependence on wealthy benefactors can also engender a culture of entitlement rather than empowerment. When government programs are propped up by donations from the wealthy, recipients come to see their support as a right rather than a temporary assistance. This mentality diminishes personal initiative and self-sufficiency, resulting in individuals who rely on external aid rather than seeking sustainable employment or developing skills. Over time, such dependency erodes the very principles of independence and resilience that many social programs strive to instill.

To this point, Benjamin Franklin made a scathing observation about England's well-intentioned but misguided attempts to care for the poor and needy: "There is no country in the world where so many provisions are established for them, with a solemn law made by the rich to subject their estates to a heavy tax for the support of the poor. Yet there is no country in the world in which the poor are more idle, dissolute, drunken, and insolent. The day you passed that act, you took away from before their eyes the greatest of all inducements to industry, frugality, and sobriety, by giving them a dependence on something other than a careful accumulation during youth and health, for support in age and sickness. In short, you offered a premium for the encouragement of idleness, and you should not now wonder that it has had its effect in the increase of poverty."

What's more, the volatile nature of philanthropic funding aggravates this issue further still. Wealthy benefactors often have their own agendas and can withdraw support at any time, which leaves government programs vulnerable. If a major supporter—say, like my professor's wife—shifts their focus to a different cause, the programs they funded suffer setbacks leading to service reductions or layoffs. This unpredictability creates instability for both providers and recipients of social services, ultimately undermining any progress made.

The Secret Agenda Behind the Call to Equity

THE PUSH for higher taxes on the wealthy isn't just a fiscal strategy; it is also a subtle disguise for expanding government control over the private sector. What looks like a benevolent effort to redistribute wealth in fact signals a deeper move toward socialism, where not only is wealth redistributed, but it's also regulated by unelected bureaucrats who are largely unaccountable. This shift raises critical questions about the future of individual freedom, entrepreneurship, and economic vitality.

First, the imposition of higher taxes on the wealthy is often justified as a way to address income inequality and fund public services, as in the case of when my professor invoked the legend of Robin Hood.[19] However, this ratio-

---

19   *The Legend of Robin Hood:* After accidentally killing a royal gamekeeper, a skilled English archer by the name of Robin of Locksley became an outlaw, and so gave birth to the legend of Robin Hood. Forced to seek refuge in the Sherwood Forest, Robin soon gathered a band of loyal followers, known as the "Merry Men," to fight against the tyranny of Prince John and his infamous henchman, the Sheriff of Nottingham. With the aid of his merry men, including Little John, Will Scarlett, Friar Tuck, and Alan-a-Dale, Robin quickly gained his legendary status by robbing the rich and giving to the poor.

The first scattered references to a figure identified as Robin Hood appeared as early as the 1370s, in poems like *Piers Plowman*, *Friar Daw's Reply*, and *Dive and Pauper*. But the earliest complete texts to tell his tale are *Robin Hood and the Monk* and *The Gest of Robin Hood*, written around 1450. Several factors came together that inevitably made Robin Hood a seminal figure in literary history. The mid-15th century was a period of national crisis for England: the loss of Normandy and the Hundred Years War added greatly to existing problems, such as the many failures of King Henry VI. Not only was law and order in total disarray at the time but the justice system was seen as being terribly corrupt— both central themes of these earliest tales of Robin Hood.

Despite the current debates about whether Robin Hood was a real historical figure, his legend remains relevant to this day because of the timeless nature of his story. As one of the most enduring folk heroes in popular culture, his tireless efforts in resisting tyranny, and championing the rights of the poor will no doubt continue to be spoken of in poems, plays, ballads, literature, and cinema for many years to come.

nale obscures a more insidious agenda—the gradual encroachment of government on private enterprise. When tax burdens are increased, any incentive for wealth creation is severely undermined. High earners, who are typically the engines of innovation and economic growth, find their financial motivations stifled. When the government claims a larger share of their income, it effectively saps the dynamism from the economy, leading to financial stagnation, not progress.

Not only that, but as taxes on the affluent are increased, the government also begins to exert more and more control over how that wealth is utilized. The argument often made is that this is for the greater good; however, the government's real goal is to empower bureaucrats so they can more effectively dictate the terms of economic engagement. So, rather than being free to invest, donate, or spend as they see fit, wealthy individuals become beholden to regulations and guidelines imposed by the state. As a result, decisions that should be market-driven are instead made by government entities, who then typically can't help but squander much of what they are entrusted with.

Additionally, the notion that wealth will simply be redistributed to uplift the disadvantaged sidesteps the reality of bureaucratic inefficiency. The machinery of government is, by nature, slow and cumbersome, and when it becomes the primary allocator of wealth, it risks prioritizing administrative processes over genuine need. In such a framework, wealth isn't merely redistributed; it is also filtered through multiple layers of bureaucracy, all of which rarely have the best interests of citizens at heart. The result isn't a more equitable society but, rather, a society where wealth is managed by officials who lack the necessary insight or motivation to handle it effectively.

Thus, we see just how this trajectory toward higher taxes and more government control mutates the nature of capitalism into something unrecognizable. The persistent expansion of government reach into the private sector stifles creativity, reduces individual agency, and ultimately leads to a system where personal freedoms are compromised in favor of a bureaucratically-managed economy. As the waters of socialism seep into the fabric of what once was a dynamic and free-market system, the essential characteristics that spark human progress—innovation, risk-taking, and entrepreneurship—are at risk of being extinguished.

Erosion of the Private Sector

IN RECENT years, the escalating government intervention in free market economies has become a pressing concern, raising questions about the impact on efficiencies essential for innovation and competition. The increasing layers of bureaucratic red tape serve as significant barriers, ultimately stifling creativity and hindering growth. As the government imposes more and more regulations, a once-thriving marketplace stalls, leading to a landscape where consumers, employees, and businesses all suffer the consequences.

To begin with, the introduction of excessive regulations creates an environment that breeds apathy among firms rather than encourages competition. Companies find themselves weighed down by a myriad of rules and administrative procedures, forcing them to divert their focus from innovation to compliance. This shift not only drains resources but also undermines the motivation to develop new, groundbreaking products or services. As a result, the vibrant competition that fuels advancements in technology and efficiency is suffocated under the weight of bureaucratic demands.

Besides that, an overly regulated marketplace often leads to monopolistic practices, further harming consumers. When smaller firms are unable to navigate the complex regulatory framework, they may exit the market, leaving larger corporations free to dominate. This lack of competition, then, results in higher prices, diminished product quality, and a stagnation of variety. Consumers are ultimately left with fewer choices, as innovation falters and the diversity of offerings diminishes in a market constrained by excessive oversight and regulation.

Employees, too, bear the brunt of increased government intervention. As companies grapple with compliance issues, they increasingly resort to practices that cut costs, leading to layoffs, reduced salaries, and diminished job security. This is particularly evident in industries that require significant upfront investment to meet regulatory standards, as many employers may decide that hiring new talent is too risky. The resulting workforce is often left vulnerable, lacking the professional growth opportunities essential for their careers, leading to widespread disillusionment within the labor market.

The Call for Economic Autonomy

THE RELATIONSHIP between individual prosperity and economic autonomy is a cornerstone of a thriving society, reflecting the original vision of the Founding Fathers who understood the importance of personal responsibility and limited government intervention. Instead of relying on governmental support, individuals should be encouraged to cultivate their own economic independence. By promoting personal accountability, minimizing taxation, and reducing regulatory burdens on businesses, society as a whole stands to benefit.

At the heart of this discussion is the principle of economic autonomy. When individuals are empowered to manage their own economic affairs without excessive governmental control, they are more likely to innovate, invest, and take risks. This focus on personal agency cultivates a sense of responsibility, urging individuals to seek out opportunities for growth and success. The Founders envisioned a nation where citizens actively engaged in their own economic pursuits, guided by the belief that freedom in commerce ultimately leads to collective prosperity. An environment that champions personal responsibility allows for a more vibrant marketplace where creativity and entrepreneurship can flourish.

Rather than deliver on its promise of equitably redistributing wealth, higher taxes only stifle innovation and deter individuals from pursuing new business ventures, as they are crushed under the weight of government's demand for a larger share of their earnings. In contrast, by limiting taxation, we create a more favorable environment for business growth, enabling entrepreneurs to reinvest their gains back into their companies, thereby creating jobs and stimulating economic development. This reflects the foundational idea that when individuals keep more of what they earn, they are more inclined to contribute to the economy in meaningful ways. Reduced taxation, then, not only rewards innovation but also empowers individuals to make choices that align with their values and aspirations.

Similarly, excessive government regulations, under the guise of instituting greater social equity, only serve as further impediments to business success. Even in their day, founding figures like Thomas Jefferson and James Madison were suspicious of government overreach. Said Jefferson: "Taxation is, in fact, the most difficult function of government and against which their citizens are most apt to be defiant." And then there was Madison, who had this to say about taxation as a means of redistributing wealth: "I cannot find a single article of the Constitution which grants Congress the right to spend, on any object of benevolence, the money of their constituents."

No wonder the Founders were so intent on limiting the government's power to interfere with the endeavors of its most valuable commodity, its most formidable economic force—its citizens. Thus, it's only through government deregulation that we'll be able to foster a more dynamic business environment, where companies are able to adapt to changing market conditions without facing daunting bureaucratic hurdles. This, in turn, allows businesses to thrive, benefiting society through job creation, increased productivity, and improved services. In this way, a regulatory framework that encourages enterprise and protects the rights of individuals also contributes to a strong economy that empowers citizens rather than constrains them.

Market-Driven Solutions

ANOTHER EFFECTIVE measure in overcoming economic stagnation is to align business practices with consumer needs, by way of market-driven solutions—an approach that has long been celebrated for creating an environment that encourages innovation and responsiveness. In a marketplace that is driven by customer demand, businesses instinctively adapt their offerings to match the desires and requirements of consumers, leading to improved products and services. This natural synergy not only benefits customers, but it also creates a thriving economy that rewards creativity and efficiency. Conversely, increased taxation only distorts these incentives, pushing businesses to prioritize compliance over innovative practices. By examining these contrasting approaches, we see why market-driven solutions hold the key to promoting a brighter economic future.

At the heart of market-driven solutions is the principle that businesses flourish when they truly understand and cater to their customers. This alignment sparks innovation, as companies invest in research and development to create products that anticipate trends and consumer preferences. When consumers express their needs, businesses are motivated to find solutions, leading to a cycle of continuous improvement. For example, the rapid advancements in technology can largely be attributed to companies that seek to enhance user experiences, responding to the demands of an increasingly savvy consumer base. This relationship not only enriches the market but also promotes a culture of accountability and agility within businesses.

On the other hand, increased taxation has a detrimental effect on this dynamic. When governments impose higher taxes, businesses often find themselves reallocating resources to ensure compliance rather than focusing on innovation. This compliance-driven mentality stifles creativity and leads companies to adopt a more risk-averse approach. As funds are redirected toward meeting regulatory requirements, potential investments in new technologies and services are sidelined. Ultimately, this shift hinders economic growth and reduces the overall competitiveness of a business landscape that thrives on innovation.

A market-driven approach also encourages competition, which is fundamental to progress in any economy. As businesses strive to outperform one another, they continuously seek new ways to add value for consumers. This competitive environment ignites the fires of progress, where new ideas are explored without the burden of compliance taking precedence. In contrast, a taxation-heavy approach leads to monopolistic practices, where established players dominate the market, leaving little room for newcomers or fresh ideas.

Long-Term Stability

IN TODAY'S rapidly evolving economic landscape, the notion that businesses can thrive without excessive governmental intervention isn't merely an ideal; it is also a necessity for sustainable growth and prosperity. The long-term stability of businesses creates an environment ripe for innovation, job creation, and enhanced living standards for average Americans. As such, it's clear that a balanced approach, where the government supports rather than controls, can yield a fertile ground for flourishing enterprises and a resilient economy.

To begin with, minimal governmental interference affords businesses the opportunity to adapt to changing market conditions. When entrepreneurs are free to innovate and pivot in response to consumer demand, they develop new products and services that better meet the needs of society. This innovation, then, leads to increased efficiency and productivity, which are essential in a competitive market. The tech industry, for example, has shown remarkable growth through minimal regulatory constraints, resulting in groundbreaking advancements that have transformed everyday life. As businesses drive innovation, they not only cater to their customers but also create new job opportunities, helping to uplift local economies and communities.

Not only that, but a stable economic environment, free from excessive governmental control, also inspires a sense of confidence among investors and entrepreneurs alike. When businesses feel secure, they are more likely to invest in expansion, which directly correlates with job creation. This growth isn't just about the number of jobs created; it is also about the quality of those jobs. As businesses expand, they require a diverse workforce, leading to higher wages and improved benefits for employees. Consequently, this elevation in living standards raises the overall quality of life for average Americans, reducing income inequality and fostering a more equitable society.

What's more, when the government plays a supporting role—such as providing education and infrastructure—it enhances the capability of businesses to thrive. Strategic investments in education and vocational training equip the workforce with essential skills, thereby aligning with industry needs. This not only aids companies in finding qualified employees, but it also empowers individuals to secure better-paying jobs. Such a robust economy generates a positive cycle of growth; as people earn higher wages, they reinvest in their communities, boosting local businesses and further encouraging entrepreneurial ventures.

Rethinking the Reach of
the Bureaucratic Behemoth

IN CONTEMPORARY discussions about government efficiency and economic competition, the size and scope of bureaucracy often come under scrutiny. As public debate rages over ever-increasing taxation and its impact on American citizens, it becomes crucial to reassess both government size and spending. By rethinking the reach of the bureaucratic behemoth, policymakers can reduce the negative effects associated with higher taxation, and ultimately drive more effective governance.

To begin with, it's essential to recognize the detrimental consequences of excessive bureaucracy. Large bureaucratic structures tend to hamper the government's ability to address citizens' needs effectively. When government spending grows unchecked, it leads to inefficiencies in delivering public services, as resources become diluted across an unwieldy network of programs and departments. This dilution, in turn, results in even higher taxes, particularly on those with greater wealth who may bear a disproportionate burden. By reassessing and downsizing government operations, a more streamlined and agile bureaucracy could emerge, reducing the financial strain on the affluent while still delivering essential services.

A reassessment of government spending is also necessary to ensure that taxpayer money is properly allocated. By focusing on effectiveness rather than sheer volume, the government could direct funds toward initiatives that stimulate economic growth and produce social benefits. This means engaging in rigorous analyses of public programs to determine which ones are yielding real results and which ones are bureaucratic relics with minimal impact. Additionally, embracing a culture of accountability and transparency could restore public trust and encourage citizens to again see the value in their tax contributions. A more judicious allocation of resources could alleviate perceptions of wastefulness and mismanagement, encouraging a collaborative approach between taxpayers and officials.

And keep in mind, reducing the size of government doesn't mean abandoning our social responsibility. Rather, it just prompts an examination of alternative approaches to governance. Innovative solutions, such as partnerships with private sector entities and non-profit organizations, could expand the effectiveness of public services without requiring large bureaucratic expansions. Such collaborations could then leverage the strengths of both sectors, driving efficiency while lessening the tax burden on every segment of society. Consequently, this could foster an environment conducive to economic investment and growth, positioning the government to be a giver rather than a taker.

Limiting Bureaucratic Regulation

ALTHOUGH GOVERNMENT regulations are supposed to protect public interests and maintain fair competition, excessive regulation stifles innovation, hinders business growth, and slows down economic progress. In contrast, by reducing regulatory burdens, we unleash creativity and entrepreneurship, and so contribute to a more dynamic and vibrant economy.

That's because excessive regulations create significant obstacles for startups and small businesses, which are often the backbone of economic growth. These entities frequently struggle to navigate complex compliance requirements that demand both time and financial resources. By streamlining regulations, we empower small businesses to allocate their resources toward development and innovation rather than bureaucratic compliance. For instance, when a startup can bypass mountains of paperwork, it can focus on refining its product or service, leading to new solutions that invigorate the market.

A regulatory environment that encourages flexibility

boosts larger corporations as well. When businesses are unfettered by cumbersome regulations, they are more inclined to invest in research and development, leading to technological advancements and job creation. A thriving innovative spirit can result in groundbreaking products and services that not only enhance efficiency but also improve the quality of life for consumers. We have seen this in various sectors, such as technology and healthcare, where reduced regulatory constraints have spurred remarkable advancements.

Limiting bureaucratic regulation also encourages more entrepreneurs to enter the market. A simplified regulatory framework cultivates an environment where individuals feel more confident in pursuing their business ideas. When aspiring entrepreneurs aren't burdened by excessive regulations, we see a surge in new startups, which contributes to job creation and economic diversity. This influx of fresh ideas and services, in turn, leads to increased competitiveness within industries, driving further innovation and prosperity.

Something else to keep in mind: when excessive regulatory barriers are reduced, there is often a renewed sense of responsibility and self-regulation among businesses. That means that when companies aren't over-regulated, they're encouraged to voluntarily adhere to ethical standards and best practices. This self-regulation leads to a more responsible and conscientious business environment where companies don't just prioritize profits and market share but also ethical sustainability and social responsibility.

Responsible Government Spending

ANOTHER CRITICAL issue that significantly impacts the fabric of our society is responsible government spending. As the government navigates the complexities of budgeting, the focus should shift from funding frivolous programs to investing in essential domestic needs. By reallocating resources in this manner, we have a greater impact on society, ultimately improving the lives of our citizens and contributing to a healthier community.

At the core of responsible spending lies the recognition of priorities. While various programs may have their merits, not all of them are equally important when it comes to the wellbeing of the public. For instance, programs that provide entertainment or luxury rather than necessary services divert funds from crucial areas such as healthcare, education, and infrastructure. By scrutinizing and potentially cutting such expenditures, government can free up resources to address pressing domestic needs. Investing in healthcare services, for example, can ensure that citizens have access to better medical treatment, improving public health outcomes and reducing long-term healthcare costs.

Allocating funds for education is also vital. An educated populace is the foundation of a thriving society. By enhancing educational programs, particularly in impoverished communities, the government empowers individuals to improve their economic prospects and contribute positively to society. By prioritizing educational investment, we would cultivate a skilled workforce that can drive economic growth and innovation. This not only benefits individuals but also strengthens the economy as a whole, creating a cycle of positive reinforcement.

Infrastructure is another area that desperately needs attention and funding. In many regions, aging or inadequate infrastructure hampers economic development and diminishes the quality of public life. By redirecting resources towards repairing and upgrading roads, public transportation, and utilities, the government would enhance accessibility and stimulate local economies. A well-functioning infrastructure system is essential for attracting businesses and ensuring that communities flourish, underscoring the importance of responsible government spending.

Encouraging Personal Empowerment

IN THE ONGOING discussion about social welfare programs and their impact on dependency, the importance of personal empowerment stands out as a critical factor. America's Founding Fathers recognized the value of self-reliance and individual responsibility, framing a society where personal initiative could thrive. That's why it's critical that we emphasize the importance of encouraging personal empowerment, rather than solely expecting more from the wealthy. Only then will we be able to effectively break the cycles of dependency that many welfare programs inadvertently perpetuate.

At the heart of personal empowerment is the belief that individuals possess the ability to shape their own destinies. By fostering an environment where people are motivated to take charge of their own lives, society cultivates resilience and innovation. For instance, programs that provide education and skills training enable individuals to find sustainable employment, reducing reliance on government assistance. Studies have shown that when individuals are given the tools and opportunities to succeed, they can break free from the constraints of poverty. Conversely, an over-reliance on wealth redistribution leads to a sense of entitlement, where individuals feel less inclined to pursue opportunities for themselves.

What's more, the foundational principles of the United States emphasized limited government intervention and the power of the individual. The Founders envisioned a society where citizens could thrive through their own efforts, which not only contributes to a stronger economy but also creates a more engaged and responsible citizenry. When people are encouraged to empower themselves, they contribute to their communities in meaningful ways. This involvement leads to the development of local initiatives and supports networks that further enhance social capital and reduce dependency on welfare.

In contrast, merely expecting the wealthy to bear the burden of social welfare creates a divisive dynamic within society. Such an approach risks inciting resentment and a culture of dependency, where individuals may believe their wellbeing depends on the generosity of others. This dependency stifles motivation and hinders progress. Instead of cultivating a spirit of entrepreneurship and innovation, an expectation of support from the affluent leads to complacency and a lack of initiative among those who benefit from welfare programs.

In conclusion, transitioning from a dependency model to one that promotes personal accountability requires a fundamental shift in perspective. Policies should focus on individuals taking ownership of their situations through education, job training, and support systems that encourage self-sufficiency. By doing this, we not only uplift individuals, but we also enhance overall economic productivity and societal health. The success stories of those who have risen above challenging circumstances through hard work and personal responsibility serve as powerful testimony to the potency of the original vision of the Founding Fathers of America.

Chapter Eight

Foreign Affairs:

The Global Consequences

LIE #8:

*In Geopolitics, as in Our Personal Relationships,
Americans Must Always Live by the Golden Rule, and
Treat Others as We'd Like to be Treated...*

ONE DAY after class, I have to say, my professor never looked so grim. Then he asked me, point-blank: "Aren't you ever worried that your work as a political science major is incompatible with the tenants of a genuine Christian faith?" Leaning back in his oversized chair, he exhaled deeply. "And when I say political science," he continued, "I'm not thinking just in terms of American politics as it relates to domestic affairs. No... You see, the thing that has invaded my thinking, intruded into my thoughts... It's not so much about our political landscape. What I'm thinking about has more to do with geopolitics. The question is... How do we—America, that is—how do we Americans fit in? I mean, what is our role in relationship with the rest of the world in general?" And when he saw the puzzled look that had materialized on my face, he chuckled. "Oh, dear," he continued, "I'm sorry for coming off so glum. It's just that my wife and I were having another one of our ...

discussions—you know the kind."

I nodded affirmatively.

"Well, anyway," he proceeded. "As usual, she was challenging me from the perspective of her faith—Catholic, you see—and we were discussing the upheaval in the Middle East, and she was asking me what I thought about our diplomatic role there."

Trying to engage with the conversation in a meaningful way, I interjected. "Maybe if you could provide me with a specific situation, I could better answer your question."

"Of course, of course," he said, with downcast eyes. Clearly, he was wrestling with an inner turmoil that was making it difficult for him to choose the right words, something I'd never seen before in the professor. "There's a humanitarian crisis there, you see," he continued, "a crisis due to recent military strikes by the various parties involved. Apparently this has triggered a sizable exodus of refugees seeking asylum in the U.S. The situation has become so dire the State Department is suggesting we temporarily suspend the normal procedure of vetting these asylum seekers; and it's creating quite a stir in Washington."

"And you say your wife is somehow involved in this," I interjected again. "How so?"

"Well, yes. Somehow, she got herself appointed to some subcommittee that's responsible for inputting their advice on the ruling in the vetting process of these refugees."

"And I suppose your wife is in favor of allowing them into our country *without* the normal vetting process. Is that why you're so upset?"

With that, the professor looked up at me in shock. "But that's the thing—that's what I *thought* she was going to say. But she completely threw me for a loop."

"A loop? What do you mean a loop?"

"Suddenly, my wife—the good and saintly Christian—is more concerned about Americans and America's national security. According to her, without proper vetting, these refugees pose a potential threat. According to her, many of these refugees come from countries that do not wish us well because of America's 'meddling,' as they see it, in their private dispute." The old man paused, as if to allow me more time to digest his words, then he blurted, "Can you believe it? The good wife?"

"Oh, I see," was all I could think of at that moment.

"I have to tell you, I could have never seen this coming, not from someone like my wife."

"You mean someone so committed to aiding the poor and needy?"

"Yes. That's why I was wondering what you think, considering your outspoken position on Christianity."

"But, sir, I'd like to know something else before I offer my take on this situation."

"Of course. What is it?"

"What is *your* opinion about the decision to bypass normal immigration procedure? Does it violate *your* moral sensibilities?"

"But that's just it. I don't have *anything* to say about it, one way or the other. What I think is meaningless. What I'm concerned with—the thing that troubles me the most— is the complete lack of consistency on the part of my wife."

"How's that?"

"Consistency, young man, consistency. While I'm certainly no Christian, I do at least subscribe to being consistent about my agnosticism. Otherwise I'd consider myself a hypocrite. Wouldn't you agree?"

"Of course. And so you're having a hard time understanding your wife's position because you see it as being inconsistent with her Christian faith."

"Naturally. I mean, don't *you* see the same thing? Are you not expected to live by the so-called 'Golden Rule'? When faced with a moral dilemma like this, aren't you supposed to put away your own personal needs, extend open arms? Even when dealing with your enemies, you're supposed to turn the other cheek, right?"

"You mean you believe loving your enemies should be

applied not just in our personal lives but also in the context of global relations. Is that it?"

"Like I said, I don't have *any* opinion regarding the idea of 'loving your enemies.' I personally think it's a lot of sentimental hogwash."

"Then what's the problem here?"

"The problem, as I see it, is: If you're going to be a Christian and hold to Christian precepts, then by all means, be consistent ... or else..." His words trailed off, as though he would regret saying what he was about to say.

"Or else what?" I asked, unable to help myself.

"Or else," he replied, slowly, "quit the game altogether."

And there it was again—my strange admiration for a man who I completely disagreed with when it came to many of the ideas I held most dear. Yet despite his agnosticism, here was a man ruled by principles, even as he struggled to understand his wife's view that challenged his own code of ethics. Besides that, I also felt an overwhelming need to avoid offering a pat answer to his question. So as always, before I did commit to an answer, I determined to further investigate both sides of this complex issue to better understand the truth of this important matter.

"Guard jealously the public liberty. Suspect everyone who approaches that jewel. Unfortunately, nothing will preserve it but downright force. Whenever you give up that force, you are inevitably ruined."

Patrick Henry

A Misfit in the World of Geopolitics

THE INTRICATE landscape of international relations often resembles a complex tapestry, woven from various threads of national interest, power dynamics, and cultural exchanges. Within this framework, the United States has historically positioned itself as a moral beacon, frequently advocating for the so-called "Golden Rule"—the principle of treating others as one would like to be treated. While this virtue is commendable in personal interactions, its application in the realm of geopolitics can be misguided and, at times, detrimental to U.S. interests and global stability.

To comprehend the implications of applying the Golden Rule to international relations, we must first acknowledge its noble intentions. Almost universally appealing as an ethical framework, the Golden Rule promotes empathy and mutual respect. As such, America has often touted this principle when addressing foreign policy issues, suggesting that by treating other nations fairly and justly, it can promote goodwill, stability, and cooperation. However, this idealistic approach overlooks the harsh realities of global politics and clashing interests, where moral posturing frequently leads to unintended consequences.

When the United States operates under the assumption that other countries will reciprocate goodwill, it risks a fundamental misunderstanding of the motives driving international actors. Nations operate based on strategic interests rather than ethical considerations. For example, in its dealings with authoritarian regimes, U.S. adherence to the Golden Rule puts us at a serious disadvantage, as these governments seek to exploit American idealism to their advantage while failing to reciprocate in kind. The consequences of such naive assumptions have resulted in numerous policy failures, where the United States found itself diplomatically and strategically marginalized.

No better example of this kind of thinking is revealed in George Washington's 1796 Farewell Address to the fledging nation: "Against the insidious wiles of foreign influence the jealousy of a free people ought to be constantly awake, since history and experience prove that foreign influence is one of the deadliest foes of a republican government. But that jealousy, to be useful, must be impartial, or else it becomes the instrument of the very influence that should be avoided, instead of a defense against it."

The application of the Golden Rule also inadvertently sends mixed signals to both allies and adversaries. What appears to be a virtuous act of kindness in one context might be seen as interference or aggression in another. Consequently, the U.S. risks either alienating allies or antagonizing adversaries, ultimately undermining its own geopolitical objectives. As such, a one-size-fits-all approach, as promoted by the Golden Rule, typically fails because it ignores the diverse motivations, histories, and power dynamics of different nations.

This is why it's so important to approach the complexities of international relationships with a more nuanced understanding of cultural and political contexts. In conflict zones, for instance, where humanitarian objectives eclipse strategic necessities, the United States may push for negotiations and conciliatory tactics, believing that kindness will prevail. However, this generally emboldens adversaries to continue aggressive behavior, interpreting diplomatic overtures as weakness rather than strength. Thus, the very principle intended to promote goodwill winds up leading instead to a cycle of exploitation and disillusionment.

The Golden Rule isn't Always Golden

THE GOLDEN Rule stands as a beacon of morality in individual lives, by encouraging empathy, understanding, and cooperation. However, when we shift our focus from personal interactions to the vast and intricate landscape of geopolitics, the beauty of this principle unravels, revealing a sobering reality that suggests a more pessimistic view of human relations on the global stage.

In our personal lives, the Golden Rule is seen as an effective tool. Families, friends, and communities often thrive on mutual respect and kindness. When individuals practice empathy, conflicts tend to be resolved more amicably, leading to harmonious relationships. This echoes the ideals of cooperation, where society benefits as members support one another. Yet, the moment we extrapolate these principles onto the geopolitical landscape, the situation becomes murky.

Just consider international relations, if you will, where reciprocity rarely works the same way as in our personal relationships. Instead of a shared understanding, we often encounter a cacophony of competing interests. When nation-states enact policies, they don't usually prioritize mutual benefit; rather, they seek to maximize their own advantage, usually at the expense of weaker nations. This reality starkly contradicts the altruism suggested by the Golden Rule. Instead of inspiring a spirit of cooperation, we witness aggression, manipulation, and exploitation on a global scale.

Not only that, but the asymmetry of power between nations also complicates the application of this moral principle. In an ideal world, nations would treat each other with respect and dignity, adhering to mutually beneficial agreements. But this, unfortunately, isn't always the case in the geopolitical arena, which is frequently marked by the imposition of will, notably by dominant countries exerting pressure on those less powerful. The resulting dynamic resembles more of a "survival of the fittest" scenario and less of a community governed by moral considerations, leaving the principles of empathy and understanding far behind.

Another point of contention is that the Golden Rule implicitly assumes a level of equality and goodwill that is often absent in international relations. Various countries operate with conflicting ideologies, histories, and values that don't easily align with the simple act of treating others as one hopes to be treated. Cultural misunderstandings and historical animosities can aggravate tensions, leading to a cycle of hostility rather than cooperation. While individuals might strive for empathy in their local contexts, global interactions rarely reflect such ideals.

A Lack of Reciprocity

POWER DYNAMICS between countries often reveal a stark contrast to personal relationships, where kindness cultivates goodwill and understanding. But in the geopolitical arena, nations operate under a framework of power that hinges on military strength, economic influence, and strategic interests, all of which underscore the idea that goodwill doesn't always beget goodwill in international relations. James Madison, writing in *Federalist* No. 41, described this dynamic as follows: "The means of security can only be regulated by the means and the danger of attack. They will, in fact, be ever determined by these rules, and by no others. If one nation constantly maintains a disciplined army, ready for the service of ambition or revenge, it obliges the most pacific nations who may be within the reach of its enterprises to take corresponding precautions."

This is because—like it or not—countries are governed by a different set of rules than those that govern personal relationships. In the realm of international politics, nations prioritize their interests and strategic advantages far above expressions of goodwill. Take for example when one country extends an olive branch through aid or diplomatic support. Does that guarantee a reciprocal gesture? Sadly, no, it doesn't. Historical instances abound where nations have sought to leverage their military or economic prowess to manipulate or dominate others, irrespective of prior kindness. The relationship between the U.S. and certain Middle Eastern nations exemplifies this; despite extensive aid and support, tensions often persist, driven by underlying strategic calculations on various sides of the conflict.

Economic power also plays a critical role in shaping these dynamics. Nations with significant economic resources can exert influence over others, often leading to unequal relationships. For instance, China's Belt and Road Initiative illustrates how economic investment is utilized not merely as a gesture of goodwill but as a tool for establishing political leverage and military dominance.²⁰ Countries that accept such investments may find themselves in debt or politically beholden to China, raising questions about the true nature of the partnership. Thus, economic power can overshadow kindness, leading to a situation where reciprocity is dictated by power imbalances rather than mutual respect or gratitude.

In addition to economic factors, military power serves as a crucial component of international relations. Nations with formidable military capabilities may respond to perceived threats or slights with aggression rather than diplomacy. Such actions emphasize how military strength dictates responses, reinforcing the notion that countries

---

20   *China's Belt and Road Initiative*: A global infrastructure development strategy, China's Belt and Road Initiative (BRI) aims to economically connect China with the rest of the world. The BRI is a series of investment initiatives that includes roads, railways, and ports, with the stated purpose of developing an interdependent market for China, growing China's political power, and creating the right conditions for China to build a high technology economy. The BRI is made up of two parts: the Silk Road Economic Belt and the 21st century Maritime Silk Road.

According to international experts, China has 3 main reasons for establishing the BRI: First, they want to counteract American dominance when it comes to maritime trading routes, considering that most of China's international trade passes by sea off the coast of Singapore, a major U.S. ally. Second, ever since China's 2008 financial crisis, they invested so much stimulus money building railways, bridges, and airports that they saturated the Chinese market in the process, and so the BRI is seen as a way to provide an alternative market beyond their borders for all these state-owned enterprises. Third, the Belt and Road is seen as an important way to stimulate the economies in their central regions, which historically lag behind richer coastal areas.

For many developing nations, the BRI is appealing because of the economic advantages it offers. The BRI offers them infrastructure development, and financial and technical assistance. For many of these countries, the infusion of foreign investment and increased trade routes also stimulates increased employment and poverty alleviation. Currently, more than 147 countries— accounting for two-thirds of the world's population and 40 percent of global GDP—have signed on to BRI projects or have indicated they intend to do so. However, despite China's insistence that their goal is primarily economic in nature, many international experts are worried that the BRI could instead serve as a proverbial Trojan horse for Chinese military expansion.

may not return kindness with kindness but, rather, with calculated measures aimed at protecting their sovereignty.

That's because, despite the best intentions of American idealists, the international system operates on principles of realism, where the chaotic nature of state interactions demands a focus on self-interest and survival. Realism posits that nations are primarily concerned with their own security, and so explains why, in the international sphere, actions are so often dictated by strategic calculations rather than the moral considerations that govern our personal relationships.

Hidden Agendas

THROUGHOUT HISTORY, nations have often presented a facade of friendliness while pursuing self-serving agendas that can render genuine goodwill ineffective. This complex interplay between perception and motive isn't a new phenomenon, and it raises critical questions about international relations and the integrity of diplomatic efforts. The Founding Fathers of America were acutely aware of the potential dangers posed by this duplicity, understanding that hidden agendas could undermine national security and the unity necessary for a thriving republic.

The notion of friendly alliances founded on shared interests is a cornerstone of diplomacy. However, these alliances often mask ulterior motives. For instance, nations may engage in partnerships or treaties that, on the surface, appear mutually beneficial, but underneath there lies a pursuit of individual national interests. This predilection for duplicity over sincerity leads to distrust among nations. When one nation perceives another as being insincere, it's difficult to establish long-term, meaningful relationships.

The wisdom of America's Founding Fathers provides important insight into this issue. Figures like George Washington and Thomas Jefferson were wary of foreign entanglements that could compromise the nation's integrity and security. Washington's Farewell Address famously cautioned against the dangers of political alliances that could draw the fledgling nation into conflicts not of its own making. Said Washington: "The nation which indulges toward another an habitual hatred or an habitual fondness is in some degree a slave. It is a slave to its animosity or to its affection, either of which is sufficient to lead it astray from its duty and its interest. Hostility in one nation against another disposes each more readily to offer insult and injury, to lay hold of slight causes of resentment, and to be arrogant and intractable when accidental or trifling occasions of dispute occur."

Jefferson echoed this sentiment by promoting the idea of "peace, commerce, and honest friendship with all nations, but entangling alliances with none." Their apprehensions were rooted in a recognition that foreign relationships might be exploited for hidden agendas, ultimately jeopardizing national safety and sovereignty.

In modern contexts, the same concerns linger. Consider, if you will, just how often nations extend aid and support in exchange for strategic advantages. Humanitarian actions can mask deeper motives, as the providing nation might simultaneously seek to expand its influence or secure favorable trade agreements. This dynamic diminishes the effectiveness of genuine goodwill efforts, as recipient nations tend to become skeptical of the real intentions behind financial or military assistance. The interplay of motives complicates international relations and raises ethical questions about the authenticity of foreign policy actions.

The prevalence of hidden agendas can also strain diplomatic relations, creating an atmosphere of suspicion. If one country suspects another of operating under the guise of friendship, it may respond defensively, resulting in increased tensions and a breakdown of trust. This cycle can lead to conflicts that destabilize not only the nations directly involved but also the broader international community.

Consequences of Misapplying the Golden Rule

IN TODAY'S world, the balance of international relations often hangs precariously between realism and idealism, with profound implications for global governance. This tension raises a fundamental question: Can ethical norms truly prevail in the face of overwhelming security interests? The chilling reality suggests that the Golden Rule, which advocates treating others as one wishes to be treated, can be overshadowed by the stark pragmatism driven by power and security needs.

Realism, rooted in the idea that nations operate primarily in pursuit of their own interests, paints a sobering picture of international relations. The relentless quest for power and dominance often leads to conflicts where moral considerations become secondary. Driven by security concerns, world leaders may feel compelled to engage in actions that starkly contradict ethical norms. This perspective implies that nations are haunted by the specter of betrayal and aggression, leading them to prioritize survival over morality.

Idealism, in contrast, encourages the belief that cooperation and mutual respect can foster a better world. Proponents of this view argue for the need of moral principles in shaping international behavior. However, the harsh reality often reveals that idealism can become a weapon of the powerful—weaponized to justify domination under the guise of benevolence. When world leaders preach about the importance of ethical norms yet employ their considerable military might to enforce their own interests, it becomes clear that the Golden Rule is being manipulated, rendering it ineffective in addressing the underlying realities of global power dynamics.

The Founding Fathers of America recognized these nuances, understanding that a singular focus on ethical norms could undermine national security. Influenced by

Enlightenment thinking and their own experiences with European power dynamics, the Founders acknowledged the importance of balancing ethical considerations with the practical need for security. They sought to create a government capable of protecting liberty while also recognizing the inevitability of conflict in a competitive world. Their writings reflect a pragmatic approach to international relations that blends ideals with the recognition of power realities. Alexander Hamilton spoke to this very point in *Federalist* No. 34, when he wrote: "To judge from the history of mankind, we are compelled to conclude that the fiery and destructive passions of war reign in the human breast with much more powerful sway than the mild and beneficent sentiments of peace; and that to model our political systems upon speculations of lasting tranquility is to count on the weaker springs of the human character."

In the context of foreign affairs, then, we can clearly see how dangerous it is to blindly adhere to the Golden Rule. Because while aspiring to treat others justly is admirable, it overlooks the underlying power dynamics at play, and in doing so fails to account for the potential consequences in geopolitical terms. As a result, a nation that naively clings to such idealistic principles, without first considering its own security and strategic positioning, is always at risk of being exploited by more realist actors in the global arena. Hence, the intricacies of applying the Golden Rule in international relations call for a more nuanced understanding of both ethical norms and power dynamics.

Realism versus Idealism

IN THE contemporary landscape of national security, the tension between realism and idealism continues to remain at the forefront of debate, particularly in relation to immigration policies. Partisan politicians often invoke the Golden Rule as a justification for lax immigration standards, even when these policies compromise national security.

As we've just seen, realism, in the context of national security, emphasizes pragmatism and a cautious approach to policies that must be grounded in the current realities of threats, both external and internal. As for the issue of illegal immigration, the present risks it poses to national security can't be overlooked or underestimated. This is particularly the case when unvetted individuals entering our country pose inherent dangers, from the potential for criminal acts, to economic and social instability. A realist perspective prompts legislators to prioritize the safety and security of citizens over an unfettered hospitality that might lead to negative consequences.

Idealism, on the other hand, focuses on moral imperatives and the belief that our country should extend compassion, even to those entering the United States illegally. Proponents of this view invoke the Golden Rule to promote a more welcoming stance toward immigrants, arguing that everyone deserves a chance at a better life. While the humanitarian angle offers a compelling narrative, idealism sometimes disregards the nuances and security implications of immigration. An uncritical application of the Golden Rule, then, can't help but overlook the potential exploitation of lenient policies by those who don't have the best interests of our country at heart.

In response to this pushback on unchecked illegal immigration, many politicians have begun to engage in a tactic of shaming opponents who have more cautious, realistic positions. By framing their discussions in terms of morality and compassion, they effectively create a narrative that casts those advocating for stricter immigration policies as lacking empathy or humanity. However, upon further review, this approach, while emotionally appealing on the surface, does clearly oversimplify a complex issue, not to mention stifles constructive dialogue.

The fear of being labeled as "uncompassionate" also leads to policy paralysis among lawmakers. They feel pressured to conform to idealistic views to maintain political favor rather than addressing the genuine security concerns that arise from unchecked immigration. The challenge, then, lies in finding a middle ground that respects both the need for compassion and for security—a balanced approach that involves the comprehensive vetting of immigrants while ensuring that those who pose a risk to national safety are effectively managed.

Assimilation versus Annihilation

THE DEBATE surrounding immigration in America has always been intense, particularly in regard to the balance between assimilation and annihilation of cultural identities. At the heart of this discussion are those partisan politicians who cite the Golden Rule as a justification for illegal immigration. While the intention behind this principle may be rooted in compassion, the potential implications for national security and domestic stability can't be ignored.

This doesn't mean the outcome of the immigration process is always negative. When immigrants adopt the values of America, they positively contribute to a more cohesive society. This willingness to assimilate promotes cultural exchange, enhanced social understanding, and economic collaboration. For example, incoming immigrants have historically brought their unique traditions while also adopting aspects of American culture. This mutual exchange has created a rich cultural tapestry, where diversity is celebrated alongside shared national values.

Encouraging unity through assimilation also leads to greater social stability. Communities characterized by a strong sense of belonging are generally more resilient in the face of challenges. When immigrants identify with the collective values of America, they are more likely to engage in civic participation, volunteerism, and social integration. This engagement not only benefits the immigrants themselves but also strengthens our social fabric, making it more robust against fragmentation.

On the other hand, there are cases where certain individuals or groups resist assimilation, choosing instead to adhere strictly to their original cultural norms. This resistance stems from various factors, including fear of losing one's identity, experiences of discrimination, or political ideologies that reject the values of the United States. In some extreme instances, such resistance leads to actions aimed at destabilizing our society, igniting division rather than unity. Such disruptions manifest in various ways, from the spread of radical ideologies, to acts of violence, creating an atmosphere of fear and mistrust.

The Golden Rule, then, while admirable in its intent, is problematic when it's used to justify unchecked illegal immigration without considering its potential risks. National security experts have raised valid concerns that not all individuals enter the country with benign intentions. So, when immigration policies fail to adequately vet individuals, they can lead to dangerous situations, such as terrorism and crime, that jeopardize the safety of citizens and the stability of our nation.

Something else to consider is how the call for compassion in regard to immigration reform inevitably blurs the lines between legal and illegal pathways to citizenship. Politicians citing the Golden Rule are always quick to argue for amnesty or leniency towards undocumented immigrants, insisting that empathy, above all else, should guide policy decisions. But in doing so, they completely ignore the sobering truth that by encouraging an unvetted flow of illegal immigration, a dangerous cycle of instability ensues that can't help but undermine national security.

The Call of Duty

THE MISAPPLICATION of the Golden Rule also undermines the efforts of soldiers who accept the call of duty to serve their country in the pursuit of freedom abroad. When this ethical guideline is improperly applied in the context of military service, it leads to a skewed understanding of duty and sacrifice, ultimately impacting the morale and effectiveness of those who serve.

One of the central tenets of military service is the idea of sacrifice for a greater good. Soldiers often face life-and-death scenarios, navigating complex moral landscapes to protect freedoms that not only benefit our nation but also uphold universal human rights. When the Golden Rule is misapplied, it suggests that all conflicts can be resolved through peaceful means, disregarding the harsh realities that soldiers face. Such a misguided viewpoint can't help but lead to a lack of support for military actions, implying that those who fight are engaging in violence rather than the noble defense of freedom. This, then, clearly diminishes the significance of their sacrifices, casting doubt on their purpose and undermining their commitment.

Not only that, but the misapplication of the Golden Rule also inflames a sense of disillusionment among service members. Soldiers are trained to understand the gravity of their mission, recognizing that freedom isn't granted without a struggle. When critics of military action invoke the Golden Rule to argue against intervention efforts, they invalidate the sacrifices of the men and women of our armed forces. This ill-advised attempt then engenders feelings of isolation and resentment within the ranks, as service members feel unrecognized or unsupported in their efforts to maintain peace and protect our republican values.

Also important to note: the complexities of warfare defy the simplistic application of the Golden Rule. Military engagements are fraught with ethical dilemmas that require nuanced decision-making. That means that blindly adhering to the principle of treating others as one wishes to be treated simply doesn't account for the reality of opposing forces that threaten life, limb, and liberty. Such a naive interpretation can't help but lead to ineffective and dangerous policies that jeopardize not only the lives of our soldiers but also the lives of those they are sworn to protect.

To Protect and to Serve

IN AN ERA where national security is increasingly threatened by foreign terrorist cells, the indiscriminate application of the Golden Rule also undermines police efforts to protect and to serve our citizens at home. While this principle promotes compassion and understanding on a personal level, misapplying it in the context of geopolitics hinders the necessary vigilance required in combating terrorism, which, in turn, provokes criticism and negative perceptions that alter public trust in law enforcement.

Law enforcement agencies daily face the challenging task of navigating the fine line between civil liberties and effective security measures. In a diverse society, the Golden Rule is supposed to encourage empathy towards individuals from various backgrounds. How sad, then, to see how often its misapplication leads to it being twisted beyond its original intent—misapplied in such a way that it becomes an excuse to overextend leniency towards foreign elements that operate with ill intent.

In short, in cases where terrorist cells threaten national security, it's the sworn duty of law enforcement to prioritize the safety of all American citizens. Yet flying in the face of this overriding need are so many ill-conceived calls for the Golden Rule, which inevitably overshadow the need for certain preemptive actions, such as surveillance, search, and seizure, and which, when foolishly thwarted, leave our police woefully handicapped in their effort to address the threats they face on the job.

Then add to that when various critics complicate matters by arguing that such proactive measures are excessive or discriminatory, particularly against minority communities, leading to an environment rife with prejudice. Such criticisms often emerge from a well-intentioned desire to uphold human rights, but unfortunately, when foreign terrorist cells see this happening they have no compunction in exploiting this criticism to gain a strategic advantage, knowing that any police action will be met with a severe backlash. In fact, terrorists thrive on this kind of division, utilizing fear and social discord as tools for recruitment and operational secrecy. That's why, in this context, strict adherence to the Golden Rule never contributes to the public welfare as its advocates assume. Far from it, actually; in cases like this, they instead allow malign actors to operate with impunity, ultimately jeopardizing the very citizens that law enforcement is tasked to protect and to serve.

Then consider how negative press surrounding police actions against suspected terrorists amplifies feelings of distrust within communities. Media outlets, in their rabid pursuit of sensationalism, conveniently overlook the necessity of tough law enforcement actions aimed at consolidating national security. Such a distorted narrative skews the perception of police work, overshadowing the rationale behind certain decisions. Rather than presenting an accurate portrayal of the risks involved, the media stirs up an environment in which reasonable national security measures are viewed as unnecessary or, even worse, oppressive.

Short-Term Gains versus Long-Term Complications

THE COMPLEXITY of foreign policy is often obscured by political rhetoric, yet a deeper examination reveals the underlying intentions that govern national interactions. As the United States navigates its role on the global stage, the contrast between short-term gains and long-term complications becomes apparent. This dichotomy not only affects international relations, but it also reflects the principles espoused by America's Founding Fathers, who understood the broader implications of policy decisions on both a national and global level.

In the realm of foreign policy, short-term gains might be won by entering alliances or imposing sanctions that yield quick results by satisfying political agendas or public sentiment, but these actions often lead to unforeseen long-term complications that jeopardize both America's national interests and international stability. A prime example of this phenomenon is the invasion of Iraq in 2003. While the immediate objective was to eliminate perceived threats, the ensuing instability and chaos led to a protracted conflict that continues to have repercussions to this day, affecting both the region and U.S. engagement across the Middle East.

To this point, the Founding Fathers, particularly figures like George Washington and Thomas Jefferson, recognized the vital importance of thoughtful diplomacy and the delicate balance of power in the world. Their warnings against entangling alliances and the pursuit of national interests underscore a timeless truth: effective foreign policy must prioritize long-term stability over short-term rewards. By focusing on mutual respect and cooperation, the United States can build partnerships that bolster both its position in the world and contribute to global well-being.

But transitioning from short-term strategic interests to long-term success is no easy task; it involves a comprehensive understanding of geopolitical dynamics and cultural sensitivities. In today's interconnected world, international actions resonate far beyond their immediate context. Fostering alliances through goodwill and collaboration can enhance America's global reputation and security. The Marshall Plan, which focused on rebuilding Europe after World War II, exemplifies how a commitment to long-term recovery and development can yield favorable outcomes not just for the affected nations, but for the United States as well, as stability fosters peace and commerce.[21]

---

21   *The Marshall Plan*: A program that provided economic assistance to Western Europe after World War II, the Marshall Plan was signed into law by President Harry Truman. Originally known as the Economic Recovery Act of 1948, it came to be known as the Marshall Plan, named for Secretary of State George Marshall.

Between 1948 and 1951, the U.S. provided $13.3 billion in aid to 16 European countries—the equivalent of about $150 billion today. By restoring agricul-

Rethinking Our Approach

IN AN increasingly interconnected world, the promotion of goodwill and understanding on an international scale has never been more crucial. However, this noble endeavor often collides with personal morality and prevailing geopolitical dynamics, leading to misconceptions that can yield dire consequences. To foster meaningful international relations, it's essential to conduct clear-eyed assessments of complex issues, prioritizing pragmatic understanding over idealistic notions.

At the heart of commendable international relations lies the concept of goodwill, which involves not only benevolence but also the capacity to engage with diverse cultures and perspectives. The promotion of understanding across borders can bridge divides and inspire cooperation, yet it's frequently clouded by personal moral beliefs that may not align with geopolitical realities. For example, while many individuals may value human rights as universal principles, the application of these values become complicated when they intersect with the political motivations of nations. The failure to comprehend the nuances of such interactions often leads to misguided efforts that ultimately jeopardize the very ideals we seek to uphold.

That's why nations that approach foreign policy with an overly simplistic view risk implementing strategies that are disconnected from the historical and cultural contexts of the regions involved. Take for example how the assumption that promoting democracy universally will yield positive

---

tural and industrial productivity, the Marshall Plan is credited with preventing famine and political chaos in Europe. In return, the plan provided markets for U.S. goods, created reliable trading partners, and supported the development of stable democratic governments in Western Europe. In 1953, General Marshall was awarded the Nobel Peace Prize for his role in establishing the plan.

Congress's approval of the Marshall Plan signaled a new era of bipartisanship in the post-World War II years. As such, the plan pioneered how economic development could lead the way in helping to advance both U.S. interests and foreign policy goals in the years to come.

outcomes has been challenged by so many countries where outside influence has led to instability and conflict. Here, the emphasis on a moral high ground, without a thorough understanding of the complexities within a region, inevitably results in unintended consequences—tyranny of the well-intentioned.

Transitioning from personal morality to a broader geopolitical strategy, then, requires a commitment to a brutally honest appraisal of international issues. It requires a comprehensive analysis that considers socio-economic variables, cultural traditions, and historical tensions. Policymakers must recognize that their decisions have far-reaching consequences, and so it absolutely requires that they tether their aspirations to an informed and realistic grasp of global dynamics. Emphasizing nuanced solutions—rather than rigid adherence to idealistic dogma—will ultimately go a long way toward cultivating a more sustainable framework for international relations.

In conclusion, American issues involving national security and foreign policy should always strive for a grounded approach that considers the multifaceted nature of global relations. After all, the world isn't simply a larger version of our personal relationships; it also requires a refined understanding that transcends simplistic ideals. Perhaps it's time to recognize that while the Golden Rule is a beautiful principle, geopolitics demands a strategy that accounts for more complex social dynamics, such as power, self-interest, and real-world concerns.

CHAPTER NINE

The Road to Redemption:

Awakening to the Truth

LIE #9:

From Israel to America, Being the "Chosen of God" Means Being Special Without any Need for Personal Responsibility...

O NE DAY, when I sat down with my professor, the first thing I noticed was the peculiar gleam in his eye and the wry smile he wore like a kid in a candy store. I irresistibly smiled back at him and said, "Professor, you're looking giddy as a school boy. Either that, or you look like the cat that ate the canary."

"Do I?"

"Yes, as a matter of fact you do. What's happening that has you so cheerful?"

"Cheerful, you say?"

I nodded affirmatively.

"Well, I wouldn't say cheerful," the old man continued, "so much as happy to see my favorite crusader."

"Really? How so?"

"Truth be told, my boy ... I envy you, in my more sentimental moments... Yes, I have to admit, I envy you."

"Envy? Who? Me?"

This time, the old man nodded back, affirmatively.

Dumbfounded, I said, "Professor, I don't know what to say. I mean, what brought all this on? Did you and your wife have another one of your *discussions*? Did she infect you with an unhealthy dose of Christian virtue?"

Letting out a raucous laugh, my professor exclaimed, "Oh, that is rich; certainly not. And what, pray tell, is so shocking about my envying you? You're a fine young man—a man of conviction, and so ... I, naturally, admire how you have maintained your stance, even in the midst of this citadel of secularism."

Embarrassed, I shrugged and sputtered, "Wow, I really don't know—uh, I just ... I don't know what to say."

Grinning at my awkward reaction, the old man continued: "And as for what brought this on, I think you might be amused. The other day I was driving down the freeway, and I noticed someone had one of those over-sized bumper stickers. You know the kind—one with big, ostentatious letters that screamed, 'Hey, look at what I believe—come what may.'"

"Yes, sir," I replied, unable to suppress a grin. "I know the kind."

"And there it was for the whole world to see: *'I'm not perfect, I'm just forgiven!'* Isn't that marvelous?"

Again, somewhat dumbfounded by this, I asked, "You think that's marvelous? But why? I would have thought you'd dismiss something like that as misguided nonsense."

"But that's just it. Maybe on a different day, I might have done so. But suddenly, quite unexpectedly, I found myself seeing things differently; maybe because I thought of you in that moment, and so I suddenly found myself 'through the looking-glass.' Suddenly I found myself reveling in the self-confidence in a proclamation like that—the sheer audacity of it. It reminded me of the reckless abandon of the old Wild West, the days of Manifest Destiny, when folks were a law unto themselves. When folks could do no wrong—in their own eyes, at least—because they were on a mission. They fearlessly carved out the American frontier on their own terms, because they saw themselves as the 'Chosen of God.' They were destined for a higher purpose—flaws and all, flaws be damned—so to Hell with accountability as the average person saw it..." The professor's words trailed off, and as if he were somewhat embarrassed at his spontaneous burst of enthusiasm, he asked furtively: "So, tell me, what's your take on the matter?"

For several awkward moments, I just sat there, trying to decide how to reply, then I finally had to say something to break the extended silence. "Wow," was all I could think of at the time, then I said, "I don't know what to say, Professor. I never would've guessed you'd have so much to say on the subject. But wow ... you ... you really do have something to say about it."

Again, the old man let out a raucous, infectious laugh that had me laughing with him.

"But what do you think?" he asked eagerly, still with that peculiar gleam in his eye. "For once, you and I might actually agree on such matters. Isn't that marvelous?"

Again, I found myself smiling, as awkward as ever, and still with no real answer to offer up yet. Truth be told: I was so amused at my professor's opinion in this, that I just didn't have the heart to tell him that, as much as I would've liked to say we were in agreement on this, I just couldn't.

Naturally, as a Christian, I was in complete agreement that God was perfectly happy to forgive humans who acknowledged their failures and sins. And of course, I also believe that for anyone who comes to a point of remorse, through an act of self-awareness, there arises within us a new desire to "never go down that road again," as it were. The Scriptures call this the act of repentance. But, of course, what my professor was describing was something altogether different.

Not that I wasn't glad to hear that the old man actually thought about such things, and that he actually considered the merits of such religiously inspired impulses like seeking God's forgiveness. It's just that, to me, at least, he was looking at the matter through what might be described as "rose-colored glasses." Of course I was all-too-familiar with this idea of Christians aligning themselves with this idea of being "forgiven," and thus no longer worried about not being "perfect." But sadly, this seemed like a huge over-simplification of a far more complicated issue. After all, if one were to assume that all Christians exist in a perpetual state of "forgiveness," then what prevents a person from assuming they therefore have no consequences to future transgressions against God's law. Clearly, the idea of be-ing the "Chosen of God" is a completely legitimate concept found throughout *The Bible*. But to anyone who reads the whole book, it's just as inescapable to see that anyone who abuses divine favor is still in danger of God's disfavor and subsequent punishment for abusing such a special status.

So, I sat there still, smiling awkwardly, trying to think of how to answer my professor so that I'd both satisfy him and avoid disappointing him at the same time. Then, quite thankfully, there was a knock on the old man's open door, and so we were mercifully interrupted by another faculty member who had stopped by to speak with the professor. I immediately rose to my feet and excused myself, at which point the old man said to me with a wry smile, "Hey, now, young man. Don't think you can escape that easily. I still expect an answer to my query. I think you owe me that much."

"No worries, Professor. I won't let you down. I'll get right on it."

"You do that, my boy, you do that. I'm looking forward to hearing from you soon."

Reprieved, at least temporarily, I nodded with a sigh of relief, and turned to go, determined as always to formulate an answer worthy of my professor who taught me so well how to investigate such matters.

"Let it simply be asked: Where is the security for property, for reputation, for life, if the sense of

religious obligation desert the oaths, which are the instruments of investigation in courts of justice?"

George Washington

The Call to Be Light and Salt in the World

THE CONCEPT of being the "Chosen of God" has permeated various cultures and societies, most notably in the contexts of Israel and America. This notion often conjures up a sense of exceptionalism—an idea that a particular group, by its divine selection, holds a unique position in the world. However, this sense of "chosenness" can paradoxically foster complacency and negligence rather than accountability and constraint. By exploring this duality, we can better understand how such beliefs shape behaviors and attitudes within these societies.

At the heart of this exceptionalism is a belief that those who are "chosen" possess a divine right or mission that sets them apart from others. In the case of Israel, this belief is deeply rooted in religious texts and historical narratives that affirm the covenant between God and the people of Israel. This covenant is perceived as a special relationship that not only provides them with a homeland but also imposes a divine destiny.

Similarly, in America, the notion of Manifest Destiny reflects a belief that the United States holds a special place in the world's affairs, rooted in a providential mission to spread the values of liberty, republicanism, and Christianity. As John Quincy Adams put it, in 1837, on the 61st anniversary of the Declaration of Independence: "Why is it that next to the birthday of the Savior of the world your most joyous and most venerated festival returns on this day? Is it not that, in the chain of human events, the birthday of our nation is perpetually linked with the birthday of the

Savior? That it forms a leading event in the progress of the Gospel dispensation? Is it not that the Declaration of Independence first organized the social compact on the foundation of the Redeemer's mission upon Earth? That it laid the cornerstone of human government upon the first precepts of Christianity?"

Ironically, though, while these ideals do inspire hope and a sense of purpose, they can also lead to a dangerous oversimplification of moral duties and responsibilities. The dilemma arises when this notion of being chosen translates into a lack of accountability. When individuals or nations believe they are inherently superior or divinely favored, it becomes easy to disregard the implications of their actions. For instance, the historical narrative of American exceptionalism has often justified aggressive foreign policies and interventions, masking the consequences experienced by other nations. Similarly, in Israel, the idea of being chosen has often inflated its sense of being privileged above all other nations as opposed to their being burdened with the call to be light and salt in the world. As such, the perceived divine right can generate a reluctance to engage with the moral complexities of these issues, leading to a sense of complacency that ultimately hinders progress and reconciliation.

What's more, when a society is steeped in the belief of divine selection, it risks encouraging an uncritical mindset. This sense of entitlement breeds apathy toward the suffering of others, eroding a collective sense of social responsibility. This sentiment is particularly relevant in discussions about social justice and equality. In both Israel and America, the narratives of exceptionalism often overshadow the urgent need for compassionate social policies that acknowledge and address historical injustices. When people view themselves as chosen, they often overlook the shared humanity that requires active participation in creating a just and humane society.

The Biblical Context of Being Chosen

THE TERM "Chosen of God" carries a profound significance rooted in biblical tradition, particularly in relation
to the status of Israel as perceived as a divine endorsement.
This notion suggests that Israel is viewed as special in the
eyes of God, set apart to fulfill His purposes on Earth.
Understanding the implications of being chosen not only
provides insights into Israel's historical identity but also
invites reflection on the broader themes of purpose and responsibility within the spiritual narrative.

In biblical texts, the concept of being chosen is first evident in God's covenant with Abraham, where He promises that Abraham's descendants would become a great nation—or more specifically, a company of nations. Said God
to Abraham: "I will certainly bless you, and I'll multiply
your descendants like the stars in the sky and the sand on
the seashore. Your descendants will possess the gates of
their enemies. And through your offspring all nations of the
Earth will be blessed, because you have obeyed My voice."
(*Genesis* 22:17-18) This covenant establishes a unique relationship between God and Israel, signifying a selection
that is both intentional and significant; it also implies that
Israel is entrusted with a divine mission, carrying the responsibility to demonstrate God's values to the world. The
sense of being chosen, then, instills a deep-rooted identity,
suggesting that the people of Israel aren't ordinary but are
part of a larger, sacred plan.

So, in light of this notion, the historical struggles and
triumphs of Israel can and should be viewed through the
lens of this divine selection. Throughout *The Old Testament*, the Israelites faced numerous challenges, from slavery in Egypt, to captivity in Assyria and exile in Babylon.
Yet within these trials, they found a reaffirmation of their
chosen status. In point of fact, none of these experiences
were ever random misfortunes; rather, they were all part
of a divine narrative that God used to forge their identity

and mission. The notion of being chosen thus signifies resilience and the capacity to overcome, instilling a strong sense of communal identity among the people of Israel.

An important aspect of this chosen status is the idea of being set apart. However, this doesn't equate to being superior in any way but, rather, it's a call to fulfilling a unique purpose—a higher purpose. For instance, being chosen invites Israel to embody values such as justice, mercy, and righteousness. Prophetic messages throughout Scripture echo this call to a higher purpose, encouraging Israel to serve as light and salt to the nations of the world. As Jesus described it: "You are the salt of the Earth, but if the salt loses its savor, how can it be made salty again? It's no longer good for anything, except to be thrown out and trampled by men. You are the light of the world. A city on a hill can't be hidden. Neither do people light a lamp and put it under a basket. Instead, they set it on a stand so it can give out its light to everyone in the house. In the same way, let your light shine before men, so they can see your good deeds and glorify your Father in Heaven." (*Matthew* 5:13-16)

As such, this broader mission, as exemplified by none other than Christ Himself, highlights the responsibility that comes with being chosen; it is nothing less than an all or nothing commitment to cooperating with God's ultimate plan for humanity, encouraging everyone on Earth towards ethical living and spiritual awareness.

The Consequences of Favor

AT THE CORE of Israel's identity is a strong sense of pride among its people, as they view themselves as the bearers of divine promise and purpose. This pride, however, was never intended as a cause for boasting, as if they were somehow superior to other nations; instead, it was intended to instill in them an acknowledgment that with such favor comes great responsibility. From their earliest teachings, the Israelites were implored to uphold justice, morality, and compassion—values clearly articulated in biblical texts. In this, Israel was charged with a dual mission: to practice righteousness internally and to exemplify these virtues to an onlooking world.

By calling the people of Israel to be the salt of the Earth and a light to the nations, they were expected to play an active role in influencing neighboring societies toward a spiritual awakening. In a contemporary context, this requirement becomes increasingly significant as Israel navigates complex political landscapes and engages with diverse cultures and ideologies. The burden of representation looms large, and the actions of Israel carry implications that resonate beyond its borders.

In this way, then, we plainly see divine favor doesn't exempt Israel from its divine obligations. Be they domestic issues such as social inequality or international concerns like conflict resolution, the challenges faced by Israel demand a serious approach to governance and ethical engagement. Fulfilling its God-ordained obligations requires acknowledging that with divine favor comes an expectation of striving for peace, justice, and mutual respect among nations. Ultimately, Israel's effectiveness as a moral compass will depend on its ability to confront internal strife and external pressures with wisdom and integrity.

The Paradox of Exceptionalism

THROUGHOUT the history of America, the concept of chosenness has significantly influenced the American identity. The phrase "one nation under God," deeply embedded within the American ethos, reflects a narrative of divine favor and exceptionalism that has evolved over centuries.

This idea was never better expressed than when, in 1777, Samuel Adams spoke to Congress while the country was still in the throes of the Revolutionary War. He solemnly addressed a convention of distressed delegates, comparing them to the Israelites as they fled the slavery of Egypt, citing *Exodus* 13, where God had guided them through the Wilderness with a pillar of cloud by day and a pillar of fire by night. He told his desperate countrymen: "We have proclaimed to the world our determination to die as freemen, rather than to live as slaves. We have appealed to Heaven for the justice of our cause, and in Heaven we have placed our trust. Numerous have been the manifestations of God's providence in sustaining us. In the gloomy period of adversity, we have had 'our cloud by day and pillar of fire by night.' We have been reduced to distress, and the arm of Omnipotence has raised us up. Let us still rely in humble confidence on Him Who is mighty to save. Good tidings will soon arrive. We will never be abandoned by Heaven while we act worthy of its aid and protection."

At the crux of American exceptionalism lies the belief that the United States is fundamentally different from other nations, bestowed with a unique role in the world. Rooted in religious and historical themes, this belief finds its origins in early colonial narratives where Puritan settlers viewed themselves as a "city upon a hill," a beacon of hope and peace. Such sentiments underscored the idea that America was divinely chosen to fulfill a unique destiny. This idea flourished as Americans forged their identity around the principles of liberty, republicanism, and Christianity, often contrasting themselves with other nations deemed less virtuous or enlightened.

As the nation progressed into the 20th and 21st centuries, the intertwining of religion and politics further reinforced this notion of chosenness. The phrase "one nation under God," added to the Pledge of Allegiance during the Red Scare of the 1950s, not only emphasized the importance of faith but also served to distinguish the United States from the perceived godlessness of communism.[22]

---

22 *The Red Scare of the 1950s*: Hysteria over the perceived threat posed by Communists during the Cold War between the Soviet Union and the United States, the Red Scare (sometimes called the Second Red Scare, not to be con-

This infusion of religious thought into our national identity solidified the belief that America wasn't just a political entity but also a spiritual one—destined to lead the world towards greater ideals. However, as confidence in this narrative grew, so did a sense of entitlement among its citizens.

This entitlement manifests itself in a variety of ways, particularly in contemporary political discourse. While the original concept of exceptionalism inspired a commitment to public good and national responsibility, it has increasingly transformed into a mindset that prioritizes individual interests over communal welfare. Political rhetoric often accentuates this sentiment, with leaders invoking the notion of an entitled America whose rights and privileges

---

fused with the First Red Scare of 1918) reached its peak in the early 1950s. Spearheaded by the House on Un-American Activities (HUAC), under the leadership of Senator Joseph McCarthy, no one was beyond the scope of their scrutiny: suspected individuals in the federal government and the Hollywood film industry were especially targeted to see if they were sufficiently loyal to America. Among the more famous targets of the Red Scare of the 1950s were Charlie Chaplin, Leonard Bernstein, Orson Welles, Lena Horne, Burl Ives, and Dalton Trumbo.

Dubbed the "Red" Scare because Communists were often referred to as "Reds" for their allegiance to the red Soviet flag, the Scare led to sweeping investigations that had a profound and enduring effect on both the U.S. government and society at large. In judicial affairs, for example, free speech and other civil liberties were significantly undermined. This trend was epitomized by the 1951 U.S. Supreme Court ruling that declared the free-speech rights of accused Communists could be restricted because their actions presented a "clear and present danger" to national security.

Average Americans were also impacted by the Red Scare on a personal level, and thousands of alleged communist sympathizers had their privacy invaded and lives ruined. They were hounded by law enforcement, alienated from friends and family, and even fired from their jobs. While a handful of the accused may have been genuine revolutionaries, most had been unfairly and falsely accused; while many of the accused were guilty of nothing more than exercising their right to join a political party.

Although the climate of fear and repression began to ease in the latter half of the decade, the specter of the Red Scare of the 1950s continues to this day to haunt and influence political debate in America. It is often cited as being both an example and a warning of how unfounded fears can threaten and compromise civil liberties.

must be preserved at all cost. This shift can be traced back to an evolving belief that being part of "one nation under God" bestows unqualified rights and privileges, usually at the expense of everyone else.

As entitlement infuses itself into our language and into our culture, it raises numerous red flags, because when a nation considers itself inherently superior, it can't help but overlook many of the republican values that are fundamental to its identity. Worse still, when the paradox of exceptionalism devolves into an attitude of unlimited entitlement, it inevitably undermines the collective aspirations of a humane society and compromises the very tenets that so many Americans hold dear.

A Toxic Sense of Superiority

THE NOTION of viewing oneself as "special" presents a profound danger that permeates individual attitudes and social norms. This mindset, often coupled with a temptation to disregard personal responsibility, incites a culture that can't help but become increasingly detached from the repercussions of its actions. This would have undoubtedly worried America's Founding Fathers, who consistently warned against prioritizing self-preservation over collective responsibility.

At its most basic level, the mindset of being "special" breeds a toxic sense of superiority. This perception encourages us to act as if our rights and our needs are all-important, leading to a lack of consideration for the rights and needs of those around us. When we view ourselves through this lens, it's so much easier to justify our selfish acts, often resulting in decisions that adversely impact others. This self-importance can be seen not only in how we see ourselves in relation to other individuals but also in how some segments of our population see themselves in relation to other segments of society—from politics to everyday interactions, where empathy diminishes and conflict rises.

Fortunately, this was something that many of the Founders were keenly aware of and something that many of them sought to address. Speaking in a time when there were so many Christian sects who had yet to reconcile their various beliefs into a viable social framework—something that would one day become known as republican liberty—John Adams wrote: "When all men of all religions, consistent with morals and equity, enjoy equal liberty, security of property, and an equal chance for honor and power, we may expect that improvements will be made in the human character and the state of society."

We also see how this sense of being "special" extends beyond the nation as a whole, as it then infiltrates the very fabric of our personal lives. Thus, the allure of exemption from typical standards of behavior soon leads to a systematic breakdown of social norms. As such, the burdens of citizenship—duty, honor, loyalty, and the like—are dramatically diminished in favor of an ideology that places personal desire above communal well-being.

As citizens succumb to this self-centered perspective, the significance of collective accountability slowly but surely fades away. In turn, the detachment from actions and their consequences fuels a society where individuals believe they can act without repercussions, undermining the very foundation of American society.

The Peril of Intolerance

IN THE LANDSCAPE of American politics, the notion of chosenness has become a pervasive ideology that inflames an exclusionary mindset, leading to a stark "us versus them" dichotomy. This belief, when left unchecked, causes certain groups to view others as being morally inferior. This polarization not only deepens social divisions, but it also threatens the foundational principles envisioned by the Founding Fathers, who warned of the dangers of intolerance and the fracturing of the republic.

That's because when left unchecked, this mindset of specialness is so prone to becoming a tool with which to negatively judge anyone outside the perceived circle of privilege. When this happens, those within the in-group are more likely to dismiss the rest of humanity and their perspectives, intensifying political and social divides.

As factions in American politics increasingly use the rhetoric of divine endorsement to stake their claims, the ramifications are alarming. This rhetoric feeds into an environment where compromise is viewed as weakness, and constructive dialogue is replaced with verbal abuse. Political leaders and their supporters adopt a binary perspective that reviles their opponents, branding them as not just different but as enemies who threaten the moral fabric of society. The consequences of this mindset are evident in the rise of extreme partisanship, which paralyzes governance and erodes trust in institutions that once sought to unify disparate voices.

The Founding Fathers recognized the peril of intolerance and the risk of creating divisions within the populace. In their writings, they stressed the importance of reasoned discourse and the necessity of acknowledging a plurality of views. They foresaw that an over-attachment to any one ideology could lead to the disintegration of the republic. As Thomas Jefferson warned us: "He that would make his own liberty secure must guard even his enemy from oppression; for if he violates this duty, he establishes a precedent that will reach to himself."

Engaging with Complexity

THE COMPLEXITY of the human experience often manifests itself in the interplay of truth and lies, and the gray areas in between. Navigating these murky waters demands more than mere acknowledgment; it requires that we sincerely question our own biases as well as seek a deeper understanding of ourselves and others. The journey towards clarity isn't a straight path; instead, it's laden with nuances that demand our attention, reflection, and open-mindedness.

In the realm of politics and personal relationships alike, the complexity of human experience signals that truth is rarely absolute. Young children often perceive the world in black and white, where right and wrong are clear-cut. However, as we mature, we encounter a spectrum of beliefs, values, and experiences that highlight the subtleties and ambiguities inherent in human interactions. This realization serves as a foundation for understanding that truth can be subjective, shaped by personal experiences and cultural contexts. Consequently, to navigate these complexities effectively, we must confront our own biases—those preconceptions that color our perceptions and judgments of others.

Understanding requires an active engagement with uncomfortable questions. When faced with conflicting perspectives, it's easy to retreat into familiar narratives that reinforce our own viewpoint. Yet, this inclination can hinder our ability to grasp the full mosaic of human experience. Accepting that our perspectives don't encompass the whole truth is a vital step toward nurturing empathy. In doing so, we enlarge our capacity to listen to others and enhance our ability to comprehend rather than to judge. The willingness to engage with different opinions and experiences not only enriches our understanding but also broadens our worldview.

It is also important to realize that clarity never emerges from a single revelation; it only arises from an ongoing dialogue within ourselves and with those around us. Asking challenging questions lead us to profound insights, but before we're able to fully apprehend those insights, it takes tremendous courage to confront the discomfort that such explorations evoke. It is through this process of questioning, reflecting, and engaging with others that we begin to unravel the intricate tapestry of human experience. This journey isn't just about seeking clarity; it is also about embracing uncertainty—recognizing that some aspects of our lives and the world may remain ambiguous.

Reshaping the Narrative

ACKNOWLEDGING responsibility is paramount in forging a society built on integrity and accountability. The notion of holding oneself to an objective standard of ethics, rather than relying on a status of divine favor, resonates deeply with the ideals espoused by America's Founding Fathers. Their vision encompassed a nation where personal accountability wasn't merely encouraged; it was also seen as essential to the fabric of societal progress.

At the heart of the Founders' philosophy was the belief that everyone is accountable for his or her actions. This principle is evident in the Constitution, which emphasizes the rule of law and the importance of civic duty. The Founders understood that a government must derive its power from the consent of the governed, which inherently requires citizens to actively participate in the political process and uphold their responsibilities. Speaking to his fellow Americans, in 1803, on the 27th anniversary of the Day of Independence, Joseph Barker declared: "Let us see that our government be kept purely republican, that is, a representative democracy. This is a duty we owe to our fathers and brethren, who paid with their blood to purchase our privileges. It is a duty we owe to posterity; we ought not willingly, or carelessly, deprive them of that goodly heritage, which God has committed to our keeping."

Just as important, the Founders also recognized that relying on this notion of being "chosen of God" brings with it the potential for a dangerous precedent—one which inevitably leads to a society where privilege overshadows merit. No less a figure than George Washington himself spoke to this point when he said: "There is no truth more thoroughly established, than that there exists an indestructible union between virtue and happiness, between duty and advantage, between the genuine rule of an honest and generous policy, and the solid rewards of public prosperity and contentment: Since we ought to be no less persuaded that the fortunate smiles of Heaven can never be expected on a nation that disregards the eternal rules of order and right, which Heaven itself has ordained."

In other words, Americans should never presume to continue to expect God's provision and guidance unless we understand what is expected from us in having this honor of receiving such gifts from Heaven above. In today's context, this principle of accountability is significant. As we navigate through various challenges in our lives and communities, whether they be societal inequalities or political discord, the need for individuals to take responsibility for their actions becomes even more critical. When people choose to acknowledge their role and the consequences of their decisions, it leads to a more engaged and conscientious society. The act of holding oneself accountable fosters trust and cooperation—key elements necessary for any community to thrive.

Not only that, but accountability extends beyond the average citizen; it also encourages leaders, organizations, and governments to act ethically and transparently. If those in positions of power don't hold themselves accountable, it sets a poor example that threatens to permeate society. The Founding Fathers understood that leadership comes with immense responsibility and should be grounded in integrity and the willingness to answer for one's choices.

Cultivating Stewardship

IN CONTEMPORARY America, the call for a narrative of stewardship over selfishness is more essential than ever. In a society often fragmented by individualism and entitlement, a renewed collective responsibility is urgently needed—one that urges us to recognize our shared humanity and the higher purpose that binds us all. By reframing our understanding of being chosen, we find a deeper obligation to serve as agents of light and salt in our communities, promoting a narrative that uplifts rather than alienates.

Because this narrative is more attuned to the biblical mandate of stewardship than of privilege, it's one that naturally invites us to take responsibility for how we frame our stories and the stories of others. It challenges us to move beyond personal gain and to consider the impact of our words and actions on society as a whole. In a world full of competing interests that often elevate division and self-interest—in short, a "pure democracy" gone mad—we must strive to create spaces where understanding and empathy flourish. This paradigm shift encourages us to see ourselves not just as individuals but as integral parts of a larger tapestry, where each thread contributes to the richness of our shared experience.

When we acknowledge that we all have common struggles, hopes, and dreams, it also becomes easier to advocate for one another. This shared purpose, in turn, transforms our interactions, enabling us to build bridges instead of walls. In doing so, we dismantle the narratives that promote isolation and distrust, and instead we cultivate a culture of compassion and solidarity. By affirming our interconnectedness, we not only create a more humane society, but we also enrich our own lives through the relationships we nurture.

The idea of being chosen is often associated with privilege or distinction. However, when reframed, it triggers a profound sense of responsibility which helps to uplift everyone around us. Embracing this notion means recognizing that our talents and resources can be used to benefit others rather than just ourselves. It challenges us to ask how we can serve our communities, to be the light that guides and the salt that adds flavor to the world. This reframing calls for action rooted in humility and service, positioning us as stewards who nourish the narratives of others as much as our own.

In conclusion, by fearlessly slicing through all the sub-tleties, ambiguities, and biases that obscure a clear-cut view of this issue, we're one step closer to embracing the realization that the road to redemption isn't just a personal journey but is one that involves humanity as a whole. To-gether, as we become the light and salt of our communities, we transform narratives of selfishness into stories that in-spire connection and compassion, shaping a more cohesive society for all.

The Conclusion

Refuting the Ultimate Lie:
God's True Purpose for the Earth

LIE #10:

Because Human Governments Will All Be Swept Away Someday, in Favor of Our Destiny in Heaven, Politics Have No Purpose in God's Plan...

A S MY GRADUATION day approached and final exams loomed on the horizon, my after-school discussions with my professor became less frequent but more cherished. One day, the old man looked at me like a beloved child, and began, "You know, I'm very proud of your accomplishments here over the last four years. Each semester, you've become more and more engaged with your studies, and I have no doubt that whatever path you choose after graduation, you'll make an important contribution to this world in the years to come."

"Thank you, Professor. Well, if that's true, then you can take a great deal of credit for your influence on my academic career."

He smiled benevolently for several satisfying moments before responding, and when he did, he spoke with an endearing sentimentality. "Still, I do have to tell you that I'm overwhelmed with a bittersweet sense of sadness in seeing you move on from here."

"Sad? How so, sir?"

"Well, to begin with, one of the things I admire most about you is the way you've excelled in a worldly pursuit like political science while still fiercely clinging, if you don't mind me saying so, to your otherworldly faith."

"Again, Professor, you can take credit more than you know."

Tilting his head curiously, he said, "You mean to say the agnostic professor aided and abetted the man of faith? How is that even possible?"

"It's possible because in all the time I've been your student, and all the time you knowing about my Christian faith, you've never made me feel intellectually inferior for not thinking like you."

The old man nodded. "That is nice to know. Still it doesn't soothe my final concern for you, because I just can't help thinking that you'd have better served your destiny going to a different kind of school. You know, like a school of divinity. Did you ever consider that?"

"Maybe a long time ago, sure. But once I got here, I never questioned that this was where I belonged."

"Belonged, you say?"

I nodded affirmatively.

"That is most intriguing," he continued, "and most unexpected. I can understand how you might feel a sense of camaraderie with your schoolmates, maybe come to appreciate your professors ... your classes. But when you use that word, 'belonged,' that denotes the kind of thinking one would only expect in a church-oriented environment."

"I never thought about it that way, but, yes, I can understand why you might think that way. But I really do mean what I say. I know in my heart of hearts, I was meant to be here."

"I'm so glad you bring that up, because now you're speaking to the very reason for my melancholy."

"Really; how so?"

"Well, the reason I have such mixed feelings about you and your time here is that—to my way of understanding, at least—you being a man of faith, I'd have thought you'd consider politics a mere triviality because you view Heaven as the real goal of every believer. Right?"

"I suppose so, sure."

"You suppose so? What is that supposed to mean? I thought the Christian worldview was that all human governments are destined to be swept away—swept away because they never had or could have any meaningful purpose in the plan of God. Am I completely off base in this regard?"

"Not entirely, no. But there is something that always had me thinking differently than most Christians on that subject."

"Oh, really. So young, and yet so wise. You never cease to amaze me. So, out of all the millions of believers down through the ages, how is that you don't see your ultimate goal as anywhere but Heaven above?"

"But that's just it. I'm sure I'm not the only one who thinks this way. It's just that most who do think differently do so without making a big deal of it."

"Okay, young man, would you mind letting me in on your little secret. Don't tell me you had some sort of special revelation, or a vision, or some such nonsense, because then I'd be truly disappointed."

"Professor, how could you think such a thing?"

"But you would agree with me that most Christians are sitting about just waiting for the Lord to split the sky and wash away this old world, as they see it. Am I right?"

"Oh, no doubt about it. And that's where most Christians have completely missed the point of the most important prayer ever uttered in *The Bible*, prayed by the most important person ever spoken of in *The Bible*."

My professor tilted his head, again, as skeptical as ever, then said, "And pray tell, what would that be?"

"Please, Professor, before you write me off completely,

hear me out. This wasn't something I figured out on my own; I just remember a lesson I heard taught at a church I once attended, where the pastor reminded us about what most Christians think of as the Lord's Prayer. But he pointed out that it shouldn't be called the Lord's Prayer; it should really be called the Disciples' Prayer."

"The Disciples' Prayer? Sounds a little sacrilegious, even to me. I mean, tradition is tradition."

"Maybe. But as I recall, Jesus did warn us that the traditions of men could destroy the word of God."

"Duly noted. Then tell me, why shouldn't we be calling it the Lord's Prayer?"

"Naturally, because Jesus never prayed it Himself, because He never had to pray, 'Father, forgive us of our sins, as we forgive those who sin against us.' You see: that was the clue that made me realize the pastor was right about this prayer, that there really is more to this prayer than meets the eye."

"Interesting. And what did you learn from that?"

"I learned that if Christians are so mistaken about that, what else about this prayer might contradict what we've been led to believe about it."

Without saying a word, my professor nodded.

"And that's when it dawned on me," I continued. "Our entire focus of this prayer has been misplaced. Most people, when they pray this prayer, are assuming it's a prayer intended to purify us so that when we die we'll be worthy of Heaven's grace. It's all about dying as soon as possible so we can go to where God and Jesus are. But that's crazy; it's all upside down, based on the simple meaning of the words of this prayer. Jesus didn't teach us to turn our backs on the world and our fellow human beings, as if this world is wholly evil. Or else why would He bother to usher in the Kingdom of God on Earth? I mean, why would the Creator go to all that trouble if the Earth itself was incompatible with His ultimate plan for humanity?"

"Interesting. And what does that mean in the context of

our discussion?"

"I think it means that when Jesus taught us to pray that God's will be done on Earth as it is in Heaven, we should start to pay closer attention to *why* He said something like that. Because maybe, just maybe, God's true purpose for the Earth involves so much more than tradition has ever led us to believe."

After several thoughtful moments, during which my professor stared back at me, I couldn't tell what he was thinking. After so many years of his appreciating the scholastic side of my personality, I wondered if I'd destroyed that in a spontaneous moment where I let my guard down and revealed a side of me that he now found repugnant and illogical. But finally, mercifully, his statue-like gaze transformed into a warm and endearing smile. "Indeed, you are a most unusual and unique young man. And I do hope you never forget just how much I'm going to miss you when you leave this place."

And that was, in fact, the last day we ever shared a smile—a smile as dear as any smile shared between a real father and son.

"Whoever believes in the divine inspiration of the Holy Scriptures must hope that the religion of Jesus shall prevail throughout the Earth. Not since the foundation of the world have the prospects of mankind been more encouraging to that hope than they appear to be at the present time. And may the associated distribution of The Bible proceed and prosper till the Lord has made 'bare His holy arm in the eyes of all the nations, and all the ends of the Earth will see the salvation of our God.'"

John Quincy Adams

The Notion of Temporary Governments

THE NARRATIVE that human governments are merely temporary institutions destined to be replaced by a divine governance can evoke a sense of hope for some individuals, presenting an idealistic vision of a utopian future. However, this perspective also has the potential to undermine critical thinking and civic engagement, essential components for a functioning society. While the promise of divine intervention may provide comfort, it risks leading to complacency and a diminished sense of responsibility among citizens regarding their roles in shaping societal outcomes.

At its core, the belief in divine governance suggests an eventual transition from flawed human systems to a perfect, celestial order. This vision can inspire hope, particularly in times of crisis when political systems appear ineffective or corrupt. When people perceive their current government as transient, they may be more willing to endure hardships in anticipation of a better, divinely orchestrated future. This notion can kindle a sense of unity among believers, providing them with a collective identity and a reason to remain optimistic in the face of adversity.

However, this same belief can also lead to detrimental consequences for critical thinking and civic engagement. When individuals adopt a mindset that relies on divine governance, they often disengage from the political processes that shape their everyday lives. The expectation of an intervention by a higher power diminishes the perceived importance of local governance and community participation. As a result, citizens begin to feel their efforts to influence policies or address injustices are futile in comparison to the grand, predetermined plans of a divine being. Inevitably, this mentality results in apathy towards vital civic responsibilities, such as voting, activism, and community service, all of which are fundamental for a vibrant public life.

The acceptance of divine governance also discourages

constructive debate and the questioning of authority. Critical thinking thrives on the examination of ideas, the challenging of norms, and the willingness to confront uncomfortable truths. When belief in divine governance becomes a dominant narrative, it can't help but stifle dissent and limit the exploration of alternative viewpoints. More and more, individuals prioritize faith-based assertions over empirical evidence or rational discourse, which, in turn, leads to polarized communities and a lack of productive conversation. Over time, this erosion of critical thinking perpetuates cycles of ignorance and dogma, weakening the very fabric of civic engagement.

The Concept of a Divine Order

THE ASSERTION that earthly governments are mere placeholders within a divinely orchestrated order raises profound questions about the nature and significance of political authority. This perspective suggests that governments, while apparently wielding power and influence, are only fleeting institutions in the grand design of existence. By examining the historical context of governance, the philosophical underpinnings of political authority, and the limitations of earthly regimes, it becomes evident that these institutions are tools of power that lack enduring significance beyond their immediate time frames.

To understand the notion of governments as temporary constructs, we must first consider the historical patterns of political systems. Throughout history, empires and governments have risen and fallen, often within short spans of time. The Roman Empire, once a colossal entity, disintegrated into fragments, illustrating that even the mightiest regimes aren't immune to decay. This cyclical nature of political authority suggests that earthly governments exist in a continuous state of flux, reinforcing the idea that they aren't permanent fixtures but rather tools that serve specific purposes during limited periods. The concept of a divine order orchestrating these transitions implies a higher purpose behind these shifts—one that transcends the mere functionality of governance.

Not only that, but the philosophical foundations of political authority also provide insights into the role of governments within a divinely orchestrated framework. Thinkers like Thomas Hobbes and John Locke grappled with the basis of authority, suggesting that governments arise either from a social contract or through the imposition of power. However, regardless of their origins, these authorities are bestowed with power that ultimately derives from the consent of the governed. As such, the shifting nature of this power, which is thus granted to these governments, is inherently limited, reflecting their brief nature and suggesting that they are vehicles of divine orchestration rather than entities of eternal significance.

In addition to their historical and philosophical contexts, the limitations of earthly governments further underscore their role as mere placeholders. Governments often face challenges that stem from their inability to fully address the complexities of human existence. Societal issues such as poverty, inequality, and injustice frequently outlast governments, revealing the shortcomings of political authority to create lasting solutions. As these issues persist beyond the life span of any given government, it becomes evident that the tools of power wielded by these institutions don't extend beyond their immediate contexts. This limitation emphasizes the notion that, in the greater scheme of things, governments serve a temporary role, fulfilling necessary functions but lacking the ability to enact permanent change.

Hopelessly Human

IN A WORLD increasingly disillusioned with political governance, many citizens find themselves grappling with political systems that seem irredeemably flawed and corrupt. The predominant response is one of waiting—not just waiting for reform but waiting for a higher power to intervene and rectify the human condition. This bleak outlook is fueled by rampant corruption, inefficient leaders, and a profound helplessness that permeates the populace. As the structures designed to serve the common good decay, hope seems a distant memory, with individuals resigned to the belief that change can only come from beyond the earthly realm.

The widespread corruption found in many political systems is a primary catalyst for this disillusionment. Leaders often prioritize personal gain over public service, leading to widespread abuses of power. Scandals and deceit frequently dominate the political narrative, making news headlines and further amplifying public skepticism. Citizens see their elected representatives engage in unethical behavior, with little to no accountability, leaving them feeling betrayed and powerless. This reinforces the notion that the very systems intended to uphold justice and equality are instead complicit in their own decay, reinforcing the belief that true change can only come through divine intervention.

More and more, the failures of these political structures are further reinforcing our sense of hopelessness. Policies intended to promote welfare and progress falter under seemingly endless layers of bureaucracy or are stymied by partisan divisions. Initiatives meant to address pressing social issues, such as poverty, inequality, and injustice, continuously fail to materialize into meaningful action. As citizens watch their hopes for improvement evaporate, the faith they once placed in these systems diminishes, leaving them with a sense of abandonment. In response to this failure of leadership to act, many people begin to look skyward in desperation, hoping against hope for a miraculous overhaul of the present world.

This descent into despair is further aggravated by the stark reality of a political landscape that offers no clear-cut solutions. Instances of violence, discrimination, and civic unrest occur frequently, further underscoring the perceived impotence of current systems. The very fabric of society begins to unravel as trust erodes among communities that have historically relied on mutual support and political integrity. This is why, in such circumstances, it becomes almost instinctual for individuals to seek solace in the idea of divine intervention, believing that only a higher power can restore order and morality to such a chaotic situation. Add to that the indifference exhibited by those in power and one can only look on in despair as a deep-seated pessimism settles in like a thick fog, as citizens grapple with the existential question: Are we actually capable of changing things for the better, or are we just helpless spectators in a grim horror story?

A Retreat into Cynicism

THROUGHOUT American history, the discourse surrounding political events has often been framed within the context of higher powers and their influence over cultural change. However, this tendency to attribute personal and political crises to external forces leads to a dangerous disregard for individual responsibility. The very essence of activism—its capacity to inspire hope, change, and optimism—is undermined when individuals relinquish their agency in favor of blaming higher powers or mysterious systems. In fact, the Founding Fathers of America warned against this dismissal of personal accountability, cautioning that such attitudes would undermine the social fabric they sought to construct. As Thomas Paine saw it: "Those who expect to reap the blessings of freedom, must, like men, undergo the fatigue of supporting it."

As nightmarish events unfold, the narrative often shifts towards a fatalistic view where individuals see themselves as victims of circumstance, overshadowed by powerful entities. This reliance on external explanations breeds pessimism and cynicism, leading to a collective psyche that views activism as futile. The ability of ordinary citizens to effect change diminishes when they see their actions as insignificant compared to the large-scale forces at play. Such a mindset not only discourages active participation, but it also stifles the necessary discourse that promotes genuine political engagement. The Founding Fathers, while championing liberty, emphasized the importance of individual action; they believed a government's power is only as strong as the citizens' willingness to participate and hold it accountable. Said Thomas Jefferson regarding the importance of civic involvement: "I know no safe depository of the ultimate powers of society but the people themselves; and if we think them not enlightened enough to exercise their control with a wholesome discretion, the remedy is not to take it from them, but to inform their discretion by education."

How sad, then, that the modern political landscape is revealing a growing trend where individuals feel increasingly detached from the consequences of their inaction. The distractions of contemporary society, combined with the overwhelming nature of global issues, lead many of us to retreat into cynicism. Worse still, movements that could rally individuals towards significant change risk being trivialized as meaningless or pointless. The pessimism surrounding the outcomes of collective efforts creates a self-fulfilling prophecy where potential activism is never realized because individuals fear their contributions will lead nowhere. This fragility of hope is in stark contrast to the intentions of America's founders, who envisioned a nation where the power of the government was an extension of the will of the people.

The Dangers of Complacency

COMPLACENCY among citizens also poses significant dangers to the stability of governments and the health of our public life. When individuals disengage from civic responsibilities, assuming that their role in the political process is negligible, they inadvertently create a vacuum that can lead to authoritarianism or totalitarianism. This passive waiting for a "divine resolution" undermines accountability and perpetuates a cycle of complacency, ultimately resulting in governments that are more vulnerable to failure.

One of the primary dangers of complacency is the erosion of civic engagement. When citizens believe that participation in governance is unnecessary or futile, they become less likely to vote, attend public meetings, or advocate for issues they care about. This lack of involvement provides political leaders with a mandate that isn't genuinely reflective of the electorate's will. As fewer voices contribute to the dialogue, decisions may skew toward the interests of a small, influential elite, sidelining the broader population. The disconnect between government action and public sentiment, in turn, leads to frustration and disillusionment, encouraging further disengagement and creating a vicious cycle.

This is why it's more important than ever that the spirit of civic duty be rekindled to counteract such dangers. Civic engagement isn't just a responsibility; it is also a vital component of a political process that supports diverse perspectives and ensures accountability. When citizens actively participate in governance—whether through voting, community organizing, or other means—they reinforce the social contract that holds our American society together. This active involvement nurtures a sense of ownership and investment in societal outcomes, compelling leaders to be more responsive and responsible. A citizenry that embraces its duty to participate creates an environment where governments are less likely to stray from the principles of a representative democracy and the rule of law. For Founders like John Hancock, that responsiveness came primarily in the form of never letting one's guard down in regard to government overreach. As he put it: "Resistance to tyranny becomes the Christian and social duty of each individual. Continue steadfast and, with a proper sense of your dependence on God, nobly defend those rights which Heaven gave us, and which no man ought to take from us."

In contrast, those who wait passively for change or expect resolution from external sources underestimate their power and agency. The belief that problems will resolve themselves or that a higher power will intervene fuels a dangerous complacency that can be exploited by unscrupulous leaders. History is replete with examples of regimes that have thrived in environments of complacency, as citizens await change instead of driving it themselves. The rhetoric of waiting for the "right moment" or "divine intervention" nullifies the proactive steps necessary for meaningful progress, thereby increasing the likelihood of governmental collapse or societal regression.

Reduced Civic Engagement

IN CONTEMPORARY society, civic engagement serves as a cornerstone of republican governance and cultural vitality. However, there is an alarming trend of reduced civic engagement among citizens, particularly when they become disillusioned because they see their governments as temporary and irrelevant. This disillusionment manifests itself in diminished participation in voting, activism, and public discourse, ultimately threatening the very fabric of society. Understanding the causes of this disengagement and its implications is essential for cultivating a more engaged and informed citizenry.

One significant factor contributing to reduced civic engagement is the perception of governmental instability. When citizens view their leaders as temporary, they may lose faith in the system itself, assuming that their participation won't make a meaningful impact. This sense of impermanence diminishes the urgency to vote or engage in political activism, as individuals feel their contributions don't translate into long-term benefit or change. Such fatalism leads to voter apathy—the belief that our votes are meaningless—resulting in lower turnout rates that compromise the political process.

What's more, the rise of social media and digital communication has transformed public discourse, complicating the relationship between citizens and their governments. While these platforms have the potential to facilitate dialogue and community engagement, they also contribute to a climate of disinformation and polarization. Citizens encounter conflicting narratives about governmental actions or political issues, leading to confusion and disillusionment. Consequently, they disengage from civic duties altogether, perceiving discussions around governance as irrelevant or adversarial. This trend not only undermines public debate, but it also erodes trust in institutions—further escalating the cycle of disengagement.

The implications of reduced civic engagement are severe. Lower participation in elections leads to a lack of representation, resulting in policy decisions that don't reflect the needs or desires of the citizenry. Additionally, the absence of active civic participation reduces accountability, allowing leaders to operate without the fear of public scrutiny. Over time, a disengaged populace sets the stage in creating a feedback loop where apathy breeds more apathy, making it even more challenging to reinvigorate public interest in their civic responsibility.

To combat this decline in civic engagement, it's imperative to foster a culture of participation and inclusion. Education plays a crucial role in equipping citizens with the knowledge and skills necessary to engage in political discourse and understand the importance of their role in society. For American founders like Benjamin Rush, James Madison, and Samuel Adams, the pursuit of knowledge was all-important. Said Rush: "Freedom can exist only in the society of knowledge. Without learning, men are incapable of knowing their rights, and where learning is confined to a few people, liberty can be neither equal nor universal." Said Madison: "The advancement and diffusion of knowledge is the only guardian of true liberty." And as for Adams: "If virtue and knowledge are diffused among the people, they will never be enslaved. This will be their great security."

As such, civic education should be prioritized within school curricula, emphasizing the significance of voting, community involvement, and informed dialogue. Not only that, but encouraging grassroots movements and local initiatives also helps citizens feel a sense of ownership over their governance, countering the perception of government as distant and meaningless.

Absence of Accountability

NEGLECTING TO hold leaders accountable allows corruption to fester, leading to decisions made without public scrutiny—a huge departure from the principles that the Founding Fathers championed. The importance of accountability in leadership can't be overstated, as it ensures that those in power are answerable to the citizens they serve. The deliberate neglect of this accountability breeds an environment ripe for wrongdoing, undermining the very foundation of a representative democracy that was envisioned at America's inception.

The lack of accountability among leaders creates a vacuum where corruption thrives. When officials aren't held to a standard of transparency and responsibility, the tendency toward unethical behavior greatly increases. Corruption comes in various forms: bribery, embezzlement, and favoritism, all of which deteriorate public trust in institutions. This erosion of trust is dangerous, as it diminishes civic engagement, leading citizens to disengage from the political process. The Founders understood that an informed and active citizenry is crucial for a healthy body politic.

They believed that public scrutiny would act as a check on power, preventing leaders from making self-serving decisions that conflict with the public good. Certainly James Madison had this in mind when he said: "I believe there are more instances of the curtailment of the freedom of the people by gradual and silent encroachments by those in power than by violent and sudden usurpation."

The absence of accountability also leads to decisions that lack public scrutiny and input, often resulting in policies that don't reflect the desires or needs of their communities. When citizens aren't involved in governance, those in power inevitably prioritize their narrow interests over those of the populace as a whole. This disconnect between leaders and constituents can be seen when legislation is passed that favors the agenda of a radical fringe element of society at the expense of the vast majority of Americans who hold to more moderate views. That's why the Founders advocated for a system where representative democracy was complemented by civic responsibility, urging the public to engage and hold their leaders accountable.

In light of these considerations, it's essential to cultivate a culture of accountability that promotes transparency and civic engagement. Encouraging public scrutiny of leaders not only helps curb corruption, but it also empowers citizens to actively participate in the political process. Mechanisms such as an unbiased free press, whistleblower protections, and community forums free of censorship are vital for fostering an environment where all leaders are answerable to the public. As we navigate the complexities of modern governance, the lessons from our Founding Fathers must guide us to reinforce the principles of proactive civic engagement.

A Culture of Passivity

WHILE THE belief that a divine hand governs the course of human history does offer hope and consolation to the faithful, there is also an unexpected downside. In many cases, it leads people to abdicate their personal responsibility in shaping the world around them. This perspective fuels a sense of complacency, where actions are dictated less by moral conviction and more by the notion that everything is predetermined. When people cling to the idea that events are guided by a higher power, they might feel justified in their inaction, which, in turn, leads to personal stagnation and inaction.

A significant consequence of this mindset is how quickly it develops into a culture of passivity. Because when we place all our hope in divine intervention as the ultimate authority, it diminishes our belief in human agency. And when we believe our choices are inconsequential, we start to believe that whatever is meant to happen will happen despite our best efforts. Consequently, this blind surrender to fate deters proactive engagement in critical issues such as social justice, ecological conservation, and political transparency.

This acute state of passivity also extends beyond personal choices to collective societal actions. When governments or institutions adopt a similar belief in divine direction, they excuse unethical behaviors or poor decision-making under the guise of their "having faith" in a higher power. This leads to a troubling dynamic where leaders evade their responsibilities, believing their actions are predestined. As a result, the interests of the populace are sidelined, and social progress is hampered. The very fabric of civil engagement unravels when individuals and leaders alike detach from the consequences of their actions, clinging to the notion that they are subordinate agents of supernatural forces beyond their control.

What's more, the impact of this belief is amplified in times of crisis. During such moments, individuals often seek solace in spirituality, holding on to the idea that a divine plan exists to guide them through hardships. While this offers comfort to many, it also dulls their sense of urgency to enact change and improve their circumstances. For example, rather than rallying against injustices, communities may retreat into fatalism, dismissing their power to reform their situations. This retreat inflames an atmosphere where problems persist and fester, as the collective willingness to combat them wanes. The result is a society that becomes increasingly disengaged from its political landscape, undermining the principles of a constitutional republic that thrive on active participation.

The Role of Critical Thinking in Politics

THE TENSION between divine governance and earthly politics has long been debated in the context of America's founding principles. The allure of passivity, often associated with a patient acceptance of authoritative rule, clashes with the critical thinking that the Founding Fathers championed. Their emphasis on discernment—the ability to distinguish between fact and fiction—paved the way for critical thinking as the cornerstone of a healthy society. Through an exploration of these themes, we can better understand the importance of active engagement in political discourse, and how it shapes the principles underpinning American life.

At the heart of the Founders' vision for America was a profound belief in the role of the individual as a thoughtful participant in their own governance. They understood that for a representative democracy to thrive, its citizens must actively engage with the information presented to them. This notion of critical thought was revolutionary, laying the groundwork for an informed electorate capable of holding their leaders accountable. In contrast, the passive acceptance of divine governance promotes a dangerous complacency, where individuals relinquish their agency and judgment to a higher authority. Such a relinquishment negates the foundational idea that governance should be "of" the people, "by" the people, and "for" the people.

In establishing the framework of the new nation, founders such as Thomas Jefferson and James Madison articulated the need for an educated populace. Said Jefferson: "If we are to guard against ignorance and remain free, it is the responsibility of every American to be informed." And according to Madison: "Knowledge will forever govern ignorance; and a people who mean to be their own governors must arm themselves with the power which knowledge gives." This perspective underscores the belief that when citizens are encouraged to think independently and question the status quo, they enrich the political landscape with diverse perspectives and debates. Independent thought fosters resilience against misinformation and authoritarianism. It enables individuals to sift through the noise of opinions, allowing a clearer understanding of the truth, which is essential for effective participation in a free and open society.

What's more, the Founding Fathers recognized that the capacity for critical thinking isn't just an intellectual exercise; it is also a civic duty. In a cultural landscape where information is often skewed or manipulated, the responsibility falls on the individual to carefully dissect fact from fiction. The discourse surrounding issues such as civil rights, economic policy, and foreign affairs requires that citizens employ critical thinking to arrive at well-informed decisions. Without this, even the most well-intentioned political framework can drift toward tyranny, with leaders using misinformation to exploit public opinion. Thus, the very fabric of American society is woven with threads of analytical engagement and independent thought.

Empowerment Through Knowledge

IN AN ERA where disillusionment with American politics is rampant, the concept of empowerment through knowledge stands as a crucial antidote. The belief that human governance is futile often stems from a lack of understanding of political mechanics and the societal structures that underpin them. By actively engaging with their political environments, individuals not only challenge this limited worldview but also contribute to a more informed and proactive citizenry.

Understanding the intricacies of political systems is essential for cultivating a sense of empowerment among individuals. Political knowledge equips citizens with the tools to assess their rights, responsibilities, and the mechanisms available for advocacy and change. For example, when individuals grasp the workings of local governance, they become more inclined to participate in civic duties such as voting or attending town hall meetings. This engagement isn't just a routine obligation; it is also a powerful means of claiming agency within a system that often seems beyond our control.

Education about American politics also enables citizens to critically evaluate the information presented to them. In a world flooded with misinformation, the ability to recognize credible sources can transform an apathetic populace into an informed one. When individuals possess the knowledge needed to challenge misleading narratives, they can hold their representatives accountable and advocate for policies that reflect their values and needs. This active participation fosters a community where discussions become rooted in reality rather than speculation, which is essential for a functioning, healthy body politic.

Of course, engagement with political environments extends beyond the immediate act of voting or attending meetings. It also encompasses being active in local community organizations, participating in grassroots movements, and engaging in open-minded dialogue with others about political issues. Through these activities, we not only enhance our understanding of governance, but we also build networks of support that can amplify our voices. As we share our knowledge and experiences, we cultivate a culture of collaboration that prioritizes informed discourse over isolation. This collective empowerment leads to tangible changes in policy and governance, demonstrating the impact of well-informed citizens on America's political landscape.

An Attitude of Stewardship

THE CONCEPT of Earth as God's domain, as articulated through biblical principles, serves as a powerful foundation for understanding and navigating the complex political issues facing America today. This perspective not only shapes ethical frameworks, but it also influences civic responsibility, encouraging citizens to engage thoughtfully in American culture. By grounding our understanding of governance and stewardship in these principles, we can better address the many challenges that confront our society.

At the core of biblical teachings is the belief that the Earth and everything in it belongs to God. This principle calls for an attitude of stewardship rather than ownership. In a political context, viewing Earth as God's domain invites citizens to recognize their responsibility to care for creation, advocate for justice, and ensure the well-being of all. This was notably emphasized in *The Book of Genesis*, where humanity was entrusted with the responsibility of cultivating and keeping the Earth.[23] Such stewardship, in

---

23 *The Biblical Mandate to Care for the Earth*: Genesis 2:15 states, "And the Lord God placed the man in the Garden of Eden, to dress it and to keep it." This single verse, rich in symbolism and meaning, encapsulates the divine relationship that God ordained between humanity and nature. It speaks of mankind's stewardship of the Earth, and the interconnectedness of all God's creation.

Two Hebrew verbs reveal all we need to know about what God desired from Adam and Eve, and so from us as their descendants: to "dress" and to "keep" the Earth. The Hebrew word used for "dress," *abad*, can be translated as both to "work" and to "serve." According to *Strong's Concordance of The Bible*, the word *abad* speaks of "the religious context that describes the worship and service of God, indicating a life dedicated to divine obedience and reverence. The Israelites' understanding of work was deeply connected to their covenant relationship

turn, extends to social justice, ecological sustainability, and ethical governance, urging citizens to approach political discourse with a sense of obligation to protect God's creation.

In addition, the biblical narrative underscores the importance of community and compassion, values that are essential in addressing contemporary political issues. For instance, the teachings of Jesus emphasize love for one's neighbor, which can guide political engagement and policymaking. When citizens prioritize compassion in political discussions, they create an environment where dialogue thrives, inspiring solutions that are inclusive and just. This communal approach encourages participation from diverse voices, leading to more comprehensive and effective policies that reflect the needs of all citizens.

---

with God, where labor was seen as a form of worship and obedience to divine commandments." Thus, we see that this God-ordained relationship with the Earth isn't one of human ownership but, rather, is one of divine partnership.

The Hebrew word used for "keep," *shamar*, speaks of protection and guardianship. According to *Strong's Concordance*, the word *shamar* implies a "sense of diligence and responsibility in maintaining what is valuable or sacred. This term also reflects the agrarian lifestyle of the Israelites, where shepherds would *shamar* their flocks, ensuring their safety and well-being." From this, we see that we are called to protect and guard the Earth and all its inhabitants, and not just to dominate it and control it for our own purposes according to the typical Christian view.

While many in the Christian tradition, then, cling to the idea that the Earth is somehow less important than Heaven, there are still other verses that speak of a more balanced view. *Psalm 24:1* says: "The Earth is the Lord's, and everything in it, the world, and all who live in it." *Psalm 25:5* says: "The sea is His, for He made it, and His hands formed the dry land." And *Psalm 89:11* says: "Heaven is Yours, and so also is the Earth; You established the world and all that is in it."

From verses like this, we see the extent to which God's ultimate purpose clearly involves the Earth as playing a much greater role than many assume. So, while you may be tempted to see the Earth as some sort of stepping stone on your way to your true goal in Heaven, remember that the Apostle Paul would want you, instead, to keep in mind, speaking of God's view of the matter: "With all wisdom and understanding, He has made known to us the mystery of His will according to His good pleasure, which He purposed in Christ, to be put into effect when the times reach their fulfillment—to bring unity to all things in Heaven and on Earth under Christ." (*Ephesians* 1:8-10)

What's more, the concept of accountability is central to biblical teachings, reminding us that leaders are also accountable to God. This understanding empowers citizens to hold their political leaders to a higher standard, demanding transparency, integrity, and justice. In a republican society, where elected officials represent the interests of the community, invoking the idea of accountability fosters a culture of responsibility and ethical leadership. Citizens can thus better navigate political issues, advocating for leaders who align with biblical values and who demonstrate a commitment to serve the common good.

Of course, this doesn't mean that viewing political issues through a biblical lens comes without challenges. In a pluralistic society, differing interpretations of Scripture and values inevitably lead to conflict. Nevertheless, by focusing on shared principles of love, justice, and stewardship, citizens can bridge ideological divides and work towards common goals. It is essential, then, to approach political engagement with humility and a willingness to listen, maintaining an atmosphere where constructive dialogue prevails over division.

God's Ultimate Plan for Creation

IN THE JOURNEY of faith, conversations about God's plan often oscillate between the immediate experiences of our earthly existence and the distant promises of a heavenly future. This dual focus can lead to profound insights into Jesus' prayer for Heaven to manifest on Earth. By contemplating the relevance of God's plan in our daily lives, we deepen our understanding of Jesus' teachings, enriching our spiritual journey and fostering a sense of communion with the divine.

At the heart of the conversation about God's plan are the realities of daily life. Jesus taught that the Kingdom of God isn't merely a distant hope, but it can also be experienced right here, right now. When we engage in discussions about how to embody God's love, mercy, and justice in our communities, we reflect on the essence of Jesus' prayer in *Matthew* 6:10: "Your will be done on Earth as it is in Heaven." This phrase invites us to consider how the principles of Heaven can be woven into the fabric of our earthly existence. Such conversations, in turn, challenge us to recognize God's presence in ordinary moments, urging us to act as vessels of His peace and love in the world.

These discussions about living out God's plan often uncover deep theological insights. For example, when we focus on the here and now, we begin to appreciate the significance of Jesus' teachings in addressing contemporary issues such as poverty, injustice, and social division. Through sincere dialogue, believers can explore how to apply Jesus' revolutionary principles in practical ways—responding to suffering with compassion, promoting healing, and advocating for the marginalized. These moments of sharing and reflection illuminate the interconnectedness of our actions and God's will, allowing us to see how our earthly struggles are an integral part of the divine narrative.

The juxtaposition of immediate concerns with the hopeful expectation of a heavenly future also invites a life-changing perspective. It encourages believers to look beyond their circumstances and to engage in acts of faith that point toward God's ultimate plan for creation. Conversations that bridge these two realities inspire a joyful anticipation of the eternal while at the same time reinforcing the importance of faith in the present. This understanding urges us to be proactive participants in this grand narrative, rather than passive observers waiting around for divine intervention.

Living Out the Faith

IN THE MODERN world, many people find themselves disheartened by the prevalence of injustice and inequality. As such, it's easy to succumb to the mindset that passively waits for God to resolve these issues, believing that only divine intervention can effect change. However, a closer reflection on the implications of Jesus' prayer urges believers to reconsider this passive approach. The call to have Heaven reflected on Earth directly implicates citizens in the realization of justice and equity. This reflects the idea that it's not enough to invoke God's authority; individuals must also embody it in their daily lives, striving to rectify wrongs and promote fairness within their communities.

The teachings of Jesus emphasize active participation in the pursuit of justice. In *Luke* 4:18-19, for example, Jesus outlines His mission to bring good news to the poor, proclaim freedom for the prisoners, and set the oppressed free. This mission statement not only reveals His divine purpose, but it also serves as a model for all who profess to follow Him. Engaging with social issues, advocating for the marginalized, and acting justly are intrinsic to living out our faith. It is through these actions that citizens become conduits of God's plan in a world so rife with division and despair.

This call, then, to "bring Heaven to Earth" is nothing less than a call to transform every sphere of society—politically, economically, personally. This means actively opposing systems that perpetuate injustice, whether they manifest in policies that neglect the poor or those in need, or in attitudes that discriminate against certain groups. A serious commitment to these ideals can enlighten how we view God's role in the world. Instead of sitting around waiting for divine intervention, we begin to understand that we're all meant to be active agents of God's love and justice, tasked with personally carrying out the work that Jesus set forth.

Of course, engaging in this struggle was never meant to be easy or swift. Many will find moments of doubt, where the disparity between the hope of justice and the reality of human suffering is stark and overwhelming. However, the assurance found in our personal faith, as well as in the community of believers, serves as an ongoing source of encouragement, inspiring us all to continue on the path of truth and justice, embodying the ideals laid out by Christ.

Embracing Civic Responsibility

IN A WORLD increasingly marked by division, apathy, and cynicism, the concept of civic responsibility stands as a vital pillar for fortifying a healthy society. Rather than resigning to the belief that human governance should be supplanted by a divine order, it's crucial for individuals to embrace the idea of civic responsibility. This approach not only enriches our communities, but it also empowers citizens to actively participate in shaping their lives and upholding republican values.

Civic responsibility is defined as the commitment to engage in the processes that govern society. It encourages people to take part in local initiatives, vote in elections, and advocate for issues that matter to them and their communities. Such engagement creates a sense of ownership over the social contract, instilling a belief that every voice matters. This direct engagement stands in stark contrast to the idea that governance is solely an act ordained by a higher power, distancing people from the consequences of their inactions. When we believe we have a stake in our communities, we're all more motivated to contribute positively rather than to lapse into passivity.

Not only that, but embracing civic responsibility also promotes a culture of accountability. When people take their roles seriously, they are more inclined to hold themselves and their leaders accountable. Participating in local government meetings, supporting advocacy groups, and engaging in dialogue about societal issues are ways citizens can ensure that their representatives reflect their values and priorities. This active involvement nurtures transparency in governance, offering a counterbalance to the disillusionment often felt towards political institutions.

By committing to civic duties, citizens cultivate a society where integrity and fairness thrive.

The concept of civic responsibility also emphasizes the importance of community. In a time when isolationism and individualism dominate, engaging in community service or local activism rekindles connections among individuals. These interactions not only strengthen the social fabric but also inspire collective efforts for social change. In this way, the shared pursuit of common goals enhances trust and cooperation, reminding people that they are all part of something larger than themselves.

Envisioning a Better Future

IN A WORLD rife with challenges and uncertainty, the belief that earthly governments will all be swept away in favor of a heavenly kingdom seems to offer humanity the hope of a better future. Unfortunately, as we've seen, it also triggers a troubling downside by discouraging the need for human action as the basis for faith in God. To move beyond this ultimate lie, we must first recognize that as much evidence as there is that Heaven is our main goal in life, there is even more evidence, biblically speaking, that Earth can be transformed through our efforts, here and now, to create a more just, compassionate, and sustainable life.

To that end, envisioning a better future on Earth begins with acknowledging the power of collective action. When individuals come together, inspired by a shared vision of a better world, remarkable changes occur. Historical movements, such as the birth of American liberty, Civil Rights, and Women's Rights, illustrate that when determined people unite, they can overcome almost anything. By fostering a spirit of compassion and cooperation, we forge an environment where positive change flourishes against all odds. And this aligns perfectly with the belief that our purpose on Earth isn't just to seek an afterlife but to invest in the well-being of ourselves and others in this world.

By focusing on our responsibilities on Earth, we promote innovation and progress. From advancements in technology that address social initiatives that uplift marginalized communities or ecological initiatives that address neglected Earth science concerns, human ingenuity shines brightest when motivated by a desire for improvement. This drive for progress reminds us that the pursuit of a heavenly existence can be intricately woven into our earthly endeavors. The more we actively participate in shaping our world, the closer we come to experiencing Heaven on Earth in the here and now.

Additionally, cultivating a mindset of gratitude and appreciation for the present transforms the way we perceive our surroundings. Instead of waiting for a promised utopia, we can embrace and celebrate the beauty and richness of our daily experiences. By nurturing a sense of wonder and belonging, we establish a deeper connection with the Earth and its inhabitants. This perspective empowers us to take action in our lives and communities, promoting a culture of kindness and empathy. In this way, the small, everyday choices we make collectively contribute to a larger vision of "Earth as it is in Heaven."

Promoting Political Literacy

THE IDEA that Heaven is the sole goal of human existence has been a deeply ingrained belief in various cultures and religions throughout history. However, this perspective detracts from the importance of creating a just and equitable society here on Earth. Instead of focusing solely on an afterlife, it's paramount that we bring aspects of Heaven to Earth by promoting political literacy and inspiring an informed citizenry. By doing so, we not only enhance the quality of life for individuals but also shape communities that reflect values of fairness, compassion, and justice.

Political literacy, then, serves as a crucial foundation for an informed citizenry. Understanding the mechanisms of governance, policies, and the rights afforded to citizens empowers us to actively participate in our communities. When people are educated about how their government operates, they become equipped to advocate for their needs and challenge injustices. This proactive engagement is essential for ensuring that policies reflect the collective values of our society, rather than being dictated by a select few. A politically literate population holds leaders accountable and contributes to a culture of transparency and responsiveness.

This bringing forth of aspects of Heaven to Earth also means that our collective efforts should be aimed at creating an environment where everyone has access to opportunities and resources. By encouraging political literacy, we allow individuals to amplify their voices and advocate for equality, justice, and sustainability. This isn't just a moral imperative; it is also a practical necessity, in forging a society that is more resilient, adaptable, and peaceful. Such a community mirrors the ideals often associated with Heaven, emphasizing that we can manifest those values in our present world, just as the prayer of Jesus urged us to do.

The challenge we face today, then, is overcoming the apathy and cynicism that so many feel toward political systems. Often, individuals perceive politics as a domain reserved for the elite or for those who are specifically trained in the art of governance. However, this only serves to perpetuate stereotypes that can't help but further entrench longstanding injustices and inequalities. In contrast, political literacy breaks down these barriers, demonstrating that everyone has a role to play in shaping our society. It invites collaboration and dialogue among all citizens, urging them to engage with ideas, challenge assumptions, and collectively work toward a better future.

Promoting political literacy also dovetails perfectly with the need for civic engagement. When individuals are informed, they are more likely to engage in activities that promote social change, such as voting, community organizing, or peaceful protest. These actions are vital in bringing about legislative changes that align with the values we wish to see reflected in our society. By prioritizing political education, we cultivate a culture of engagement that resonates with the vision of a harmonious community, thus transforming our earthly existence into a reflection of heavenly ideals.

Honoring the Original Vision

THROUGHOUT HISTORY, the role of human governments has often been debated, particularly in relation to their perceived purpose in fulfilling a higher destiny. The argument that political systems are temporary or ineffective is compelling, but it oversimplifies a complex reality. While it's tempting to claim that divine plans exist independently of human governance, we must recognize the potential of earthly governments—especially like that of America—to champion progress and serve as instruments to fulfill God's purpose for humanity.

The Founding Fathers of the United States envisioned a government that would uniquely empower citizens and reflect their aspirations for liberty, equality, and justice. Their revolutionary ideas laid the foundation for a political system designed not only to maintain order but also to inspire progress. Central to this vision was the belief that human beings are capable of shaping their destinies. These ideals weren't merely secular in nature; they also echoed a profound understanding of a divine purpose that guides humanity towards greater freedom and fulfillment. Thus, to dismiss political structures as irrelevant in favor of spiritual aspirations undermines the potential for human agency to align with divine intent.

Not only that, but governments also have the capacity to effect positive change and address the pressing issues faced by societies. Through legislation, social programs, and public policy, governments can uplift the marginalized and create opportunities for everyone. History is replete with examples of how political movements have led to substantial advancements—be it civil rights, ecological protections, or economic reforms. Each of these achievements exemplifies a manifestation of collective will, driven by a sense of purpose that transcends mere politics. So, rather than viewing governments as barriers to divine destinies, we should see them as tools for actualizing communal aspirations.

The notion that politics lack purpose—in this case, American politics—can also be countered by the idea that human beings are inherently social creatures. We thrive in a community setting and seek to govern our interactions in ways that promote harmony and progress. It is through this collective engagement that we fulfill our responsibilities to one another and to the divine vision that underpins our existence. In recognizing the interdependence of individuals within a society, we can appreciate the role that governments play in reflecting shared values and working towards a common good.

So, while it may seem appealing to anticipate a time when all human governments are swept away in favor of God's heavenly kingdom, such a view overlooks the significant progress that political systems have made in the wake of Christ's mandate concerning His true purpose for Earth in the here and now. In line with this, it's clear that our Founders set a clear precedent for a governance structure that champions "life, liberty, and the pursuit of happiness," one which undoubtedly reflects Christ's prayer that we partake in the manifestation of His Kingdom on Earth, from age to age.

In conclusion, then, rather than seeing American politics as being devoid of any heavenly purpose, we should embrace the transformative potential of our government as it strives to embody a hopeful vision for the future. Ultimately, it's through our engagement in the political arena that we actively contribute to a meaningful legacy aligned with God's plan for humanity. Clearly, the ideals espoused by the Founding Fathers were aligned with such a vision of progress that invites us to engage, innovate, and work together towards a better world. By embracing this approach, we can manifest a reality that reflects the harmony and fulfillment often associated with the concept of Heaven. And so, as we strive to bring Heaven to Earth, as Jesus taught His disciples to do, we not only fulfill our civic duty to our fellow Americans, but we also honor the original vision of the Founding Fathers, ensuring that the spirit of progress that inspired them will endure both in our time and for generations yet to come.

THIS CONCLUDES *Lies My Professor Told Me About American Politics.* To get the eBook or audiobook version of this work, go to *The Lost Stories Channel* at loststorieschannel.com or *Amazon Books.*

Additionally, for those of you who are so inclined, please post a positive review on Amazon so that others might become aware of its valuable contents. Because this book was not published by a conglomerate-style publishing house, we rely more heavily on word-of-mouth to advertise its importance to others who, like yourself, are searching for books like this. Thank you for your support.

QUOTING THE FOUNDING FATHERS

FROM THE PREAMBLE

"I've lived a long time, and the longer I live, the more convinced I am of this truth—that God governs the affairs of men. And if a sparrow doesn't fall to the ground without Him noticing, then how is it possible that an Empire can rise without His aid?" Benjamin Franklin

"God Who gave us life also gave us liberty. And are the liberties of a nation secure when we remove their only firm basis—a conviction that these liberties are the gift of God? That they can be violated without incurring His wrath? Indeed, I tremble for my country when I reflect that God is just, and that His justice cannot sleep forever." Thomas Jefferson

"Posterity—you will never know how much it has cost my generation to preserve your freedom. I hope you will make good use of it." John Quincy Adams

FROM AN INTRODUCTION - UNVEILING THE TRUTH: SHEDDING THE BLINDFOLD

"He who permits himself to tell a lie once, finds it much easier to do so a second and third time, till at length it becomes habitual; soon he speaks lies without realizing it, and truths without the world believing him. This falsehood of the tongue, then, leads to that of the heart, and in time corrupts all its good intentions." Thomas Jefferson

FROM CHAPTER ONE - INHERITED IGNORANCE: LIES FROM THE PAST

"The highest glory of the American Revolution was this; it connected in one indestructible bond the principles of civil government with the principles of Christianity." John Quincy Adams

"Of all the tyrannies that affect mankind, tyranny in religion is the worst." Thomas Paine

"Religious institutions and government shall operate independently of one another, in order to establish effectual barriers against the horrors of spiritual tyranny, and every species of religious persecution." George Washington

"The accumulation of all powers, legislative, executive, and judiciary, in the same hands, whether of one, a few, or many, and whether hereditary, self-appointed, or elective, may justly be pronounced the very definition of tyranny." James Madison

FROM CHAPTER TWO - THE BROKEN MACHINE: A CORRUPTED BODY POLITIC

"Never forget the religious character of our origin. Our fathers were brought here by their high veneration for the Christian religion. They journeyed by its light, and labored in its hope. They sought to incorporate its principles into every aspect of American society, and to diffuse its influence through all their institutions—civil, political, and literary." Daniel Webster

"If you would rule well, you must rule for God, and to do that, you must be ruled by Him. Those who will not be governed by God will be ruled by tyrants." William Penn

"Pure democracies have always been spectacles of turbulence and contention; have always been found incompatible with personal security, or the rights of property; and have, in general, been as short in their lives as they have been violent in their deaths… A republic, by which I mean a government in which the scheme of representation takes place … opens a different prospect, and promises the cure for which we are seeking... The influence of factious leaders may kindle a flame within their own particular states, but will be unable to spread a general conflagration throughout the other states." James Madison

"It is in the man of piety and inward principle that we may expect to find the uncorrupted patriot, the useful citizen, and the invincible soldier.

May God grant that in America, true religion and civil liberty may be inseparable." John Witherspoon

From Chapter Three - The Myth of Pure Democracy: The Real Story of American Governance

"Democracy is like when two wolves and one sheep vote on what they will eat for dinner. Liberty is a well-armed lamb contesting the vote." Benjamin Franklin

"It has been observed by an honorable gentleman that a pure democracy, if it were practicable, would be the most perfect government. Experience has proved that no position in politics is more false than this. The ancient democracies, in which the people themselves deliberated, never possessed one feature of good government. Their very character was tyranny; their figure deformity." Alexander Hamilton

"The republican is the only form of government which is not eternally at open or secret war with the rights of mankind." Thomas Jefferson

"Between a balanced republic and a democracy, the difference is like that between order and chaos." John Marshall

"Real liberty is neither found in despotism or the extremes of democracy, but in moderate governments." Alexander Hamilton

"Remember, democracy never lasts long. It soon wastes, exhausts, and murders itself. There never was a democracy yet that did not commit suicide." John Adams

"The people are the ultimate guardians of their own liberties. In every government on Earth, there is some trace of human weakness, some germ of corruption and degeneracy... Every government degenerates when trusted to the rulers of the people alone." Thomas Jefferson

From Chapter Four - The Media Mirage: The Truth Behind the Headlines

"Human nature is the same on both sides of the Atlantic, and will be influenced by all the same causes. The time to guard against corruption *and tyranny is before they have gotten hold of us. It is better to keep the wolf out of the fold than to try withdrawing his teeth and claws after he has got you." Thomas Jefferson*

"The only thing more expensive than education is ignorance." Benjamin Franklin

"What is government itself but the greatest of all reflections on human nature? If men were angels, government would be unnecessary. And if angels governed men, no external or internal controls on government would be needed." James Madison

"Whenever the people are well informed, they can be trusted with their own government; that whenever things get so far wrong as to attract their notice, they may be relied on to set them to rights." Thomas Jefferson

"Our liberty depends on the freedom of the press, and that cannot be limited without being lost." Thomas Jefferson

"Nothing can now be believed which is seen in a newspaper. Truth itself becomes suspicious by being put into that polluted vehicle." Thomas Jefferson

"Men are ambitious, vindictive, and rapacious." Alexander Hamilton

FROM CHAPTER FIVE - DIVIDE AND CONQUER: THE WEAPONIZATION OF IDENTITY POLITICS

"I walk on untrodden ground. There is scarcely an action of mine whose motives is not subject to a double interpretation. There is scarcely any part of my conduct which may not hereafter set a precedent." George Washington

"Complaints are everywhere heard from our most considerate and virtuous citizens, that our governments are too unstable; that the public good is disregarded in the conflicts of rival parties; and that measures are too often decided, not according to the rules of justice and the rights of the minor party, but by the superior force of an interested and over-bearing majority." James Madison

"There is no act, however virtuous, for which ingenuity may not find some bad motive." Thomas Jefferson

"A popular government without popular information, or the means of acquiring it, is but a prologue to a farce or a tragedy, or perhaps both. Knowledge will forever govern ignorance; and a people who mean to be their own governors must arm themselves with the power which knowledge gives." James Madison

FROM CHAPTER SIX - THE PUPPET MASTERS: UNVEILING HIDDEN PERSUADERS

"I am all for doing good to the poor, but I do not think the best way of doing good to them is to make them easy in poverty but to lead or drive them out of it." Benjamin Franklin

"To take from one person because it is thought he has acquired too much from his hard work, to give to others who have not exercised equal industry and skill, is to arbitrarily violate a fundamental guiding principle: that everyone is guaranteed to maintain ownership of the fruits of their own labor." Thomas Jefferson

"In my youth, I traveled much, and I observed in different countries that the more the poor were given public provisions, the less they provided for themselves, and of course they became poorer. And on the contrary, the less that was done for them, the more they did for themselves, and so they became richer." Benjamin Franklin

FROM CHAPTER SEVEN - TAKING FROM THE RICH: AN ECONOMIC RIPPLE EFFECT

"To compel someone to contribute money for the promotion of opinions for which they disbelieve is sinful and tyrannical." Thomas Jefferson

"A wise and frugal government is one that restrains men from injuring each other, that leaves them free to regulate their own pursuits of industry and improvement, and that does not take from the mouth of labor the bread it has earned. This is the sum of good government, and this is necessary to close the circle of our contentment." Thomas Jefferson

"There is no country in the world where so many provisions are established for them, with a solemn general law made by the rich to subject their estates to a heavy tax for the support of the poor. Yet there is no country in the world in which the poor are more idle, dissolute, drunken, and insolent. The day you passed that act, you took away from before their eyes the greatest of all inducements to industry, frugality, and sobriety, by giving them a dependence on something other than a careful accumulation during youth and health, for support in age and sickness. In short, you offered a premium for the encouragement of idleness, and you should not now wonder that it has had its effect in the increase of poverty." Benjamin Franklin

"Taxation is, in fact, the most difficult function of government and against which their citizens are most apt to be defiant." Thomas Jefferson

"I cannot find a single article of the Constitution which grants Congress the right to spend, on any object of benevolence, the money of their constituents." James Madison

From Chapter Eight - Foreign Affairs: The Global Consequences

"Guard jealously the public liberty. Suspect everyone who approaches that jewel. Unfortunately, nothing will preserve it but downright force. Whenever you give up that force, you are inevitably ruined." Patrick Henry

"Against the insidious wiles of foreign influence the jealousy of a free people ought to be constantly awake, since history and experience prove that foreign influence is one of the deadliest foes of a republican government. But that jealousy, to be useful, must be impartial, or else it becomes the instrument of the very influence that should be avoided, instead of a defense against it." George Washington

"The means of security can only be regulated by the means and the danger of attack. They will, in fact, be ever determined by these rules, and by no others. If one nation constantly maintains a disciplined army, ready for the service of ambition or revenge, it obliges the most pacific nations who may be within the reach of its enterprises to take corresponding precautions." James Madison

"The nation which indulges toward another an habitual hatred or an habitual fondness is in some degree a slave. It is a slave to its animosity or to its affection, either of which is sufficient to lead it astray from its duty and its interest. Hostility in one nation against another disposes each more readily to offer insult and injury, to lay hold of slight causes of resentment, and to be arrogant and intractable when accidental or trifling occasions of dispute occur." George Washington

"Peace, commerce, and honest friendship with all nations, but entangling alliances with none." Thomas Jefferson

"To judge from the history of mankind, we are compelled to conclude that the fiery and destructive passions of war reign in the human breast with much more powerful sway than the mild and beneficent sentiments of peace; and that to model our political systems upon speculations of lasting tranquility is to count on the weaker springs of the human character." Alexander Hamilton

FROM CHAPTER NINE - THE ROAD TO REDEMPTION: AWAKENING TO THE TRUTH

"Let it simply be asked: Where is the security for property, for reputation, for life, if the sense of religious obligation desert the oaths, which are the instruments of investigation in courts of justice?" George Washington

"Why is it that next to the birthday of the Savior of the world your most joyous and most venerated festival returns on this day? Is it not that, in the chain of human events, the birthday of our nation is perpetually linked with the birthday of the Savior? That it forms a leading event in the progress of the Gospel dispensation? Is it not that the Declaration of Independence first organized the social compact on the foundation of the Redeemer's mission upon Earth? That it laid the cornerstone of human government upon the first precepts of Christianity?" John Quincy Adams

"We have proclaimed to the world our determination to die as freemen, rather than to live as slaves. We have appealed to Heaven for the justice of our cause, and in Heaven we have placed our trust. Numerous have been the manifestations of God's providence in sustaining us. In the

gloomy period of adversity, we have had 'our cloud by day and pillar of fire by night.' We have been reduced to distress, and the arm of Omnipotence has raised us up. Let us still rely in humble confidence on Him Who is mighty to save. Good tidings will soon arrive. We will never be abandoned by Heaven while we act worthy of its aid and protection."
Samuel Adams

"When all men of all religions, consistent with morals and equity, enjoy equal liberty, security of property, and an equal chance for honor and power, we may expect that improvements will be made in the human character and the state of society." John Adams

"He that would make his own liberty secure must guard even his enemy from oppression; for if he violates this duty, he establishes a precedent that will reach to himself." Thomas Jefferson

"Let us see that our government be kept purely republican, that is, a representative democracy. This is a duty we owe to our fathers and brethren, who paid with their blood to purchase our privileges. It is a duty we owe to posterity; we ought not willingly, or carelessly, deprive them of that goodly heritage, which God has committed to our keeping." Joseph Barker

"There is no truth more thoroughly established, than that there exists an indestructible union between virtue and happiness, between duty and advantage, between the genuine rule of an honest and generous policy, and the solid rewards of public prosperity and contentment: Since we ought to be no less persuaded that the fortunate smiles of Heaven can never be expected on a nation that disregards the eternal rules of order and right, which Heaven itself has ordained." George Washington

FROM THE CONCLUSION - REFUTING THE ULTIMATE LIE: GOD'S TRUE PURPOSE FOR THE EARTH

"Whoever believes in the divine inspiration of the Holy Scriptures must hope that the religion of Jesus shall prevail throughout the Earth. Not since the foundation of the world have the prospects of mankind been more encouraging to that hope than they appear to be at the present time. And may the associated distribution of The Bible proceed and

prosper till the Lord has made 'bare His holy arm in the eyes of all the nations, and all the ends of the Earth will see the salvation of our God.'" John Quincy Adams

"Those who expect to reap the blessings of freedom, must, like men, undergo the fatigue of supporting it." Thomas Paine

"I know no safe depository of the ultimate powers of society but the people themselves; and if we think them not enlightened enough to exercise their control with a wholesome discretion, the remedy is not to take it from them, but to inform their discretion by education." Thomas Jefferson

"Resistance to tyranny becomes the Christian and social duty of each individual. Continue steadfast and, with a proper sense of your dependence on God, nobly defend those rights which Heaven gave us, and which no man ought to take from us." John Hancock

"Freedom can exist only in the society of knowledge. Without learning, men are incapable of knowing their rights, and where learning is confined to a few people, liberty can be neither equal nor universal." Benjamin Rush

"The advancement and diffusion of knowledge is the only guardian of true liberty." James Madison

"If virtue and knowledge are diffused among the people, they will never be enslaved. This will be their great security." Samuel Adams

"I believe there are more instances of the curtailment of the freedom of the people by gradual and silent encroachments by those in power than by violent and sudden usurpation." James Madison

"If we are to guard against ignorance and remain free, it is the responsibility of every American to be informed." Thomas Jefferson

"Knowledge will forever govern ignorance; and a people who mean to be their own governors must arm themselves with the power which knowledge gives." James Madison

ABOUT THE AUTHOR

FOR MORE than forty years, W. Kent Smith has immersed himself in the teachings of the greatest biblical scholars of the ages—William Barclay, C.S. Lewis, W. Gene Scott, *et al*. More importantly during that time, he has immersed himself in *The Bible* itself. Add to that, Kent's unique perspective on history, humanity, and life, and the result is a one-of-a-kind take on biblical history

and theology. What that means to you as a fellow truth seeker is a message unhindered by many outmoded traditions of biblical interpretation.

Beholden to no deacon board or school of thought, Kent has remained free to tread where others are unwilling to tread, and because of that, a brand-new view of Scripture has emerged. Not some new revelation, mind you, in the sense of it being above and beyond *The Bible* itself. What we are talking about is a fresh understanding of what Scripture has been saying all along, one that's been hidden in plain sight, waiting for someone to connect the dots, to reveal a picture that's been lying dormant until now.

Kent lives in West Covina, California, an eastern suburb of Los Angeles. He can be contacted at wkent@loststorieschannel.com or lodestarcinema@msn.com.